Under Army Orders

TEXAS A&M UNIVERSITY MILITARY HISTORY SERIES

74

Under Army Orders

The Army National Guard during the Korean War

William M. Donnelly

TEXAS A&M UNIVERSITY PRESS
College Station

First edition

The paper used in this book meets the minimum requirements
of the American National Standard for Permanence of Paper
for Printed Library Materials, Z39.48-1984.
Binding materials have been chosen for durability.

∞

Library of Congress Cataloging-in-Publication Data

Donnelly, William M., 1962–
Under Army orders : the Army National Guard during the Korean War / William M. Donnelly.—1st ed.
p. cm.—(Texas A&M University military history series; no. 74)
Includes bibliographical references and index.
ISBN 1-58544-117-1
1. Korean War, 1950–1953—United States. 2. United States. Army—History—Korean War, 1950–1953. 3. United States—National Guard—History—Korean War, 1950–1953.
I. Title. II. Series.
DS919.D658 2001

00-011803

IN MEMORY OF

Corporal John Creed

Battery B, 319th Field Artillery Regiment

American Expeditionary Forces

Citizen Soldier

CONTENTS

PREFACE

The U.S. Army National Guard played a sizable role in American mobilization for the Korean War, providing 138,600 guardsmen in eight divisions, three regimental combat teams, and numerous separate battalions, companies, and detachments for service throughout the world.[1] Yet the army guard's participation in the war passed, for the most part, into historical obscurity soon after the 1953 armistice. Works on the war and on the National Guard offer little detailed discussion of the army guard's role in the conflict. What discussion there is usually focuses on one of four areas: army guard units deployed to Korea; military effectiveness; manpower problems during the war; or effects of the war on reserve component policy.[2]

This historical shadow under which the National Guard's role during the Korean War resides is, in part, the result of the general shadow that fell over the entire Korean War. Many Americans, conditioned by World War II to destruction of the opposing regime, saw the Korean War as an aberration. Since it would not be repeated, the consensus was that it did not need to be examined in any great detail. Moreover, in the wake of the trauma of the Vietnam War, the Korean conflict became trapped between two giants that soaked up most of the attention devoted to America's twentieth century wars.[3] Further complicating the army guard's role in the war is the fact that only about one-third of its units were mobilized, and less than half of those units saw service in Korea—although many guardsmen were sent to Korea as individual replacements.[4]

Nevertheless, guard units that deployed to Korea have been the focus of most of what slim attention has been paid to the guard in discussions of the war. This is not surprising. Official histories of American wars focus on learning from the past to improve future performance. Units in combat are a rich source of examples, both good and bad, and their performance is the ultimate test of unit and institutional effectiveness.[5] The army and the Department of Defense (DOD) after 1953 produced or commissioned several studies for internal use examining the mobilization of guard and reserve units. The focus of these works, too, is the question of military effectiveness: What can be learned from past mobilizations to improve future reserve component mobilizations?[6]

Unofficial histories of the war generally follow the same pattern as the army's official history: a brief discussion of the 1950 decision to mobilize the guard and a brief discussion of the decision to deploy two guard divisions to Korea. The major exception to this pattern is William Berebitsky's *A Very Long Weekend.* Using mainly interviews with veterans, supplemented with unit after-action reports, Berebitsky looks at mobilization, post-mobilization training, and operations in Korea. The book touches on the major problems mobilized guard units faced, such as equipment, personnel, and training shortfalls; racial integration; guard–Regular Army relations; adjusting to combat; and the phase-out of guard personnel from units that remained in federal service. Still, because it focuses only on units that deployed to Korea, the book does not cover the entire army guard experience during the war.[7]

John K. Mahon's and Jim Dan Hill's National Guard histories devote little attention to the army guard during the Korean War. Mahon devotes just three pages to the topic. He provides a brief outline of the guard's role during the war, but offers no details of unit experiences. Hill has twelve pages on the subject, but almost all this space is taken up by an extended critique of American strategy and personnel policies during the war. Hill, a guard major general, argued that the correct American strategy in Korea should have been the total mobilization of the guard, followed by a campaign to destroy Kim Il Sung's regime using all or most of its units, and the creation of a unified Korea, allied to the United States, with its northern border on the Yalu River.[8] Most histories of state National Guard forces only sketch their units' federal service during the war.[9] Others provide a more detailed narrative, and a few, such as Jerry Cooper and Glenn Smith on North Dakota, and Richard C. Roberts on Utah, offer a comprehensive examination of the units mobilized in those states.[10]

This book will survey the various experiences of army guard units mobilized during the Korean War, sampling units by type, by home state, and by postmobilization assignment. In doing so, it will look at several questions. First, how effective was the army guard in meeting the demands placed upon it by the Korean War? Units faced considerable obstacles before and after mobilization. Before the war, Congress and the president failed to adequately finance the guard's post-1945 force structure. By 1950, units were on reduced personnel authorizations and entered federal service with major equipment shortages. Units between 1945 and 1950 suffered extensive personnel turbulence, and leadership was of uneven quality. Both these conditions significantly affected a unit's ability to train, as did the format of weekly two-hour drills. The army in 1950 did not expect to use guard units at the start of a war, recognizing that they would need time to prepare for deployment. During postmobilization training, units encountered considerable friction, mostly because the army had planned only to fight World War III.

Despite these difficulties, army guard units generally performed well when they possessed the traditional ingredients of military success: good leadership, good training, good equipment, and a belief in the cause—or at least an acceptance of service. Nondivisional units deployed to Korea in late 1950 and early 1951 equaled or surpassed the performance of like-type Regular Army units. The two infantry divisions deployed to Korea in late 1951 also did as well as their regular counterparts, although the war of limited movement that had developed by the time they arrived did not fully test their skills.[11] Units that deployed to Europe or remained in the United States were never tested in combat, so they cannot be judged by this most exacting of methods. Additionally, extensive personnel turbulence buffeted the units. Generally, however, units sent to Germany performed well in the role given them by the army: building up the North Atlantic Treaty Organization's (NATO) military strength as part of the army's "long-pull" approach to the Cold War. Units that remained in the Zone of the Interior (ZI), the army's name for the continental United States, are another matter. Personnel turbulence ripped apart units assigned to the general reserve and to continental air defense. Units had their guard character greatly weakened or even destroyed by the end of their first year of federal service. Many units left in the ZI spent their second year on active duty as little more than way stations in the manpower pipeline funneling troops to and from overseas units as the army scrambled to supply personnel for the hot war in Korea and the cold war in Europe. It is fortunate that these units were never tested in combat.

This study also provides another window on early Cold War American society, and another way to examine the effects of the Korean War on the United States. The National Guard's dual state-federal status, its strong local ties, and its powerful lobbying organization gave it an extensive presence in American society during this period. As units were mobilized, the costs of the Truman administration's decisions during this period were felt in a large number of American homes and communities.

For the most part, communities in 1950 and 1951 saw mobilization of their guard units as an undesirable but necessary measure in the struggle against communism. In areas where much emotion had been invested in a guard unit, there was a sense of pride that the unit had been selected. Protests of the mobilization centered on two issues: perceived unfairness and fears the Regular Army would mistreat guard units. The first mainly concerned the recall to active duty of World War II veterans serving in the guard. While guardsmen's bitterness over this issue never approached the intensity found among involuntarily recalled inactive reservists, it did increase after the war stalemated and college draft deferments were introduced—especially among guardsmen deployed overseas.

The second issue was a hardy perennial. There were a number of concerns: the purging of senior guard officers; ignoring the integrity of larger units; and stripping guardsmen from their units to provide individual replacements for other units. All three, but especially the last one, once again flared up during this war.

Guardsmen, their communities, and their lobbyists were not shy about seeking political assistance in redressing their grievances. Families and friends often contacted state political figures on issues concerning mobilized guardsmen. Some guardsmen in federal service maintained back-channel communications with their state adjutants general and political figures, who in turn kept watch over their mobilized units. In Washington, the National Guard Association maintained its vigil against what it saw as attempts by the Regular Army to use the war as a tool in weakening the guard as a key institution of American society.

What is clear from this study, however, is that the army guard's experiences during this war are a part of what both Jerry Cooper and Martha Derthick have pointed out: the increasing weakness during the twentieth century of the guard vis-à-vis the Regular Army. During the Korean War, guardsmen and their advocates could only successfully work the margins of influence in a reactive manner, hoping to block actions by the Regular

Army. On the major issues, such as total mobilization of the army guard and preventing the stripping of units not sent to Korea, guardsmen and their advocates always lost. As Maj. Gen. James C. Styron pointed out in 1951 when orders arrived sending his 45th Infantry Division to Japan, a guard unit inducted into federal service was "under army orders, and will go wherever it is assigned."[12]

Many people helped make this project possible. Staff at all the archives I visited responded patiently and efficiently to my requests for sometimes very dusty file boxes. I want to note especially the assistance of Richard Sommers and David Keough at the U.S. Army Military History Institute; their knowledge of army history is breathtaking and their desire to aid researchers is inspiring. The staff at Ohio State's Interlibrary Loan Office quickly obtained newspaper microfilms and obscure publications from across the nation. The National Guard Association allowed me to spend a day browsing in its well-stocked library. A Dissertation Year Fellowship from the Harry S. Truman Library Institute was crucial to the completion of this project.

Major General Bruce Jacobs (AUS, Retired), Prof. Edward Coffman, Prof. Jerry Cooper, and Prof. William Childs all graciously gave of their time to review various drafts and offered many useful comments. William Berebitsky generously sent me a draft copy of his book on army guard units in Korea. Professor Allan Millett, my adviser at the Ohio State University, provided a critique that did much to improve both the history and writing in this work.

The members of the 3d Battalion, 92d Field Artillery, of Akron, Ohio, never suspected that in the four years we served together that they were providing a historian numerous insights into the reserve components. The lessons continued with the soldiers of the 660th Transportation Company of Cadiz, Ohio—particularly on those marathon motor marches to North Dakota. While serving in both units, I benefited greatly from the advice and encouragement of Maj. Keith Sousa. I also want to thank Maj. David Brooks, Royal Logistics Corps, Territorial Army, for his friendship and insights during his stay with my unit under some very trying conditions.

Krista Donnelly's love and encouragement helped me see this project through to its end and gave me a deeper understanding for the sorrows of separation and the joys of reunion felt by citizen-soldiers called away from home "under army orders."

Under Army Orders

CHAPTER 1

Rearming the Minutemen, 1945–50

The National Guard played an important part in the success of the Army of the United States (AUS) during World War II. From the mobilization that began in the fall of 1940 to victory in 1945, the guard provided eighteen infantry divisions, hundreds of separate units and almost three hundred thousand officers and men. In 1945, prewar guardsmen looked back at this performance with great pride, believing it justified the sacrifices and slights they had endured during the 1920s and 1930s. Major General Robert S. Beightler, commander of Ohio's 37th "Buckeye" Infantry Division, informed the chief of the National Guard Bureau (NGB) in April, 1945, that the "Guard has made an incalculably valuable contribution to the building of our great armed forces of today. The preservation and strengthening of the National Guard in years to come must be assured."[1]

However, many guardsmen looked forward to the postwar world with trepidation. The AUS's success had not stilled traditional National Guard–Regular Army tensions. Many guardsmen complained of what they perceived as the condescension and contempt of most regulars. Beightler advised the president of the National Guard Association (NGA) in 1945 that Regular Army officers during the war had "succeeded in alienating and embittering the civilian component officers and particularly the National Guard." On the other hand, many regulars believed that the war had demonstrated what they saw as critical flaws in the guard and the need for a single federal reserve force. Shortly before his death in 1944, Lt.

Gen. Lesley J. McNair, chief of the Army Ground Forces, submitted a plan to the army chief of staff to abolish the National Guard after the war.[2]

Complicating this volatile emotional situation was the fact that on V-J Day there were no units in the National Guard. Every guard unit had been ordered to active duty in 1940–41 or disbanded. All that were left in the states were the adjutants general's office staffs and some "home guard" units made up of overage and unfit men raised by states for internal security duties. While in federal service, many guard units had been reorganized to meet new tactical demands and filled with nonguardsmen to replace casualties and bring them up to strength. After V-J Day, the army inactivated all guard units and discharged all surviving guardsmen. The only equipment returned to the states was their units' colors. The guard would require a massive rebuilding effort in the postwar period.

Campaigning With Walsh

Even as guard units campaigned around the globe, back in Washington, D.C., other guardsmen waged what they saw as their own crucial and hard-fought campaign for the guard's postwar future. Their objective was to prevent the National Guard's enemies from using the war as a means either to abolish the guard or to bring it under the Regular Army's total control. For these guardsmen, the enemy was the traditional one: Regular Army officers like General McNair and their allies in the U.S. Army Reserve. The friendly forces were the National Guard Association and its supporters in Congress.

Guardsmen found much to worry about when considering the postwar future of their institution. There was, for example, the precedent of World War I. After that war, the War Department had attempted to do away with the guard and replace it with the Uptonian dream of a single federal reserve force based on universal military training.[3] Many guardsmen believed the relief of guard senior officers and the reorganization of guard units in 1940–41 had been part of a conspiracy by regulars to weaken the guard and to deny guardsmen the power and prestige of senior positions. The continuing hostility and condescension from regulars that many guardsmen encountered in federal service was another major source of irritation. Finally, the guard's advocate on the army General Staff, the National Guard Bureau, suffered a dramatic decline in its influence when the chief of staff, Gen. George C. Marshall, reorganized the General Staff in early 1942.

The National Guard Association, a private organization representing guard officers, quickly stepped in on the guard's behalf. In January, 1942, George E. Lynch, mayor of Minneapolis and vice president of the NGA, wrote to Marshall and asked that a committee of guard, regular, and reserve officers be appointed to study the question of how to organize the postwar army. However, the NGA made little progress in shaping the postwar army until 1944, when several developments came together.

First, Maj. Gen. Ellard A. Walsh, Minnesota's adjutant general, became president of the NGA in 1943. Born in 1887, Walsh joined the Minnesota National Guard in 1905. Commissioned during World War I, Walsh served thirteen months overseas. After returning home, he was appointed assistant adjutant general of Minnesota in 1921, and in 1927 he became adjutant general. Walsh took command of the 34th Division in 1940 and was called into federal service the following year, but health problems forced him to give up command before Pearl Harbor. He returned to Minnesota and again became the adjutant general.

Walsh watched the use of the guard in the war effort and became increasingly concerned about its treatment by the Regular Army. He invigorated the NGA with his energy and determination to protect the guard from what were, in his opinion, the General Staff's efforts to destroy it. Walsh set out to rally the NGA to what he saw as a struggle to save the guard.[4]

A skilled political and bureaucratic operator, Walsh exploited the NGA's considerable support in Congress. This support rested on certain characteristics of the guard. Many communities had strong emotional ties to their guard units, which had become, particularly in small towns, major local institutions. This made issues affecting the guard matters of concern to politicians. The involvement of guard officers in state politics reinforced this concern at the state level. This provided the foundation upon which rested the NGA's influence with Congress. That a number of members of both houses had been guard officers also helped the NGA when it came to Capitol Hill. This influence allowed Walsh to inform the War Department in 1944 that Congress would not look favorably upon any effort to shape the postwar army without first consulting the NGB and the NGA.

Finally, the guard received important, if unexpected, support from Brig. Gen. John McAuley Palmer. Marshall had called his close friend Palmer out of retirement to advise the army staff on the direction the postwar army should take. Palmer had long been an advocate of a small standing force, backed up with a very large reserve of citizen soldiers produced by a system of universal military training. His ideas greatly influenced the army's post–World War I reorganization plan, although Congress never provided the funds to implement it. In 1944, Palmer wrote and Marshall signed War Department Circular 347. This document argued that a small regular force, backed up with a large reserve produced by universal military training, should form the basis for planning the postwar army. However, in a reversal of Palmer's earlier views, the circular stated that the reserve force should consist of organized units ready for use rather than individuals who would be called up to augment Regular Army units.

War Department Circular 347 did not mention specifically the National Guard. It did, however, give the NGA a much firmer footing upon which to base its claims for continuing the guard's role as the army's first-line reserve combat component. The bureaucratic struggle ended in early 1945 with a victory for the NGA. A joint Regular Army–National Guard committee established the year before reported that the guard should be an "integral" part of the postwar military. Furthermore, it reported that the guard's postwar strength should be based on the army's M (Mobilization)-Day requirements. Finally, the committee concluded that the National Guard Bureau should be returned to its prewar position as a special staff agency.

In mid-1945, Marshall merged the joint guard-regular committee with a similar committee working on the postwar reserve. To reassure Walsh and the NGA, Marshall appointed as committee chairman Maj. Gen. Milton A. Reckord, a Maryland guardsman then serving as provost marshal of the European theater of operations. Born in rural Maryland in 1879, Reckord enlisted in the guard in 1901. A guard major by 1917, Reckord returned home in 1919 as a decorated colonel after commanding his regiment in combat. That same year he became Maryland's adjutant general. Because of his proximity to Washington and connections made during World War I, Reckord became the NGA's primary lobbyist. He soon was the man to see in Washington about guard matters, and he wrote most of the interwar legislation dealing with the guard. In 1940, Reckord entered federal service as commander of the 29th Division, which he had led since 1934. However, General McNair evaluated Reckord as a "good administrator, but should go." And go Reckord did, relieved of command in January, 1942, and assigned to a series of administrative posts before Marshall selected him to head the postwar reserve committee.[5]

It thus was no surprise that in October, 1945, Reckord's committee reaffirmed the earlier findings of the guard-regular committee. It based its findings on two assumptions: that large numbers of World War II veterans would join the guard, and that all postwar guard recruits would be graduates of a universal military training (UMT) system. The General Staff agreed to these findings because it concluded the NGA's support in Congress was too strong for it to overcome. Also, General Staff officers believed that any guard based on these findings would be dependent on UMT, thus ensuring the guard's support in trying to get congressional approval of UMT.[6]

How Big a National Guard?

As army chief of staff, George C. Marshall advocated a small (330,000) postwar Regular Army training large numbers of UMT draftees who would then fill guard units and the reserve. Marshall based this plan on the assumption that the nation would have up to a year's warning to fully mobilize. When Gen. Dwight D. Eisenhower succeeded Marshall as chief of staff in November, 1945, plans for the postwar army changed. Eisenhower believed the next war would be another total war lasting up to five years, and that the nation would have little time to mobilize before hostilities began.

These assumptions meant that the army would face two difficult tasks: be prepared to field a significant force quickly, and be prepared for a lengthy conflict requiring a mobilization on the same scale as World War II. These tasks would require a much larger army than the one Marshall envisioned. Eisenhower wanted an army that could put into the field 27 2/3 divisions, with supporting units, within thirty days of M-Day—a mission that would depend heavily on guard and reserve units being able to deploy quickly. Furthermore, while fielding this force, the army had to retain the capability of significant further expansion as the war continued.

To meet these objectives, the postwar army plan approved in September, 1946, called for a Regular Army of 1.121 million men in ten divisions and seventy air groups, and assumed that UMT would begin in 1948 and overseas occupation duties would end by 1951. The plan envisioned a National Guard of 680,000 men providing the army's first-line combat reserve force. This force, more than twice as large as the one mobilized in 1940–41, would be composed of twenty-five infantry divisions, two armored divisions, twenty-one regimental combat teams, hundreds of nondivisional combat and support units, and twenty-seven air groups. This ambitious plan, with its increased size and responsibility, reaffirmed for guardsmen their belief in the guard's importance to national defense.[7]

Over the next few years the guard reinforced its success in shaping the postwar reorganization plan with other bureaucratic and political victories. Again, its success rested in large part on its influence with Congress as expressed through the NGA. In 1947, Congress funded a major three-year public relations effort by the guard at a cost of $1 million a year. Also in that year, the NGA made sure the National Security Act, which created a separate air force, contained language insuring that the air force would have to administer the new Air National Guard through the National Guard Bureau.

The following year saw continued triumphs. Congress established retirement benefits for guard officers. When Congress approved resumption of conscription, though not in the form of UMT, the guard benefited; the NGA made sure that inserted into the Selective Service Act was a provision providing an exemption from the draft for seventeen to eighteen-and-a-half year olds who enlisted in the guard. Also in 1948, a special DOD committee on reserve policy, the Gray Board, recommended that the guard and reserve be merged into a single force. Walsh, Reckord, and the NGA mobilized for what they called "the Battle of Washington," a battle they considered so crucial that they ostracized one of the guard's greatest officers, Lt. Gen. Raymond S. McLain. One of two prewar guard general officers given a postwar commission in the Regular Army, McLain had served on the Gray Board and approved its recommendations concerning the guard. However, the threat of the NGA's influence with Congress prevented the DOD from implementing the board's recommendations.[8]

Chief of the "New Minutemen"

The postwar blueprint for the guard was impressive and ambitious, and would require an impressive and ambitious level of funding and skill to implement. Generals Walsh and Reckord, as officials of the NGA, could lobby for and promote the guard's interests. However, their public, official power was limited to their roles as adjutants general of Minnesota and Maryland. Responsibility for building the postwar guard fell upon the National Guard Bureau. A special staff agency of the General Staff, the

NGB acted as the army's supervisor of the various state guard organizations and as the guard's advocate on the General Staff. While the NGB's staff was a mix of guardsmen on extended active duty tours and regulars, the chief's position was reserved for a senior guardsman. Major General Butler B. Miltonberger held that post in 1946, but he was forced to retire the following year because of poor health.

Connecticut's Maj. Gen. Kenneth F. Cramer, commander of the 43d Infantry Division—which had units in Connecticut, Rhode Island, and Vermont—replaced Miltonberger in September, 1947. Cramer's National Guard experience differed significantly from that of generals like Walsh and Reckord. Born in 1894, Cramer received his bachelor's and master's degrees from Princeton. He enlisted in the army in 1917, earned a commission, and served with a draftee division in France. After leaving active duty in 1919, he founded a coal company in Hartford, joined the Organized Reserve Corps (ORC), and served twice in the state House of Representatives and twice in the state Senate. Cramer left the ORC in 1931 and joined the Connecticut National Guard, where by 1941 he commanded an infantry regiment. Cramer had a much more professionally satisfying time in World War II than did Reckord or Walsh. Promoted to brigadier general in 1942, he spent most of the war in the Pacific as assistant commander of the 24th Infantry Division, a Regular Army division, and emerged with a reputation as a tough disciplinarian and a "frontline" general. Cramer left federal service and returned to Connecticut in 1946, where he was promoted to major general and given command of the 43d Infantry Division.

Cramer's scrappy character, reflected in his wartime reputation and three Silver Stars, did not make him a subtle or patient chief of the NGB. His final efficiency report praised his "high integrity and moral courage" and his "high professional competence," but noted that his "inflexible adherence to his own views" detracted from "that maturity of judgment" expected of an officer of his rank and experience. These qualities were most noticeable in Cramer's determination to safeguard what he saw as the proper sphere of the NGB's interests. In 1949 he embarrassed Walsh and the NGA by engaging in a public feud with the air force over control of the Air National Guard. On other occasions, Cramer and the NGA disagreed on issues because of his and Walsh's different backgrounds. Cramer, who did not spend his formative years as an officer in the guard, focused on preparing the guard for M-Day, including the 43d Infantry Division, which he continued to command while serving as chief of the NGB. If that meant sacrificing some power or control to the Regular Army to achieve that goal, Cramer would not reflexively oppose doing so. This was not so for Walsh, who saw himself and the NGA as standing firm against the efforts of Uptonian regulars to destroy the guard. As with the rest of the army staff, the NGA's political clout usually made it the winner in any disputes with the NGB and its chief.[9]

As army chief of staff, General Eisenhower had supported Cramer's appointment. Cramer brought a drive and determination to the post that Eisenhower believed vital to the success of the army's ambitious plans for the postwar guard. Although Cramer was often difficult to get along with, he enthusiastically supported the postwar guard's role. Soon after taking over, he published a series of articles outlining the guard's expanded role in national defense, all stressing the idea of the guard as "Our Modern Minutemen."[10] Cramer linked the colonial militiaman with his 1940s descendant when he wrote, "the United States is indeed fortunate that succeeding generations have followed the traditional concept of national defense." He claimed that with the "volunteer spirit, local leadership, and the guardsman's sure knowledge that he fights for his own home and family," it was "obvious that America has the essentials of an indomitable defense."[11]

"Bring Back Our Old Company K"

The first task in building the postwar National Guard was assigning units to the states. This was a cooperative process involving the NGB and the states that was largely completed by 1947. The NGB staff analyzed the force structure established for the guard in Army Mobilization Plan I (AMP I) and how many and what types of units each state could support. It then would offer units to the states, which could either accept or reject them, based on what the states needed and thought they could support. This process continued until all the units called for by AMP I had been assigned.[12]

Assigning units to the states often involved the NGB in negotiations with state adjutants general. The strong ties that linked company-sized units with their communities, and sometimes an entire division with a state, meant state officials often found themselves under pressure to return units to their prewar location. Complicating this process were other factors. The much larger postwar guard required many more units than did the 1940 guard. Population distribution had shifted during the war, often changing an area's ability to support a unit. Changes in army doctrine and tactical organization also affected the process. The changes eliminated the need for some units, such as horse cavalry and coast artillery, and increased the need for others, such as tanks and antiaircraft artillery. Other prewar units, which in 1940 had been part of larger units, now found themselves operating as independent units.

The NGB and the states dealt with these considerations in a number of ways. Infantry divisions traditionally associated with one large and politically influential state, such as Texas' 36th, Ohio's 37th, and Pennsylvania's 28th, retained their prewar connections. Other divisions that before the war had connections to several states were given new homes.[13] Some separate companies, battalions, and regiments were simply converted to another type of unit needed under AMP I.[14] Also a problem was the need to activate units that had not existed in the prewar guard. Often, the solution was to redesignate units. Parts of several large new units, such as divisions and regimental combat teams, thus were drawn from prewar organizations.[15] However, smaller new postwar units, particularly support units, often had no formal links to the prewar guard.

Once a state accepted units from the NGB, the adjutant general had to assign subunits to communities within the state. This often resulted in another round of negotiations, this time between the adjutant general and communities. Many communities felt a strong attachment to "their" longtime company, battery, or troop affiliations and resented any changes. This process often required much time and discussion until both the communities' demands and the demands of the state's assigned troop list were satisfied or at least reconciled.[16]

A major problem for both the National Guard Bureau and some states in developing the new troop lists was the question of what to do with African American guardsmen. African American guardsmen and the communities from which they were drawn also felt deep attachments to "their" unit. Three segregated guard regiments had been mobilized during World War II, but in keeping with the Regular Army's conventional wisdom about African Americans' abilities, no black unit larger than a battalion was established in the postwar guard, although battalions of each regiment were used to form new units. In addition, the postwar atmosphere of heightened civil rights activism placed the NGB and the states under increasing pressure to desegregate the guard. This pressure only intensified with Pres. Harry S. Truman's 1948 executive order calling for an end to segregation in the armed forces. The NGB's policy in this period was that of the Regular Army, which moved with glacial speed to comply with Truman's order. Given the NGB's attitude, and without pressure to integrate coming from higher echelons, the issue defaulted to the state level. Some black units served within larger guard formations, such as the 137th Antiaircraft Artillery Battalion of Ohio's 37th Infantry Division.[17] A few northern states began the process of desegregating their forces, but by 1950 there were few integrated units. Most African American guardsmen, about 2 percent of the force in 1950, served in segregated battalions and companies, limited to fourteen states and the District of Columbia.[18]

"Not Ordinary Men"

Once a state adjutant general and the NGB had agreed on the assignment of units, their next task was recruiting men to fill them. Particularly important was the selection of commanding officers, since they would bear the main burden of building the unit. The Regular Army before and during the war had often complained about the uneven quality of the guard's officer corps. Guard officers, proven in battle, also warned of this problem in 1945. General Beightler, the most successful guard division commander of the war, wrote, "I have seen too many officers given advancement in rank simply because they were friends or favorites of the regimental commander or the Adjutant General of the state."[19]

Sometimes the senior guard officers still with a unit began the selection of officers between the end of the war and the unit's demobilization. However, given the high levels of guard personnel turbulence most units experienced, this process usually did not begin until the unit colors returned to the state. Then the adjutant general and other senior officers in the state would ask officers to take command of units. Political considerations also contributed to this process, particularly in regard to command of the largest units (divisions, brigades, and regiments) in a state. In some cases, officers would lobby for positions, particularly if they had served with a unit before or during the war. Often, the new commanders, particularly of larger units, would personally recruit officers for key command and staff positions. Routine assignment procedures were followed when filling other officer billets, especially company grade ones.[20]

Company commanders were especially important, as they led the recruiting effort. Selecting a man whose community respected him and who had regular contact with young men was crucial to bringing in recruits. Guard senior officers especially liked having teachers and coaches as junior officers. Robert Stockton enlisted in the 45th Infantry Division's band in 1949 at age seventeen. His high school band director was the warrant officer in command of the band. Marine Corps lieutenant LaVern Weber returned home to become a high school teacher and Marine reservist. An Oklahoma guard general officer visited Weber twice in 1948, trying to get him to take command of a company that had failed its second annual inspection. Despite Weber's protests of "I'm a Marine," he finally capitulated and took command of the company.[21]

By 1950, the guard contained a mix of three different generations of officers. The first came of age shortly before or during World War I. This generation dominated the general officer ranks and filled many of the colonel slots. A number of senior officers had served with guard units during the Mexican border campaign and World War I. Almost all had continued to serve with the guard during the interwar years. They had witnessed what they saw as the shabby treatment of their seniors by regulars in 1917–18 and the efforts to destroy the guard after that war. Their dislike of the regulars was further inflamed by what they saw as continued discrimination during World War II. Given other characteristics these men shared—small town or rural background, politically conservative, and significant involvement in state politics—they tended to be predisposed to distrust the federal government in any case. They also tended to be middle class professionals or businessmen, for only with these civilian careers could they afford to concentrate on their "exclusive hobby." These officers usually had a significant emotional investment in the guard. The only major split within this group tended to be between those officers who had spent most of their careers with troop units (as did General Cramer) and those who had spent much of their careers with the state's adjutant general office (as did Generals Walsh and Reckord). The latter group tended to be the most vociferous in their defense of the guard against any perceived encroachment by regulars.[22]

The second generation came of age during World War II. This group of officers consisted of some colonels, the majority of the other field grades, and most of the company grades. During World War II, these officers had received much more on-the-job training and active duty experience than did the World War I generation. Guard senior officers vigorously recruited them, believing this experience would be crucial to the greatly expanded postwar guard's success. Unlike their seniors, members of this group had more diverse experiences and had three subdivisions: prewar members of the guard (either as officers or enlisted men), officers commissioned during the war, and wartime enlisted men who received postwar guard commissions.

Those who had served in the prewar guard, while not a majority of this generation, provided a strong bridge of continuity for guard traditions. Many of the higher-ranking members of this group had begun their guard careers in the late 1920s or early 1930s, and the resulting socializing process gave them much the same outlook about the guard as the World War I generation. These officers filled many of the key command and staff positions at regimental, group, and battalion levels.

Officers commissioned during World War II usually were graduated from one of the many wartime officer candidate schools. However, these officers often found themselves accepting guard commissions in an arm or service different from the one they had served in during the war. The most dramatic examples of this were former air and naval officers who became ground combat officers. This posed problems since few of these officers were able to attend active duty branch schools. They received most of the training in their new specialties on drill nights, at summer training camps, and by taking correspondence courses.

Many of these officers did not immediately join the guard after demobilization. Some remained in the inactive reserve, into which many wartime officers had been demobilized, or the active reserve for two or three years before joining the guard. These officers joined the guard for a number of reasons: an interest in things military sparked by the war, Cold War tensions, pay and benefits, and social status—a most powerful motivation in small towns. Because of their lack of prior guard experience, the World War I generation often suspected these officers' commitment to the guard as a historic and crucial American institution.

Enlisted veterans who received commissions in the postwar guard were the last group of the World War II generation. These men usually enlisted in the postwar guard and, after completing a course of study and appearing before an examination board, were granted commissions. They shared many of the same characteristics as officers commissioned during World War II, including often finding themselves in a branch different from the one in which they had previously served. In addition, they often had to learn how to be effective leaders and trainers—roles their wartime experience usually had not included.

Likewise lacking experience as troop leaders and trainers was the third generation of guard officers: men who had been too young for World War II service. These men, the smallest of the three groups, usually became guard officers either by enlisting in the guard and following the same procedure as enlisted veterans, or by graduating from college with a Reserve Officer Training Corps (ROTC) commission. This group, with the exception of chaplains and doctors, filled lieutenants' billets, and few of them had attended their branch officer basic course before mobilization.[23]

Most units were unable to fill all of their company grade officer billets. To fill some of these vacancies, units alerted for mobilization during the Korean War gave commissions to a number of enlisted guardsmen—mostly World War II veterans. Other vacancies were filled by guard officers recalled from inactive status, or by reserve officers who resigned their federal commission for a commission in a guard unit, usually to escape involuntary recall and shipment to Korea as an individual replacement.[24]

Once the state adjutant general found officers for his units, the next step was filling the enlisted ranks. Enlisted personnel remained a source of concern for the guard throughout the 1945–50 period because of recruiting and retention problems. As with officers, enlisted men fell into one of three generations: prewar guardsmen, World War II veterans, and those too young for service in the war. Overall, by 1950 youth dominated the guard's enlisted ranks: 25.8 percent were age 17–19, and 50.4 percent were age 20–25.[25]

Not many prewar enlisted guardsmen returned to the guard's enlisted ranks after the war. Many had been killed or disabled. Some had failed to perform during the war and were not welcomed back. Others either had grown tired of military life or had found a new calling and enlisted in the Regular Army. A number of them received commissions during the war. Those enlisted men who did return to the guard were welcomed for their experience and commitment. Although they remained a small part of the force, they often recruited family members to join their units.

Guard leaders sought World War II veterans to serve as noncommissioned officers (NCOs), the backbone of the enlisted force. These men possessed the needed maturity and experience and also could quickly form the cadres required to train the large number of young nonveterans the guard recruited. In many units, up to 25 percent of the enlisted men were veterans, and they dominated the NCO ranks.

The majority of enlisted guardsmen by 1950 came from the postwar generation, men too young for service during World War II. They joined for a variety of reasons: adolescent fascination with things military, to learn a skill, the pay, the fellowship, and patriotism. In 1948, the draft became another motive because it exempted young men from active duty service if they enlisted in a guard unit before they were eighteen and a half. (The army did not require non–prior service guard recruits to attend active duty training until after the Korean War.)

While this generation often brought great enthusiasm to their units, they were also a source of many difficulties. Because they lacked prior service, they required extensive training. Many left units before their enlistments expired as college, jobs, families, or enlistment in the Regular Army pulled them away. This resulted in significant personnel turbulence in many units. Some young enlistees were underage and thus nondeployable if mobilized. Finally, many from the World War I generation suspected that these youngsters did not share their dedication to the institution.[26]

The National Guard Bureau under General Cramer made recruitment one of its top priorities between 1947 and 1950. The guard's success at this forced the states in early 1950 to limit recruiting to replacing losses when the guard reached its budgetary strength ceiling of 350,000.[27] The NGB used the $1 million a year authorized by Congress in 1947 to mount a sophisticated effort to convince Americans that the "The New National Guard" was "giving the nation 'the thing that counts!'"[28]

The NGB combined a national campaign with efforts by state officials and unit leaders that took advantage of the guard's strong local ties. At the national level, the NGB hired an advertising firm and orchestrated publicity campaigns that used mass-market magazines and sponsorship of radio programs. The bureau also sought to build bridges to other groups in American society in the hopes that they could help spread the word about the guard. This effort included educators, businessmen, labor unions, and clergy, and yielded valuable endorsements, publicity, and collateral advertising.[29]

The most significant single recruiting period was between August, 1947, and August, 1948. During that time, the guard's strength rose from 96,815 to 309,322. "Operation 88,888" conducted from September to November,

1947, became the high point of this period. Designed to add 88,888 men to the guard and raise the public's awareness, it began on 16 September with the proclamation of "National Guard Day" by President Truman, himself a former guardsman. The campaign, which integrated a national print and radio advertising effort with the activities of local units, brought in 81,648 recruits.[30]

The guard stressed several themes in its recruiting campaigns. Trying to downplay bad publicity generated during the 1940–41 mobilization, the guard stressed that it was now a "new" organization, with plenty of up-to-date equipment and methods. In the atmosphere of a deepening Cold War, the guard noted that in "this era of world uncertainties, peace cannot be governed by wishful thinking." Guard ads proclaimed that "The basic insurance against future war is national preparedness," and the "new" National Guard had a vital role in maintaining that preparedness.

The ads told potential recruits they could learn new skills that would be useful for the nation and for their own improvement. "Members of the National Guard are not ordinary men," said a message from Dwight Eisenhower, and ads stressed the fellowship one could find in such company. Not neglecting its dual nature, the guard also stressed its status as a "federally supervised" state institution that played an important role in communities. Drawing on its militia roots, which extended back more than three hundred years, and the strong guard traditions existing in many communities, ads pointed out the continuity across generations and the glorious heritage created by past members. Finally, the guard stressed the practical benefits of pay and retirement benefits. While the ads did not openly state that guard service was a way to avoid the draft, the guard did appeal to young men to serve with buddies or neighbors, with the implication clearly being that they would not have to serve with strange draftees in far away places for two years.[31]

"Giving the nation 'the thing that counts!'"

With units assigned to the states and soldiers recruited, the next priority was training. The National Guard Bureau originally had developed a six-year program for preparing units for M-Day. However, in 1948 the NGB replaced this with a three-year plan, keyed to the three-year enlistment of soldiers and focused on the essential items required to make units as ready as possible for M-Day—a day many thought was closer than ever thanks to the growing Cold War tensions. Recruits would learn basic soldier skills during their first year of service, begin specialist training in their second, and master advanced skills in the final year of their enlistment. This change placed a heavy burden on units by forcing them to run a number of different classes during each drill period for the different skill levels within the unit. The personnel turbulence within many units, particularly among young enlistees, caused further problems in training management. This was particularly troubling since the plan rested on the assumption that there would be little turnover. An Army Field Forces (AFF) report in early 1950 noted that with this turnover, "it is doubtful if the training and overall efficiency of the Guard will ever reach its desired standards." The new three-year plan also meant that the only time many units could do collective training was during their two-week summer camp.[32]

Guard units faced additional difficulties in conducting effective training. They depended on the Regular Army to assign officers and sergeants as instructors to guard units. These instructors helped plan and present training, advised guardsmen, and inspected to insure that units met the standards required for federal recognition and thus federal funding. However, Truman administration budget cuts left the Regular Army far under the strength planned for it in 1946 and badly overcommitted. As a result, many guard instructor slots remained unfilled and reserve officers on extended active duty tours filled others. In addition, guard instructor duty was not considered a career-enhancing assignment. Thus, many instructors were men an already shorthanded army felt it could spare from other duties. Moreover, even competent, motivated instructors often had difficulty making the cultural transition from serving with regulars to serving with guardsmen.[33]

The guard also suffered from inadequate armories. Construction and maintenance of armories was a state responsibility. When units returned from World War II, they often found their armories taken over for other purposes. With the great expansion of the guard after the war and major changes in weapons and equipment from prewar organization, even units that reclaimed their armories often found them inadequate for the "new" guard. An extreme example of this problem occurred in Hastings, Nebraska. The rifle company commander there received his unit's full load of equipment shortly after federal recognition. Unfortunately, the company's armory at the time was a barn leased from the county. Until more satisfactory storage could be arranged, the commander kept the equipment on the unit's cargo trucks at his home, which ruined his driveway.[34]

The guard could not find an answer to its greatest training problem, the lack of sufficient time. This had always been a major criticism of the guard, most recently by the 1948 Gray Board. Units trained for only ninety-six hours a year at home station and then spent two weeks each summer in field training. This schedule could not make units, particularly higher echelon staffs, ready on M-Day for the stressful demands of modern combat operations, no matter how often the guard was extolled as the "new Minutemen."[35]

Shortages of equipment further aggravated shortages of time. The stockpiles of World War II equipment and the small procurement budgets of the Truman years did not allow the army to purchase much new equipment. What equipment it did have was, like its manpower, stretched thin. While guardsmen did not usually suffer a shortage of individual equipment, their units often lacked a complete allotment of major items like heavy weapons, electronics gear, and vehicles. In 1950, Pennsylvania's 628th Tank Battalion had only fifteen of twenty-two tanks authorized for each of its three companies. Most firing batteries in the 28th Division Artillery fielded only four of six authorized howitzers. The 121st Transportation Truck Company had only two of fifty-six authorized trucks. Shortages affected training, which in turn meant that units were not fully prepared for M-Day.[36]

The Limits of Influence

Despite the National Guard Association's influence, neither President Truman nor the Congress ever authorized enough money to fully fund the ambitious plan of a 680,000-man guard. While the guard was cheaper to maintain than an equivalent force of regulars, it was still beyond the pale for a president and Congress determined to keep the military on a very lean diet. By June, 1950, the Congress had appropriated only enough funds for an Army National Guard of 324,761 officers and men.

This ceiling did not allow units to be manned at their full wartime strength. To become combat ready, they would have to spend time after mobilization absorbing filler personnel and would have to receive large shipments of equipment. The guard and the Regular Army both understood this situation, and made plans for postmobilization expansion of guard units to full strength, followed by a training program to prepare units for deployment. However, this situation did not provide the Regular Army with a combat-ready force it could tap on or shortly after M-Day, nor did it fit with the image the guard had projected since 1945 as the "new Minutemen."[37]

CHAPTER 2

Limited Mobilization during a Limited War

When M-Day arrived in July, 1950, there were significant differences between what planners had expected to happen and what actually happened. The army called on the guard not for World War III with the Soviet Union, but for a limited war in defense of a nation most guardsmen probably could not point to on a map. The army did not call out the entire guard, but only a portion of it. And, with few exceptions, most units mobilized did not proceed quickly to the theater of operations. The first guard units to reach Korea, transportation truck companies, did not arrive until five months after M-Day. Instead, the army ordered guard units to posts across the nation for a lengthy training period in an atmosphere charged with rumors and uncertainty over their eventual use.

Unexpected War, Unexpected Demands

These developments flowed naturally from a set of interrelated factors: stopping the North Korean invasion of the South was not the type of war the army had been planning to fight, and the army's efforts to do so in the summer of 1950 proved embarrassingly more difficult and costly than its leaders had expected. The Regular Army's flaws and weaknesses, which left the service ill-prepared for war—even a limited war in Korea that fell short of the final showdown with the Soviet Union that had driven contingency planning in the postwar period—are well described elsewhere.[1]

In order to prevent Pusan from joining Dunkirk on the list of ignominious withdrawals from a continent, the army had to strip its General Reserve in the Zone of the Interior to send reinforcements and replacements to Eighth Army. Infantry divisions, field artillery and tank battalions, and separate service support companies were hastily prepared and shipped to Korea. At posts and stations across the nation, individuals received orders to ship out as replacements for Eighth Army's growing number of casualties. By early August, the cupboard in the ZI, not very full to begin with, was nearly bare.[2]

The stripping of the General Reserve affected the guard's mobilization in several ways. First, it meant that the army ordered many more guard units to active duty than could be prepared for combat and transported to Korea in time to influence the course of events during the remainder of 1950. These units were needed instead to reconstitute the General Reserve, which had to be rebuilt in case the Soviets, as many feared, used Kim Il Sung's reunification drive as a cover for mischief elsewhere in the world. This fear also led the army to mobilize large numbers of guard antiaircraft artillery (AAA) units to build up the nearly nonexistent air defenses of the ZI.[3]

Second, tight budgets had left Eighth Army without many of the nondivisional combat and support units called for by army doctrine and which were sorely missed during the early fighting in Korea. The small prewar General Reserve, also affected by the same tight budgets, had run short of these types of units before filling Eighth Army's needs. As a result, guard units would have to be deployed to Korea as fast as possible.

Third, the use of so much of the General Reserve's trained manpower in Korea meant the army would find it exceedingly difficult to expand its relatively small training base to meet the demands of mobilization. Thus, those guard units not designated during the autumn of 1950 for deployment to Korea received mostly untrained draftees for enlisted fillers, creating a very heavy load on these units' already overstretched trained, experienced personnel.

Struggling to keep Eighth Army supplied with men and material, the army staff made another decision that had a significant effect on the guard's mobilization during 1950. Casualties in Korea soon outpaced the Regular Army's ability to provide trained replacements. The army turned to the volunteer and the inactive components of the reserve to provide quickly the thousands of trained, experienced officers and enlisted men Eighth Army needed. Unfortunately, army mobilization planning had designated many of these reservists to fill key vacancies in guard units ordered to active duty. As a result, most mobilized guard units would experience shortages of junior officers and qualified technical specialists during their first year of active duty because they did not receive the expected number of reservists.[4]

As the situation in Korea worsened during July, senior army leaders in Washington debated what the guard's role would be in this unexpected conflict. The Selective Service Extension Act, passed at the end of June, had given the president the authority to order to active duty for a period not to exceed twenty-one months whatever portions of the various civilian components he believed were needed to deal with the emergency.[5]

There was, however, an initial hesitation among senior army leaders, especially the chief of staff, Gen. J. Lawton Collins, to mobilize guard units. The hesitation arose from worry over the economic and political repercussions of ordering large numbers of guardsmen to active duty; concerns that the already overtaxed army could not supply the equipment, fillers, and training sites needed by guard units to make them combat ready; uncertainty over whether guard units could be ready in time to influence the course of events in Korea; and fears that guard units deployed to Korea would not be available for use elsewhere if the conflict escalated into a global confrontation.

By mid-July army leaders came to the conclusion that at least a portion of the guard would have to be ordered into federal service, a decision based on the continuing bad news from Korea, together with the realization that stripping the General Reserve had left the army with little ability to respond to some other crisis, and that there was no effective AAA defense of the United States if the crisis became a third world war.[6]

To address this last concern, AAA units dominated the first two increments of guard units alerted for mobilization on 22 and 23 July. Army Field Forces recommended guard units for active duty based on estimates of units' training and leadership and their equipment status. Thus the army, over the National Guard Bureau's objections, did not maintain the command relationships between guard AAA groups, brigades, battalions, and detachments. Instead, higher-ranked battalions and detachments were sent them to various training sites where mobilized group and brigade headquarters batteries took command of gun battalions, operations detachments, and radar maintenance units they had never worked with before.[7]

Two other groups of guard nondivisional units were alerted for mobilization in July. One was of types needed in Korea that the General Reserve had run out of before filling Eighth Army's requests. The other was of types needed to help in rebuilding the depleted General Reserve. These units included field artillery battalions, maintenance companies, truck companies, engineer battalions, signal battalions, and several different types of battalion and group headquarters detachments and companies. By the end of the month, a total of sixteen battalions, twenty-five separate companies, and eleven battalion and group headquarters detachments had been alerted for active duty service. These were joined in three more increments during early August by a further twenty-nine battalions, thirty-three separate companies, and eighteen headquarters detachments, companies, and batteries. The army also increased the number of mobilized guard AAA units, adding a further two gun battalions, three headquarters batteries, and six operations detachments.[8]

Whether or not to deploy guard nondivisional units to Korea remained uncertain for several months. Initially, the army G3 earmarked for service in Korea a number of units that entered active duty during August and September. These units were filled to full strength with reservists and a few regulars, and many went to training sites west of the Mississippi from which it would be easier to ship them to the Far East.

However, after the successful Inchon landing in September and invasion of North Korea in October, the army put on hold the decision to deploy guard units to the combat theater. Then, in early November, in order to improve Eighth Army's increasingly creaky logistical system as it advanced farther north, six truck companies and two truck battalion headquarters detachments received orders to sail. That same month, the Chinese launched a massive offensive that highlighted, among other problems, Eighth Army's shortage of crucial types of nondivisional units. As a result, the army G3 in December and early January issued movement orders for Korea to nine field artillery battalions, six combat engineer battalions, three bridge companies, one engineer group headquarters, three maintenance companies, one ordnance battalion headquarters, and one quartermaster group headquarters.[9]

The use of divisions was the thorniest decision concerning guard mobilization in the summer of 1950. Senior army leaders had doubts about the usefulness of guard divisions and the political and economic ramifications of mobilizing guard divisions. Mobilization of guard divisions would present the army, already straining to support the war in Korea, with some difficult problems in finding fillers and equipment to bring the divisions to full Table of Organization and Equipment (TO&E) strengths. In addition, mobilized guard divisions would not be ready for deployment in time to influence Eighth Army's immediate fate, and many regular officers still doubted the skills of senior guard commanders and staffs to competently operate a formation as large as a division in combat.

These divisions formed the core of the guard's twentieth century heritage. Guardsmen attached much emotion and symbolism to these formations, particularly the sensitive issue of how the Regular Army treated guard general and senior field grade officers. As the biggest guard units, their mobilization would generate the greatest fallout—particularly with divisions that drew all their members from just one state (like Oklahoma's 45th) and with divisions that were located in America's industrial heartland (like Pennsylvania's 28th, Illinois's 33d and Ohio's 37th). These political ramifications would escalate greatly if a guard division suffered casualties on the same scale as suffered by some regular divisions in Korea during July and August, 1950.[10]

In spite of these concerns, the empty General Reserve and fears of a possible wider war with the Soviets led the army staff to conclude that it would have to order some guard divisions into federal service. The question then became how many and which ones. After examining several proposals generated by the G3, the chief of staff on 31 July decided, and the Joint Chiefs of Staff (JCS) agreed, that four divisions and two separate regimental combat teams (RCT) should be ordered to active duty on 1 September. None were initially designated for use in Korea.[11]

The second question became much more complicated. Earlier in July, General Collins had ordered Army Field Forces to prepare recommendations on which guard divisions should be ordered into federal service. As was the case with smaller units called up in July and August, Army Field Forces ranked the guard divisions based on their equipment status and AFF's evaluations of their training status and the quality of their leadership. Using these criteria, AFF recommended, in order, the 28th Infantry (Pennsylvania); 29th Infantry (Virginia and Maryland); 31st Infantry (Mississippi and Alabama); 37th Infantry (Ohio); 45th Infantry (Oklahoma); and 50th Armored (New Jersey) Divisions.[12]

The army chief of staff believed that other criteria also had to be considered, including nearness to ports of embarkation for deployment overseas and geographical spread across the United States, so that one or several sections of the country did not bear a heavier burden than did others. The chief, Army Field Forces, Gen. Mark W. Clark, disagreed, arguing that the two key considerations in selecting divisions had to be their personnel strength and the quality of senior leaders. As a result, the only modification the army staff initially made to the AFF list was to substitute the 40th Infantry Division (California) for the 50th Armored Division in the belief that an armored division was unsuited to conditions in Korea.

General Collins, however, continued to insist on using more than just military effectiveness as the selection criteria. On 31 July, the chief of staff selected the 28th, the 40th, the 45th, and the 43d (Connecticut, Rhode Island, and Vermont) Infantry Divisions. Collins also picked two Regimental Combat Teams: the 196th (South Dakota) and the 278th (Tennessee). Alert orders went out to the state adjutants general, and the secretary of the army telephoned each of the governors in the affected states on 1 August.[13] A probable additional reason for selecting the 43d over Massachusetts's 26th for First Army's contribution was that mobilizing the 43d would get its commander, the prickly NGB chief, General Cramer, out of Washington.[14]

M-Day: The Reality

As senior army leaders pondered the role the guard would play in this unexpected war, and bad news continued to dominate reports from Korea, guardsmen across the country braced themselves for the call, some mocking recruiting slogans with a new version: "There's a Korea in the Army for You." Some units, especially during early July, believed that they would only be called if the crisis in Korea escalated into a global conflict. Other guardsmen were not so sure. Those at summer training watched for unusual activities, such as conspicuous visits by senior regular officers and extra attention from the AFF training inspection teams that visited summer training—clues that perhaps their unit was being considered for mobilization.

For many guardsmen, the distinct possibility of mobilization for a war that was not going well for the United States gave field training an urgency lacking in previous summers. A reporter at Indiantown Gap in early July found nondivisional units from Pennsylvania "grimly serious." When the 28th Infantry Division arrived at Indiantown Gap later that month for summer training, the division commander advised his soldiers "that we must lose no time in getting ourselves in the best possible state of readiness." In late July, on the eve of departure for summer training, the commander of Rhode Island's Battery C, 243d AAA Battalion, said that since the war began, there had been a "spirit of determination and seriousness in their weekly drills."[15]

Some guardsmen, mainly those boys and young men who had not served during World War II, looked forward to the adventure and excitement of active service. A first sergeant in the 163d Military Police (MP) Battalion told a reporter that his young soldiers "were full of ginger." A reporter visiting Battery D, 705th AAA Gun Battalion, noticed that "there's no hiding the eagerness" among the young soldiers in the battery. Their families did not usually share this eagerness, as they were fearful of sending their boys and young men off to war. The 43d Infantry Division, which was at summer camp when it received its alert notice, reported "many anxious calls" from the mothers of the division's large contingent of seventeen- and eighteen-year- old soldiers.[16]

The 45th Infantry Division had recruited heavily among high school boys, and most of the division's enlisted soldiers were either still in school or recent graduates. The *Daily Oklahoman* estimated that only 20–21 percent of the enlisted men were veterans of some type of military service during World War II. Oklahomans, particularly parents of these junior enlisted soldiers, could only grow more and more concerned during August as newspapers carried an increasing number of reports of Sooners serving in the Regular Army and the Marine Corps being killed, wounded, or missing in action. The paper did point out that about 60 percent of the enlisted men were veterans of at least one summer training camp and a year of armory drills, which did little to reassure those familiar with how much training could be accomplished in that amount of time.[17]

The *Daily Oklahoman* added that "many parents may be glad to know" that the 45th's staffs and commanders had "lots of service experience."[18] General Clark offered his own reassurance about the mobilized National Guard divisions: "We can shorten the length of training to five months instead of nine. It doesn't take long to make killers of them." From his position as a company commander, LaVern Weber was less sanguine. Mobilization "was a traumatic time for me because of the fact I had worked with the parents of the local community to recruit all of these youngsters into my unit and now I was taking them from their community, and from their homes and families, off to something."[19]

Also not looking forward to mobilization were the many World War II veterans in the guard. They watched the news reports from Korea and Washington with a mix of apprehension and resignation, wondering if their civilian lives, only recently reestablished, would again be disrupted by active duty. A *Daily Oklahoman* reporter and longtime guardsman told readers "You knew all the time world conditions might one day result in another spell of active army duty yet it's still somewhat a shock when it actually happens." A *Providence Journal* reporter found Battery C, 169th AAA (AW) Battalion's, veterans "in no hurry to see action again" and quoted a lieutenant in the 43d Infantry Division: "We all had a stomachfull of war last time. None of us want to go back in very much, but we know the country is in a bad spot and we are willing."

Some, like Maj. James Christie, the 51st AAA Brigade's radar officer, expected orders for active duty when he heard of the North Korean invasion and, while "not overly happy" when the orders did arrive, looked forward to the challenges of active service. Also reassuring for some veterans was the comfort of going with those that they knew. A sergeant first class in Oklahoma's 279th Infantry said: "[I]t's a job that has to be done. I'm not eager but I'm not going to twist anyone's arm to get out. I like the old outfit. There's still some of the old guys in it and I'd like to see a lot more of them."[20]

Meanwhile, the uncertainty of which units would be called to active duty generated discrimination against guardsmen during the summer and autumn of 1950, as some employers shied away from hiring men who might soon disappear into federal service. This problem with employers would continue to affect guardsmen remaining in state service through the end of 1951.[21]

Guardsmen who had come to distrust the Regular Army's use of guard units in federal service carefully watched the Regular Army's decisions concerning the guard's role in Korea, determined to prevent any efforts by the regulars to mistreat the guard—as they believed the army had done during the world wars. The major fears were that guard divisions would be broken up and their components scattered throughout the army; that senior guard officers would be replaced by Regular Army officers; and that the Regular Army would violate the guard's major selling point, "Go With

Those You Know," by stripping units of men and sending them as individual replacements to regular units. The friends and families of some guardsmen, particularly in New Mexico, also feared that their hometown unit would be destroyed in this new war as its predecessor had been during World War II.[22]

Oklahoma, which had invested substantial amounts of state pride in its 45th Infantry Division, saw a significant level of concern about active service. Local political leaders quickly intervened. Congressman Mike Moroney reported that "top Defense officials" had reassured him that "under no circumstances" would the 45th be broken up in this way. Despite the official reassurances gained by Oklahoma politicians, news in August of the 45th's selection for mobilization rekindled fears. A *Daily Oklahoman* editorial reviewed the proud history of the Oklahoma guard, with an emphasis on the mistreatment of guard units by the Regular Army while serving on active duty. The editorial observed that "many of the officers who recruit the guard and train it are not privileged to command its units in active service."[23]

Many state officials and many guardsmen—regardless of their age, experience, and enthusiasm about mobilization—expressed a great deal of pride in their units. The 715th Transportation Truck Company's commander proudly told a reporter in July that "they were ready to go." Governor James H. Duff said that the army's selection of the 28th Infantry Division was "the highest tribute that could be given the splendid leadership and caliber of the officers and men of our Keystone Division." A lieutenant in the 987th Armored Field Artillery Battalion who had served in the British army during World War II said of his outfit after it received orders for active duty, "there just aren't enough good adjectives to describe them." A corporal in the 705th AAA Gun Battalion boasted, "I've been in four different outfits, including 22 months in the ETO during the war, and this is the best yet."[24]

As more and more units received alert notices, state officials, particularly in industrial states, became increasingly concerned that the war would result in the complete mobilization of the National Guard, leaving them vulnerable to sabotage and civil disturbances. As Pennsylvania governor Duff put it: "the day-to-day news makes it clear that anything can happen. It also should be an additional incentive for communities throughout the Commonwealth to prepare themselves for internal security." In many states, officials began making plans to raise state guard units for internal security duties, as had been done during World War II.[25]

Failure to select a unit that believed it should have been selected could create hard feelings and generate a political squall. When the army chief of staff passed over the 31st Infantry Division, a Mississippian wrote his senator and complained that "in the minds of the public, the thought will lie forevermore that the four divisions called were the best four divisions—this being untrue and unfair to the name of the 31st."[26]

Generally, newspaper editorial opinion presented the partial mobilization of the guard as a necessary, if unwelcome, development in this odd war. The *Logan Herald-Journal* portrayed the departure of Utah's 204th Field Artillery (FA) Battalion for Fort Lewis, Washington, as part of "a great conflict today between the people who believe in Democracy and those who spread Communism all over the globe." One questioning voice came in a 30 July *Washington Post* analysis piece that charged that the guard was not ready on M-Day for combat operations, and that its units were "far under strength, ill-trained, partly equipped and, most important of all, unprepared morally for the task which confronts it now."[27]

However, much more common was a celebration of the guard's citizen-soldier tradition. Discussing the 378th Combat Engineer Battalion's imminent departure from North Carolina, the *Charlotte News* said that the battalion was "imbued with the high tradition of the National Guard established in four previous wars. They realize—as we all do—that the National Guard is an invaluable reservoir of strength to this nation in time of need." The *Raleigh News and Observer* pointed out that the mobilizing 449th FA Battalion's North Carolina guardsmen "once again join the ranks of civilians who have taken up arms in times of stress when freedom was threatened." The caretaker of Westerly, Rhode Island's, armory told a reporter: "this'll be the third outfit I've seen leave the armory. First the old 5th Company, then Battery E in '41 and now Battery D. The other two were corking outfits and this one can hold its own with either of them."[28]

Nondivisional guard units that shared their state with a division sometimes lost out in press coverage. In Rhode Island, mobilization orders arrived for the 705th AAA Gun Battalion and for the state's portion of the 43d Infantry Division (three battalions, four separate companies, and the Division Artillery headquarters). Between 21 July and 30 September there were thirteen articles about the 705th in the *Providence Journal* and fifty-two articles about the 43d; the newspaper even sent one of its reporters to Camp Pickett, Virginia, to see how the division was settling in at its training site. Wives of two 705th AAA soldiers wrote to the newspaper accusing it of bias in favor of the 43d. The second pleaded for "more news about the 705th. They're R.I. boys too." Saint Paul's 216th AAA Group headquarters had the misfortune to be mobilized just before Minnesota's 47th Infantry Division went off to summer training, and the *Saint Paul Dispatch* carried more stories on the summer training than on the 216th's preparations for active duty. New York City's 715th AAA Gun Battalion and 955th FA Battalion also suffered in press coverage compared to New York's 27th and 42d Infantry Divisions' summer camps. Coverage of the battalions by the *New York Times* consisted of one short notice, whereas the newspaper published five much longer articles on the divisions during August.[29]

In areas where local or state pride had been deeply invested in a guard unit there also was an element of chauvinism in coverage of the mobilization. Nowhere was this more evident than in Oklahomans' attitudes toward "their" 45th Infantry Division. The division commander on 1 August told Oklahomans, "there's a rich heritage in the Thunderbird history and, although it may be a dubious honor, it still is an honor to be considered one of the nation's best outfits." The Oklahoma Press Association launched a drive for contributions to a division welfare fund, reminding Oklahomans that "this outfit belongs to the whole state and we should show our appreciation for it. . . . No matter who comes in the division later it always will be the 45th from Oklahoma." To help maintain those ties between the division and the state, the *Daily Oklahoman* arranged for its daily and Sunday editions to be delivered to Camp Polk, Louisiana, and nearby towns.[30]

From Alert to Farewells

As the shock of receiving alert notices passed, guardsmen began the hard work of preparing their units for active duty. Army Field Forces in mid-August brought commanders and key staff officers of alerted divisions and RCTs to AFF headquarters for a conference outlining the plan for postmobilization training.[31] All alerted units had many tasks to accomplish in the thirty days allotted by AFF between alert and entry into federal service.

With all guard units understrength, one of the first and most pressing tasks was recruiting. With the alert notice came authorization for guard units to recruit to their full wartime TO&E strength. The states launched aggressive recruiting drives, reminiscent of the Operation 88,888 campaign in 1947. The theme also was reminiscent of the 1947 recruiting campaign, or, in the words of a *Providence Journal* editorial cartoon: "If You've Got To Go, Go With Friends!" Battery C, 705th AAA's, commander stressed that enlisting in his battery permitted "area men to train with their friends and other local enlistees. Members of the batteries will not be separated." Major General James Styron, commander of the 45th Infantry Division, told reporters: "Men who are subject to draft probably would rather be with other men they know, particularly those from their home town. We would rather have Oklahomans in the 45th because we know what they can do. There's a rich heritage in the Thunderbird history and, although it may be a dubious honor, it still is an honor to be considered one of the nation's best outfits.[32]

The success of these campaigns varied, with divisions benefiting the most because they could offer the widest variety of positions to potential recruits and because their greater visibility tended to monopolize the public's attention. Other units faced different problems. Despite the "handicap" of the Kansas State Fair, the 130th Field Artillery Group headquarters added thirty new recruits before induction.[33]

As in many other aspects of the postwar guard, Oklahoma's pride in its Thunderbirds led the state to outdo others. Across Oklahoma, newspapers, radio stations, and prominent citizens accepted the division's request to spread the word. Oklahoma Gas and Electric, with forty-three of its employees serving in the division, saluted the 45th and wished for them "a soldier's 'Best O' Luck' and an American hand shake on their new adventure." The new medium of television joined in, with WKY-TV airing a program combining a history of the 45th and interviews with current Thunderbirds.[34]

Across the state, the emphasis was on recruiting junior officers and enlisted men to go with those they knew. A major asset for this campaign was Lt. Col. Roy P. Stewart, the division's military government officer and a senior reporter for the *Daily Oklahoman.* Stewart's newspaper ran sixty-seven stories concerning the 45th between 2 and 31 August, and a large ad warned young men that this was "the best military opportunity you'll ever have—a chance to serve with your *hometown outfit, a combat organization that performed heroically on the battleground of World War II . . . a chance to serve with your* hometown friends and neighbors, to *train* with the people you've lived with all your life!"[35] (emphasis in original)

The "Go With The Men You Know" theme proved very appealing—

especially to those who had already received their draft notices. In early August, the Oklahoma Selective Service found forty-one men enlisted in the 45th who had not answered their draft calls. Some draft boards gave their local guard unit lists of those men most likely to be called up next. William Craig passed his physical in mid-July and returned home to await his notice to report for induction. However, after being "propositioned many times" by Thunderbird recruiters, Craig enlisted in the 179th Infantry after a friend joined the regiment. "I knew in my heart that I was violating the draft laws by enlisting, but the 45th Division recruiter, a silver-tongued devil, convinced me that it was completely legal."[36]

Along with recruiting new enlisted guardsmen, alerted units moved to fill key vacancies. One of the most important positions was the unit administrator, a warrant officer slot in each company or battery that rarely was filled while the unit was in state service. However, the great administrative demands of mobilization led many units to promote senior noncommissioned officers, often battery or company first sergeants, into this position.[37]

Many vacancies existed in battery and company officer positions. Many of these vacancies were filled by officers drawn from the inactive guard, by commissioning promising guard enlisted men (usually World War II veterans), by 1950 ROTC graduates, or by officers in the inactive reserve who wished to avoid going to Korea as individual replacements. The 28th Infantry Division's reconnaissance company, a descendant of Philadelphia's elite City Troop, provided twelve new officers to various units of the division. The 45th Infantry Division's 180th Infantry Regiment received twenty officers commissioned after the alert notice arrived, while the division's 158th FA Battalion received six. New York's 715th AAA Gun Battalion commissioned two officers after the alert and received five officers from the inactive guard.[38] Oklahoman Charles Rice had served in Europe with the 69th Infantry Division's reconnaissance troop. After the war he attended college and was commissioned in the Organized Reserve Corps. Going to Korea as an individual replacement, Rice decided, "wasn't for me. . . . I did not want to go as a replacement, I wanted to go with a unit." He called the division reconnaissance company's commander and asked if the unit could use another lieutenant. The company could, and Rice quickly obtained a guard commission.[39]

In addition to commissioning new officers, a number of guard units promoted some of their officers and enlisted to the next higher grade after receiving their alert notices. This was easier to accomplish while still in state service because once they were on active duty, they would be governed by the Regular Army's more stringent promotion policies. However, some regulars believed this hurt units by elevating some guardsmen above their level of competence.[40]

Some recruiting campaigns were quite successful. The 45th Infantry Division enlisted 2,321 men. The other divisions and the two RCTs did not match Oklahoma's turnout, but they did bring in significant numbers of recruits. Nondivisional units usually measured their recruiting success in the tens, although some small units added significant numbers. However, with the exception of Alabama's 107th Transportation Truck Company, no guard unit examined was able to reach full TO&E strength before departing its home state. All needed additional officer and enlisted fillers to become combat ready.[41]

One reason that these recruiting campaigns did not significantly increase unit strength before induction was that the mobilization process both subtracted and added guardsmen. As a result, the gains in new personnel achieved by the four divisions and two RCTs were canceled out by losses. The six units added a total of 6,458 new personnel after the alert notice, but lost 6,210 guardsmen during the same period. Nondivisional units suffered from the same phenomenon, but on a smaller scale.[42]

A major source of personnel losses during mobilization was the guard's success after 1945 in recruiting among boys, especially in rural and small-town America, where the local guard unit often was one of the main social centers in a community. Army regulations prohibited calling anyone younger than seventeen to active duty. Once again, the 45th Infantry Division led the way, discharging 1,218 underage boys (16 percent of its enlisted strength). California's 40th Infantry Division was a close second with 1,114 (12.7 percent of enlisted strength). The 45th suffered an additional loss when Gov. Roy Turner announced that he would offer discharges to boys under eighteen who wanted to finish high school; 565 accepted the offer. Together, these two sources cost the Thunderbird division 23 percent of its 1 August enlisted strength.[43]

Another reason many guardsmen did not enter active duty was failure to pass the induction physical. Army regulations required a physical examination by an army doctor to certify that a guardsman was fit for service. Among the divisions and RCTs, the 28th Infantry Division suffered the greatest losses from induction physicals, with 673 guardsmen failing the exam (6.7 percent of total strength). The next highest attrition rate was in the 43d Infantry Division, with 505 (6 percent) failing the exam.[44]

Trying to arrange these exams consumed a great deal of time and effort after alert notices were received, as most military districts did not have enough doctors on hand to smoothly process units through this phase of mobilization. The Regular Army's response was to use doctors stationed at active military installations and to order reserve doctors to serve short active duty tours. Nevertheless, conducting tens of thousands of physical exams significantly slowed the mobilization process.[45]

Other sources of manpower losses were guardsmen granted deferments based on either hardship or because they filled irreplaceable positions in key sectors of the economy needed for industrial mobilization, such as the 705th AAA's chaplain, a forty-year-old World War II veteran with five children, and the commander of the 145th FA Battalion, who was quickly returned to Utah because he was a senior executive in a steel corporation.[46]

Unfortunately, there was extensive confusion concerning deferments. Units often lacked copies of the appropriate army regulations and received conflicting guidance from military districts, continental armies, and the NGB. Governors and state adjutants general usually tried to insulate the process of granting deferments from politics by appointing a board of officers to hear requests.

These measures did not prevent guardsmen and their families, encouraged or angered by the conflicting policies they heard about, from appealing to their governors and congressmen for assistance. Governors usually referred these requests back to the state adjutant general's office, while congressmen's requests for assistance went to the National Guard Bureau, which in turn referred cases back to the appropriate state adjutant general's office. The number of deferral requests dismayed some senior guard officers. Michigan's Brig. Gen. George C. Moran believed that many request were from "dollar-wise patriots" who were perfectly willing to accept drill pay until there was the possibility of mobilization, whereupon they began "seeking ways to avoid their responsibilities."[47]

Physical exams and applications for deferment only added to the daunting administrative workload created by mobilization. A major problem for guardsmen was that the guard and the Regular Army operated two different and incompatible administrative systems. Clerks and personnel officers struggled to transfer personnel records from the guard system to the Regular Army system, one with which guardsmen had little experience and for which most units lacked the appropriate forms and references. To handle the workload, some units rented typewriters or hired civilian typists. Another source of friction in this process was some personnel officers' "initial failure to grasp the necessity for night work in their sections."[48]

To prepare for induction, many units ordered key administrative and logistical personnel to active duty early. Units' Regular Army instructors worked closely with these personnel. Because they were more familiar with Regular Army systems, these instructors proved especially useful in dealing with staff officers at military districts and in the continental armies headquarters. Military districts created administrative support teams for alerted units, but the districts lacked the manpower to provide every unit with all the support it needed. Rivaling the transfer of personnel records in administrative complexity and consumption of time was the transfer of equipment provided by the federal government, through the U.S. Property and Disbursing Office in each state, to unit property books.[49]

Most state adjutants general authorized alerted units to hold three drills a week instead of the normal one. While some units hoped to use this time for extensive training, these hopes were crushed under the combined weight of administrative processing and preparing equipment for movement to the training site. As a result, most training during the alert period was on less-complex skills, such as close order drill and first aid. Also covered during this period were army regulations and military law.[50]

On the appointed day, units mustered at their armories early in the morning. There an officer would read the orders bringing the unit to active duty, formally inducting it into federal service. Some units performed the requirement with ceremony, whereas others, like some in the 28th Infantry Division, did so with "a note of informality, which found many of the former civilian soldiers in the Pennsylvania National Guard wearing street clothes."[51]

The days between entry into federal service and departure for the training site were filled with more of the same: the seemingly endless administrative work; the completion of preparations for shipping unit equipment and loading onto cars those items to be shipped by rail; and what individual training that could be squeezed in. Those who lived near enough to the armories could return home at night, while those who did not were housed at the armory. Some guardsmen in every battalion or larger sized unit left their communities for the training site before the rest to act as an advance party, coordinating for billets and support at the training site.[52]

As units prepared for departure, so did their communities. Local governments and private groups arranged farewell dinners, picnics, and dances—often coupled with fund-raising events to build up company and battery unit funds. Speakers at these events stressed the sad necessity of mobilization to fight the new foe, communism, and pride in their guardsmen's continuation of the citizen-soldier tradition. At the farewell barbecue for Statesboro, Georgia's, 101st AAA Gun Battalion, each soldier received a silver cigarette lighter as a token of the community's affection.[53]

While other areas of the nation often had enthusiastic farewells for their units, Oklahoma's pride in the 45th Infantry Division led to a massive show of support as citizens rallied to support their Thunderbirds. Shortly after the alert notice, Governor Turner declared that Saturday, 26 August, would be "45th Division Day" in Oklahoma. Between the alert notice and induction, cities and towns across the state set aside days to honor their local units. Ardmore, home of Company H, 179th Infantry, and the 179th's medical company, held a special service and dinner for its guardsmen on 19 August at the Missionary Baptist Church. A few days later, the town held a stag party, charging a dollar a ticket to help raise money for the two companies' unit funds. During the weekend of "45th Division Day," there were farewell parties across the state.[54]

Soon, too soon for many, the day to depart arrived. Units generally marched from their armory to the nearest train station, usually behind a guard or reserve band not yet mobilized, or a local high school band. Local or state political leaders often addressed the units. Before leaving its armory to march to North Station, Boston's 272d FA Battalion heard Gov. Paul Dever convey the commonwealth's pride in the state's first guard outfit to leave. For many of the young men in departing units who had no prior active service, it was the beginning of the great adventure of their short lives, and they acted more like boys going off to summer camp than soldiers who might soon find themselves on the battlefield.

At the railroad station, however, often under bright TV lights in larger cities, families and friends said their final farewells in an atmosphere usually described as tearful, grim, and apprehensive. In East Greenwich, Rhode Island, for Battery B, 705th AAA Gun Battalion, came "all too soon the train's warning whistle—the hurried goodbyes—the crowd of youngsters cheering as the train disappears in a blur which handkerchiefs cannot seem to clear. The 705th was on its way!" In Charlotte, North Carolina, home of the departed 378th Combat Engineer Battalion, "long after the station was deserted, a pretty, teen-aged girl in a brown sunback dress stood beside the track, her face buried in her hands."[55]

The Army National Guard, at least a sizable part of it, was again going off to war. But this war was unlike anything the guard, the army, and the American people had been expecting since 1945. As the troop trains moved out of the stations they headed into a future clouded by a mist of uncertainty and concern. Newspapers carried more and more articles reporting the death, wounding, and disappearance of hometown boys and men in Korea. In Oklahoma, a Regular Army corporal, back home from Korea to mend from his wounds, warned that this was a very different war, and that the "Gooks" were a more cruel and dangerous foe than the Nazis America and its allies had defeated just five years earlier. What would happen in Korea? Was World War III just down the tracks? And, most importantly for them, what would the army do with these modern minutemen?[56]

CHAPTER 3

Postmobilization Training

Army National Guard units during the Korean War, particularly combat units, were less ready for action than their regular counterparts. This made unit training prior to deployment crucial to how well they would perform. Five considerations influenced the effectiveness of postmobilization training during the Korean War: the training plan, the unit's cadre, the quality of the fillers sent to a unit, the level of external support provided to the unit, and how well the postmobilization training was protected from other demands on a unit's time and resources.

Army Field Forces had postmobilization training programs ready for guard and reserve units to use, but they encountered significant friction in attempting to follow these programs. This friction was the result of both internal and external factors. The greatly expanded National Guard force structure established after World War II never reached full strength before 1950 because the two key assumptions undergirding it, universal military training and adequate budgets, failed to materialize. Units in 1950 thus were essentially cadre formations with serious equipment shortages, and they often had significantly uneven levels of expertise among their officers and NCOs. All units had major problems with the junior enlisted force, and most units had been unable to do much effective training above the squad, crew, and section level.

The major external factor that interfered with postmobilization training was the assumption guiding all mobilization planning in the army: the next war would be World War III with the Soviet Union, with the initial American response coming from the sea and the air. As America mobilized its resources to counterattack, Army National Guard units would be ordered into federal service, provided sufficient personnel and equipment to reach their full TO&E strength, and given enough time to train so they could reach a minimum acceptable level of proficiency before deploying to the combat zone. What President Truman committed the United States to in 1950, however, overturned these planning assumptions. The army, not the air force and navy, became the key component of America's response to the North Korean invasion, and the regulars turned out to be poorly prepared for combat. Eighth Army's immediate and relentless need for reinforcements and replacements destroyed the meager General Reserve in the ZI, overwhelmed the army's enlisted training system, made serious inroads on the pool of individual reservists, and quickly consumed much of the existing equipment and supply stockpiles. Nevertheless, the Truman administration declined to order a total national mobilization and, believing Europe to be the primary theater of operations, decided on a major expansion of Seventh Army while Eighth Army was fighting in Korea. Under these conditions, the army had to do much improvising on the run, with considerable negative effects on guard postmobilization training.

Postmobilization Training Plans

Unit postmobilization training programs were based on the principles developed in World War II by Army Ground Forces, AFF's predecessor. Cadre for a unit would be given special training both in their specialties and in how to conduct training. In guard units, special emphasis was placed on having officers and technical specialists attend army schools. Mobilized reservists would join units to fill leadership vacancies and technical specialties. Untrained enlisted fillers would then arrive at the unit, be processed in, and then assigned to a position. Training would commence with basic soldier skills, followed by advanced training for each soldier in his specialty. Collective training would follow, starting with the lowest echelon—squad, crew, or section—and progressing to the highest echelon of the unit. Each phase of the training program concluded with standardized tests, administered by either a higher echelon within the unit or by the unit's higher headquarters. Individuals or units that failed a test had to undergo remedial training and retake the test before moving on to the next phase of the program.[1]

Army Field Forces had prepared a specific Army Training Program (ATP) for each type of unit, and a Master Training Program (MTP) for infantry divisions. The ATPs varied in length, depending on the type of unit, but they all followed the same pattern: basic and advanced individual training, then collective training at each echelon, with Army Training Tests (ATTs) administered at the conclusion of each phase. The MTP took twenty-eight weeks to complete, divided into three phases: eleven weeks of basic and advanced individual training; thirteen weeks of unit training that progressed from lower to higher echelons; and four weeks of combined arms training at the RCT and division level. The MTP only outlined the division's training program; ATPs provided specific guidance to regiments, battalions, and separate companies on subjects and the sequence in which they were to be taught.

In addition to individual and collective training, mobilized units conducted "Cadre and Pre-Cycle Filler Training" from the time they arrived at the training site until the start of basic individual training. This period varied in length, depending on how long it took the fillers to arrive. The purpose of this phase was to prepare the guardsmen to conduct postmobilization training and to integrate reservists and regulars assigned to the unit. Units ran courses in technical and tactical skills and in how to conduct training for the cadre, while junior enlisted guardsmen began setting up housekeeping and underwent an abbreviated version of basic training. During this period, units also would send officers and enlisted men to attend various army schools. Although this meant these guardsmen would not be present to assist in conducting some or most of the postmobilization training, depending on the length of the course, guard commanders saw this as a wise investment that would improve the unit's capabilities in the long term, given how few guardsmen were graduates of army schools. Most officers attended their branch basic or advanced courses, whereas enlisted men were sent to the course for their specialty. Those tabbed as potential NCOs were sent to leadership courses.[2]

In late 1950, AFF analyzed the induction of guard units during the summer. The study concluded that mobilization had been impeded by conflicting directives from higher headquarters; the disruptive effects created by changing over from guard to Regular Army administrative and supply procedures; insufficient numbers of trained fillers for technical and leadership positions; and, most notably, by the absence of guardsmen attending service schools, which had a significant effect on the unit's ability to conduct postmobilization training. In response, AFF introduced a four-month period between the time a unit received its mobilization alert notice and when it reported for duty. This provided enough time for guardsmen to attend service schools and return before their unit entered federal service. The press of events following the shock of Chinese intervention prevented AFF from using this modified timeline and increasing the number of trained fillers for units mobilized in early 1951, but it did use the four-month interval between alert and induction with the 37th and 44th Infantry Divisions later in 1951, and provided each division thousands of men already in the service, mainly soldiers returning from Korea.[3]

Cadre

One major difference between activating new regular units and the postmobilization training of guard units was that AFF had much greater influence over the cadre of new units. For the most part, it had to accept what a guard unit brought with it into federal service. As discussed in chapter one, guard units varied considerably in the quality of their officers and NCOs. Army Field Forces was well aware of this, as were realistic guard commanders. Once units arrived at their training site, both AFF and unit commanders took steps to improve the abilities of guardsmen, particularly those holding key leadership, staff, and technical positions. Special instructor teams arrived at training sites, sent by branch schools or continental army headquarters. The teams' mission was to train the trainers, preparing guardsmen to conduct the ATP. Instruction focused on skills that had atrophied or never been developed because of the many problems units faced in training at their home stations. Teams from the AAA School at Fort Bliss, Texas, visited guard AAA units, covering such topics as radar operations, fire control procedures, and operating an AAA firing range. Fourth Army sent instructor training teams to Camp Polk in 1950 and 1952 to assist the 45th and 37th Infantry Divisions, respectively. The teams covered field artillery topics, the 4.2-inch mortar, recoilless rifles, tanks, signal, ordnance, engineer, antiaircraft artillery, food service, and the information and education program. In 1950, ten teams assisted the 28th Infantry Division at Camp Atterbury, Indiana.[4]

Thousands of guardsmen left their units to attend army schools in temporary duty status. Most commanders eagerly filled the quotas allocated to them for various schools. During the period September through December, 1950, the 163d Military Police Battalion sent 10 percent of its enlisted men and 20 percent of its officers to attend courses, mainly at the Provost Marshal General School. By the end of December, 1,629 officers and enlisted men from units of the 51st AAA Brigade had been ordered to various schools. Two months after entering federal service, the 28th Infantry Division had sent 1,215 guardsmen for training. In the 45th Infantry Division at the end of 1950, 142 officers and 524 enlisted men had graduated from schools, 197 officers and 700 enlisted men were still undergoing training, and 117 officers and 927 enlisted men were scheduled to go. The 37th Infantry Division took vigorous advantage of the four-month interval between alert and induction added to the mobilization procedure by AFF. When the division left Ohio in January, 1952, 516 officers and warrant officers and 2,222 enlisted men had graduated from or were completing courses.

Some guardsmen were unable to grasp the material presented and failed to graduate from their service schools. Others discovered that their units did not possess the equipment on which instruction at the school was based. Officers sent to the AAA School found their courses included instruction only on the latest AAA equipment, not the obsolete weapons most guard units used, which meant much of the training was useless to their current situation. While school quotas often left units short of officers and NCOs in the initial phases of their ATP, most commanders believed the resulting difficulties were well worth the return of school-trained soldiers. The 168th MP Battalion's commander believed these courses "helped considerably in refreshing" the skills of his NCOs.[5]

Units conducted their own schools on a wide variety of subjects. Although these schools varied in length and complexity, their primary purpose was to prepare guardsmen to serve as trainers during the ATP. The 45th Infantry Division conducted a number of schools at battalion, regimental, and division level. Units assigned to the 51st AAA Brigade at Camp Stewart, Georgia, in 1950 operated a system of schools in various subjects at battalion, group, and brigade level, providing "much needed and valuable training." The most important courses were the brigade ones on radar and the 90-mm gun, designed to standardize later training in subordinate units during the ATP; 120 men attended the gun school and ninety the radar school. Units of the 28th Infantry Division held classes on training methods for officers and NCOs.[6] Some units, unable to obtain seats for technical specialists at service schools, created and ran their own courses of instruction during the ATP. The 50th Ordnance Group established its own technical school at Fort Knox, Kentucky, in November, 1950, for the guard and reserve ordnance companies assigned to it, drawing on subordinate units for instructors and equipment. While better than nothing, this solution was "not adequate because of the lack of trained personnel and training equipment as well as training facilities."[7]

Another method for improving the quality of the cadre was on-the-job training. Military police battalions, for example, detailed soldiers to the provost marshal at their training site for experience in garrison policing tasks. Most guardsmen had never performed in their position during wartime or with a full-strength unit in peacetime. Federal service now gave them, especially those in leadership positions, the opportunity to practice their craft daily. Commanding an infantry battalion headquarters company, LaVern Weber at first "really didn't appreciate what a full 283-man company can be." This process could at times be rough on those serving under men—especially NCOs with no active duty experience—learning their craft, but it allowed guardsmen with the ability and desire to become proficient in their duties.[8]

A unit's cadre did not always remain fixed. As discussed in chapter two, some guardsmen failed to qualify for federal service because of age, health, or hardship. Some field grade and general officers left their units for other assignments. One month after being called up, the 45th Infantry Division had a new chief of staff. Colonel Ross H. Routh, who had spent World War II as the division's finance officer, was transferred to First Army and replaced by Col. Preston J. C. Murphy. Murphy, like Routh, was a longtime Thunderbird, but he had served as a line officer during the war and commanded one of the 45th's infantry regiments in 1944–45. Integrated into the Regular Army after the war, Murphy left the AFF plans and training section to rejoin the Thunderbirds. Sent on temporary duty status to sit on a promotion board in Washington, the 28th Infantry Division's assistant commander was transferred permanently to staff duties in Washington and replaced by Brig. Gen. J. G. Van Houten, a regular who had commanded the Ranger Training Center. Van Houten, seven years younger than his predecessor, had commanded an infantry regiment and served as chief of staff and assistant division commander of the 9th Infantry Division during World War II. While not explicitly stated in surviving records, this change may have been because Van Houten's wartime duties and experience running the Ranger Training Center were thought to be useful for getting the Keystone division's infantrymen into shape after AFF and VI Corps inspectors filed sharply critical reports.[9]

Some guard commanders deliberately shuffled their subordinate leaders. This was sometimes an attempt to fit the best man into a position, as active service revealed abilities more clearly than could weekly drills and a few summer training periods. On other occasions, it was an effort to break or weaken hometown ties existing separately from and sometimes contradicting official relationships. Regulars had often noted the detrimental effects of these ties on official military relationships within guard units during World War II. In the new war, some guard commanders agreed—usually those whose units came from small towns. In the 168th MP Battalion, because "many of the officers knew enlisted men under them too well as all were from the same locality, and in many instances were relatives," the battalion commander reassigned all his platoon leaders to different companies soon after the 168th arrived at Fort Meade, Maryland. The 279th Infantry's commander shuffled all his battalion and company commanders. The commander of the 158th FA Battalion offered this explanation for doing the same: "I devised this procedure to break up the circles of personal friendship that naturally exist in small communities among officers and enlisted men, especially non-commissioned officers; these warm friendships—natural and, to a great extent, beneficial among guardsmen—are prejudicial to good order during periods of active service. Such a decision also tends to inure both officers and men to accept the personnel changes that are bound to occur in service."[10]

Some leaders were fired because they failed to perform to expected standards. This usually occurred after outside inspectors visited a unit and found it unsatisfactory, or when a unit conspicuously failed an Army Training Test. In the summer of 1951, reports by AFF and VI Corps inspectors led to the relief of a number of commanders and staff officers in the 28th Infantry Division. The most noticeable casualty was the 109th Infantry's commander, the oldest of the division's three guard regimental commanders. A regular who had commanded two infantry regiments in Europe during World War II replaced him. Another casualty was the commander of the 103d Medical Battalion. The 28th's commander, Maj. Gen. Daniel B. Strickler, found relieving officers a painful, but necessary duty: "this we had to do, and we dropped a number in spite of our friendship because we knew we had to have top notch officers in every instance."[11] The 272d FA Battalion's commander had been an infantryman before taking over the unit, created in 1946 from the 372d Infantry's Massachusetts battalion. The battalion performed very poorly on both battery- and battalion-level ATTs in the spring of 1951, and an AFF inspector evaluated the battalion as needing a minimum of four to six months training under a new commander before it "may conceivably pass the tests." The battalion commander's failure to graduate from the Field Artillery Officer Advanced Course reinforced that conclusion and in August Fifth Army relieved him and his operations officer.[12]

Fillers

Army Field Forces did not have much control over the cadre a guard unit brought with it, and guard units had little say in the number and quality of fillers they received. The most desirable fillers were personnel already trained in their specialty. These were available from three sources: the Regular Army, the Organized Reserve Corps, and the National Guard. In 1950 and early 1951, Eighth Army's need for such personnel trumped all others, and with some exceptions, mobilized guard units, particularly divisions, did not receive their full quota of these officers and men before completing postmobilization training. The importance of these men during postmobilization training was pointed out by the 746th AAA Gun Battalion, which noted that enlisted reservists assigned to it filled key NCO positions "with excellent results." The 196th RCT's commander believed that reserve officers and NCOs sent to his unit became "invaluable" and the 196th had been "very fortunate" to receive them. The 37th Ordnance Battalion headquarters detachment had "very little difficulty" bringing its enlisted ranks to full strength since it only required thirty-five men and it entered federal service with eleven. Its enlisted fillers—a mix of draftees, reservists, and regulars—were of high quality; only five had Army General Classification Test (AGCT) scores below a hundred, with the result that "excellent" progress was made during postmobilization training.[13]

Other exceptions were units tagged in the late summer of 1950 for possible deployment to Korea. Those outfits were sent sufficient regulars, reservists, and even a few guardsmen stripped from other units. The 715th Transportation Truck Company received thirty-three recalled inactive reservists and twenty-one fillers from a regular unit at the 715th's training site, Fort Eustis, Virginia.[14] Nine field artillery battalions also benefited from this status. In January, 1951, just before shipping out to Korea, five of these battalions had 17, 20, 26, 31, and 42 percent of their enlisted strength composed of reservists. Lieutenant Colonel Joe E. Whitesides, commander of the 204th FA Battalion, recalled that the enlisted reservists in his battalion "were badly needed and were very welcome replacements. In most cases they had served during World War II and were excellent soldiers." The remaining personnel needed before deployment by these field artillery battalions came from a variety of sources: regular field artillery units, other regular units, and several other mobilized guard units—including the 28th Infantry Division. The 936th FA Battalion received a group of "real good artillerymen" when the army disbanded a 75-mm pack howitzer unit at its training site, Camp Carson, Colorado. The arrival of regulars in guard units often resulted in culture shock for both sides. A Regular Army corporal found that most of the officers and enlisted men were related to each other in the battery of the 936th Field Artillery to which he was assigned, and only the regular enlisted men in the battery addressed the officers as "sir."[15]

As the war continued, another source of trained personnel appeared: soldiers rotating back to the ZI from tours overseas. The Army Field Forces believed these trained and experienced men could be used to fill critical technical and leadership positions in mobilized units, providing units the benefits of their recent operational experience and thus helping to more effectively conduct postmobilization training. The use of these troops as fillers was one of the revisions to mobilization plans made by AFF after the 1950 inductions, but the press of events prevented their use in 1951. Only with the mobilization of the 37th and 44th Infantry Divisions in early 1952 did AFF have the opportunity to use these men as fillers. The 37th received 3,950 personnel transferred in from other units, about half of them returnees from Korea. The division's advance party proved too small and was too overwhelmed by its many other tasks to properly supervise these men. Some returnees, with less than a year left to serve in the army, had bad cases of short-timer's syndrome. Others carried a grudge against the army, since while in Korea they had been promised their choice of station in the ZI and few wanted to be at the 37th's training site, Camp Polk, Louisiana. Others received a Military Occupational Specialty (MOS) from their former units for which they were not school trained and for which their Korean experience had only the faintest of connections, such as infantrymen who had been company radio operators receiving Signal Corps MOSs. This was often done as a way to promote men, but the result was that school-trained guardsmen found themselves working for NCOs who knew less about their MOS than they did. A freeze on promotions for enlisted guardsmen during the first eighteen months of the 37th's federal service did not help this situation. Fourth Army, under which the 37th served, had the responsibility for screening and processing overseas returnees, but it did not do a very good job. The administrative paperwork on many of these men was a shambles; some were technically Absent Without Leave (AWOL) or found that their pay stopped. Some had pay deductions made because of incorrect or missing clothing and equipment records. Other returnees found themselves assigned to MOSs for which they were physically unqualified, often as the result of wounds received in Korea. Finally, a significant number of the returned combat veterans drank heavily and openly resented assignment to a National Guard division. The 37th's commander evaluated these men as "not uniformly excellent," and noted that "many returnees became problems either through violations of discipline or in less spectacular but equally effective ways."[16]

The press of events in 1950 and early 1951 meant that for the majority of guard units, the bulk of their enlisted fillers were untrained draftees and enlistees. The 37th Infantry Division, mobilized in the less hectic 1952, received 4,050 enlisted fillers who had received basic training at a replacement training center before being shipped to the division. The quality of fillers varied. The AFF's Maj. Gen. John O'Daniel, after visiting the 28th Infantry Division in October, 1950, commented on the fillers sent to the division: "I have never seen a better appearing group of recruits." The 45th Infantry Division found its enlisted fillers "to be of even higher type than anticipated, physically capable, mentally alert, and eager to learn." The fillers sent to LaVern Weber's company "turned out to be great soldiers."[17]

Other units were not as impressed with their fillers. In early October, 1950, the first group of 230 arrived at the 163d MP Battalion; the battalion complained these men "had not been carefully screened as concerns their qualification for performing military police duties." The 171st MP Battalion's first fillers also arrived in October, and it, too, complained that not all its new soldiers had the necessary AGCT scores or the "high sense of individual moral responsibility, and a desire to be a part of the Military Police Corps."[18] A total of 315 untrained enlisted fillers arrived between October and December, 1950, in the segregated 272d FA Battalion. The initial shipments, drawn from urban black areas in the Midwest, were "desirable," but 95 percent of the men in a later shipment of 195 fillers from the rural South had less than a fourth grade education. After receiving its fillers, the 272d's enlisted strength, as measured by AGCT scores, was 32 percent from Category I, 14 percent from Category II, 17 percent from Category III, and 37 percent from Category IV. The AFF standard for a field artillery battalion was 33 percent from Category I, 34 percent from Category II, 33 percent from Category III, and none from Category IV.[19]

The army did not attempt to use mobilization to racially integrate guard units inducted in 1950 and 1951, in accordance with its segregation policies and from fears that to do so would create political storms. Five white officer fillers assigned to the 171st MP Battalion were soon transferred out of the battalion, even though at the time the battalion had only 60 percent of its authorized officer strength. When reception centers sent the 45th Infantry Division sixteen black soldiers in 1950, the 45th quickly transferred them to another unit at Camp Polk. The question of integrating mobilized guard units in the ZI later became a political issue as the army moved to integrate units overseas. Mobilized in early 1951, the 31st Infantry Division (Mississippi/Alabama) attracted a good deal of press attention while in federal service, with a band in Confederate army uniforms and no black fillers assigned to it until the majority of its guardsmen had been levied from the division. Unnamed "Pentagon officials" told *Army Times* that there had been no written orders not to integrate the 31st, "'it just worked out that way.'"[20]

In 1952, as the army began moving to end racial segregation in the ZI, it modified its practice with the 37th and the 44th Infantry Divisions. By September, the 37th's batteries and companies, with the exception of the segregated 137th AAA Battalion, averaged 5 to 7 African American enlisted men out of a total of between 85 (in artillery batteries) and 247 (37th Ordnance Company). There is no evidence of African American officers in these units. The 137th AAA Battalion remained segregated until it had lost most of its guardsmen to levies. No reasons for this battalion's exemption from integration are in the surviving documents, but it may be the result of the battalion's separation from the division for eight months while training at the AAA School, and of a widespread reluctance in the army at that time to whites, particularly white officers, serving under the command of black officers.[21]

Another question of integration concerned integrating fillers into a guard unit. This could be a delicate procedure, given the often strong ties among guardsmen who had known each other for years, with fillers of all ranks afraid that guardsmen would receive preferential treatment. General Styron addressed this concern in his welcoming talk to fillers for the 45th Infantry Division, telling them they shared in "international communism" a common foe with the guardsmen. He added that everyone in the 45th was "giving up much and we here in the 45th want you to share with us on equal terms everything that lies ahead." Successful integration of guardsmen and fillers in LaVern Weber's company was largely the work of his first sergeant, a World War II veteran of the 45th and "super troop leader" with extensive experience dealing with fillers during the previous war. Smart guard commanders followed the example of the 158th FA Battalion, which sought "to imbue our old men with a spirit of hospitality toward the new men and a feeling of tolerance for their ways (our fillers were from the North Atlantic and Northwestern States). It worked. A fortnight after their arrival, the new had blended with the old so that one could not discern a stranger in the organization."[22]

External Factors

A number of factors external to mobilized units affected the course of postmobilization training. An early problem in planning and conducting training was that many units did not have copies of the ATP at their home station. In the 45th Infantry Division, ATPs began arriving in Oklahoma as the division was packing for its move to Camp Polk. Only after setting up at Polk could the division's operations staff and subordinate units begin to examine the ATPs and plan to implement them.[23]

The army in 1950 and early 1951 was hard-pressed to find sufficient training sites to meet the needs of mobilized units, especially combat units. Many of the sites used during World War II had been sold, reduced in size, or placed in caretaker status since V-J Day. Few installations, no matter what their status, were prepared for the large number of mobilized guard and reserve units and newly activated regular units that they now had to host. But AFF had few options and was pressed for time, so units made do the best they could.

Units assigned to the 51st AAA Brigade at Camp Stewart in 1950 found that the post was in many ways obsolete and worn out, like much of the brigade's equipment. Stewart had been an AAA training center during World War II, but in the postwar period it was used mainly for guard and reserve training. Third Army operated an AAA training center at Stewart, but by September, 1950, the post's facilities were in poor shape and its staff was not prepared for the challenges of supporting an entire AAA brigade for more than summer annual training. Nevertheless, it was the best available site east of the Mississippi for large numbers of AAA units, even though, as one guardsman wrote home, it was "very common place" to see cows, pigs and mules grazing on the lawn of post headquarters. By the end of the year, troops were still living under canvas, without proper winterization, leading to an above average number of men on sick call with respiratory ailments. The need to rebuild Stewart's small-arms ranges meant that some units finished the ATP's individual training phase without soldiers firing their personal weapons, forcing them to insert weapons qualification into later phases.[24]

The experience of the 51st AAA Brigade was common to most units during 1950 and early 1951. The 45th Infantry Division found the process of "housekeeping and rehabilitation of troop areas" a "major undertaking." But there were some limitations at training sites units could not overcome. At Camp Atterbury, the weather was miserable during the first three months of 1951, with temperatures so low at times that the tracks on the 628th Tank Battalion's M4 Shermans would freeze to the ground in the battalion's unpaved motor pool. A shortage of classroom space forced units to conduct much training outdoors, where a lack of adequate cold weather clothing left troops, in the words of the 628th Tank Battalion's commander, "too concerned with keeping warm to concentrate on the instruction." A thaw in February, coupled with heavy rain, made many of the dirt roads in training areas impassable to wheeled vehicles until freezing weather returned in March. The AFF's Maj. Gen. G. D. Shea, visiting the 28th in mid-January, commended the division for its performance under such harsh conditions. Camp McCoy, Wisconsin, was also unprepared for the number of units stationed there during the winter of 1950–51, as AFF inspectors pointed out.[25]

At McCoy, the IX Corps Artillery, a regular headquarters activated in August, 1950, and assigned two group headquarters and eight battalions from the guard and reserve, discovered the post's artillery ranges were too small and encumbered with restrictions for efficient training of so many artillerymen.[26] Camps Atterbury and Polk were too small for the task of training an entire infantry division. Limitations on firing hampered field artillery training at the posts, while the 112th Infantry complained that Atterbury lacked "adequate training areas of sufficient size to conduct battalion problems properly." Tankers from the 28th Infantry Division traveled to the Armor School at Fort Knox, Kentucky, to fire on tank ranges unavailable at Atterbury. The automatic weapons AAA battalions from the 28th, 37th and 45th Infantry Divisions had to travel to Fort Bliss, Texas, to find ranges they could use for firing their crew-served weapons and completing the battery and battalion portions of the ATP. In early 1951 there were so many AAA gun battalions at Bliss that the 28th's 899th AAA Battalion had to continue on to the Oro Grande AAA Range in New Mexico.[27]

Those installations that had not had a significant Regular Army presence after 1945 also were poorly prepared in other ways. They lacked sufficient morale and welfare activities such as furnished company day rooms, service clubs, and exchanges. Many guardsmen with families who brought them to the training site were shocked to find a serious shortage of rental housing in surrounding communities to supplement the scarce post housing. They were also shocked by the poor condition and high rents of what was available off post. For guard units from urban areas, the isolated nature of training sites located deep in rural America was a shock of another type. African American units faced the extra burden of racial prejudice, both on and off post, in adjusting to active duty life. At Camp McCoy in rural Wisconsin, where by early 1951 three black guard battalions had been stationed, many soldiers complained of racist treatment by the post commander and his staff. The climate was no better off post. The assistant commander of the IX Corps Artillery at the end of 1950 wrote, "though there is little local hostility to them, they are not understood and there are no provisions for them." An AFF inspection team visiting McCoy in early 1951 noted that "inter-racial social contacts are not accepted by the indigenous population," and the 171st MP Battalion's commander told AFF inspectors that McCoy was "entirely unsatisfactory for this particular unit."[28]

Arriving at Camp Polk in January, 1952, the 37th Infantry Division found that eighteen months of war had changed some things, but not others. The division's billets were in good shape, but not much money had been invested in Polk's morale support activities—a major problem at an isolated post filled with many men used to the amenities of city life. While relations with local civilians were generally good, the area's economy since late 1950 had become dependent on various methods of separating soldiers from as much of their paychecks as possible. This included off-post housing of poor quality for soldiers' families, a number of which had come to Louisiana to join their men. Those who got a spot in the post trailer park considered themselves lucky.[29]

The support that units received from the installation staffs at their training sites also affected the quality of life and could interfere with training. The 163d MP Battalion found "excellent co-operation of all staff and installation officers" at Fort Custer, Michigan. Upon arriving at Fort Meade, Maryland, the 168th MP Battalion briefly found itself the post police force, as the Regular Army MP unit assigned there had just received orders to move overseas. This distraction from the ATP ended with the arrival of a mobilized reserve MP company. Unfortunately for the 51st AAA Brigade, as an AFF inspection confirmed in February, 1951, the Camp Stewart signal and ordnance repair facilities were poorly managed and lacked a sense of urgency about their work, preventing them from providing effective support to units on post. The 145th AAA Battalion, training at Fort Bliss, found the AAA School there to be "extremely cooperative" in assisting the battalion, including assigning an instructor team drawn from the school's cadre that was "invaluable in the conduct of training."[30]

Far less helpful were the post staffs at Forts Bliss and Eustis. At Bliss, the 107th Transportation Truck Company was ordered to detail men to support the replacement training center. In October, 1950, 60 percent of the 107th's personnel spent twenty-four days practicing for and performing in parades honoring the outgoing and incoming post commanding generals. Morale and training in the company suffered further when the trucks the company had brought to Bliss, all in good condition and with low mileage, were taken and replaced by old trucks scraped together from other units at Bliss. Finally, a request for leave before deployment to Korea was denied, but a "considerable number of relatives" traveled from Alabama to spend Thanksgiving with their soldiers. The 715th Transportation Truck Company's experience was similar at Fort Eustis. The company spent most of its time in post support duties, including performing in several parades, and a number of its personnel were placed on detached service with the 1st Transportation Replacement Training Group.[31]

The prize for most blindly bureaucratic treatment of a unit must go to Fort Lewis. The 300th Armored Field Artillery (AFA) Battalion arrived there in September, 1950, received its fillers, and began training. Even though the battalion had been alerted for deployment to Korea, the Lewis post personnel section began stripping men from the 300th AFA Battalion, transferring them to both field artillery and non–field artillery units leaving for Korea before the 300th. The post staff justified this drastic action by citing army regulations requiring that deploying units be filled to 100 percent strength before departure. This action gutted the 300th AFA Battalion, taking almost 40 percent of its enlisted strength. Fort Lewis replaced the men with whatever it could scrape up from other units on post—including musicians, firefighters, and fresh graduates of basic training—since the post staff transferred personnel based on the rank required, not the MOS required. Although the battalion commander believed his unit had been rendered combat ineffective, the 300th AFA Battalion deployed to Korea at the end of January, 1951, as scheduled. Before departing, the battalion commander appealed to state authorities for assistance. Wyoming's adjutant general traveled to the Pentagon, where he threatened the army chief of staff with a massive publicity campaign if the 300th suffered losses in combat because of the personnel turbulence inflicted upon it before deployment. The army promised the battalion would receive six weeks of additional training after arriving in Korea before being committed to combat.[32]

Higher echelon commanders and staffs could also influence the course of postmobilization training. At Camp McCoy, the IX Corps Artillery initially controlled the field artillery groups and battalions assigned there. But in November, 1950, Fifth Army—upset that this headquarters could not handle the administrative workload—removed the units from IX Corps Artillery's control and placed them directly under the post commander, an infantryman with neither the time nor the knowledge to supervise their training. This left the groups and the battalions on their own in conducting their ATPs. The 300th AFA Battalion at Lewis was assigned to a guard field artillery group, and a study of the 300th suggests the inexperience of this headquarters in supervising battalions exacerbated the difficulties the battalion faced because it had no links to a field artillery unit in the 1940 troop list.[33] At Camp Stewart, the 51st AAA Brigade headquarters soon clashed with the Third Army AAA training center over how to supervise subordinate units' ATPs, creating what an AFF inspector diplomatically called "a problem of command relations that adversely affects training." The problem was resolved in March, 1951, by transferring the brigade headquarters to take command of the Chicago area AAA defenses. With the 51st's departure, the Third Army AAA training center took charge of training and the 197th AAA Group took over many of the brigade's administrative functions.[34]

At Camp Atterbury, Major General Strickler and the 28th Infantry Division established a close and effective relationship with VI Corps's headquarters, activated in January, 1951, and commanded by Maj. Gen. Withers A. Burress. The same could not be said for the Fifth Army's headquarters, which supervised the 28th during 1950. Strickler recalled that they "were a tough crowd of officers at Fifth Army, and their top commanders were not any too friendly to the National Guard." When General Burress left in May, 1951, to take command of VII Corps, Strickler found his replacement, Maj. Gen. Paul Kendall, "a tough, unreasonable commander, who did not like the Guard. He rode us hard and his demands were harsh. The result was that he got everyone mad at him and a spirit of we'll show you gripped the soldiers."[35] The XV Corps's headquarters at Camp Polk became a problem for Maj. Gen. Leo Kreber and his 37th Infantry Division. Fourth Army was responsible for the division's training, but this did not stop XV Corps from exercising its rank. Kreber reported "unnecessary harassing by Corps' inspectors located at this post making inspections for lack of anything else to do" and that the corps's "constant inspection defeated its own purpose." He added that "(c)omplaints to the XV Corps Commander changed only methods." An AFF inspection team visiting the 37th in July, 1952, noted that the division was conducting infantry battalion ATTs "without obvious support from Fourth Army or XV Corps."[36]

In addition to these local influences, certain armywide conditions affected the course of postmobilization training. Because of prewar NGB-reduced TO&Es and general shortages created by tight prewar budgets, guard units arrived at training sites with significant equipment shortages. Unfortunately, the small prewar stockpiles, difficulties in building up production capacities, and heavy losses in Korea meant that much of what already existed or was being produced went to Eighth Army. The army in late 1950 made de facto conditions official by placing units in postmobilization training on reduced TO&Es, and the authorization for some major pieces of equipment in short supply fell to as low as 30–50 percent of full strength. Units were to receive a full issue when they deployed. What equipment units did possess was often obsolete, worn out, or both. Typical was the situation in the 28th Infantry Division, where AFF inspectors found significant shortages of major pieces of equipment, and what items the division did have were so badly worn that their use in combat was "questionable." The 899th AAA Battalion had none of the M19 self-propelled twin 40-mm guns and few of the M16 self-propelled quad–.50 caliber machine guns required by its TO&E, although it did have a number of the obsolescent M15 systems. While training in New Mexico, the battalion had to borrow a number of M16s and M15s from the AAA School. The 145th AAA Battalion was in the same condition, and to complete its ATP drew weapons (on which the 145th had to do much maintenance to make them useful) from the AAA School and other units at Bliss.[37]

At Camp Stewart, the 51st AAA Brigade's commander, determined to bring the brigade's units to combat readiness as soon as possible, ordered cross-leveling of equipment and personnel within the brigade. Those units that mobilized with a high percentage of equipment and qualified personnel had to give up some of these to less fortunate units. This order caused considerable grumbling from many of the units forced to transfer equipment. A warrant officer in the 703d AAA Gun Battalion wrote to Maine's assistant adjutant general in February, 1951, complaining that "we are left in a bad way and have to borrow equipment when we fire—it just doesn't work out." The 197th AAA Group, however, believed the equipment transfers eased the maintenance burden on the well-equipped units, as absences at schools and the demands of training fillers had left few qualified mechanics available to work on the equipment.[38]

For the 45th Infantry Division, the greatest equipment shortage was in tanks. The 245th Tank Battalion's TO&E called for three companies with twenty-two M46 tanks per company, yet in January and February, 1951, the battalion usually had just one platoon of tanks on hand. Company B developed a field expedient by using the company commander's private automobile during training on tank formations, but "even with that some people had to walk, waving the flags to change from one formation into another." Regimental tank companies also were supposed to have twenty-two M46s, but they never did during this period. The 179th Infantry, for example, had only one M26 and five M4A3 tanks.[39] Other significant shortages in the 45th included motor vehicles, counterfire equipment, and radios. While these shortages made life difficult, one guard company commander did find this period "quite enjoyable because of the challenges. Every day was kind of a new world in that we didn't know what kind of equipment we'd be getting tomorrow." Temporary equipment shortages developed when additional recruits were sent to the 45th in January and

February. As these fillers brought the division over its authorized TO&E strength, the provisional training battalions had to borrow rifles and other items from their parent units in order to train the new men.[40]

Field artillery battalions training at Fort Lewis, Camp Carson, and Fort Hood, Texas, reported serious equipment shortages. Some units were issued either older models or similar types of equipment—especially radios and vehicles—in lieu of what was called for by their TO&E, but most units did not receive the equipment needed to bring them up to full TO&E strength until they reached the port of embarkation. Equipment shortages were, an AFF inspector noted, a "definite handicap" to training. Shortages of howitzers and prime movers forced gun crews in some battalions to take turns training on the equipment. Shortages of vehicles made supporting training in general, and training on displacing elements of the battalion—a key skill during the first year of the war in Korea—very difficult. Shortages of radios made it more difficult to conduct service practices and to train on coordinating fire support. An AFF inspection of battalions shortly before deployment found significant shortages: the 176th AFA Battalion was short eleven howitzers and thirty-six cargo trucks; the 196th FA Battalion had all its howitzers, but was short eleven prime movers for the howitzers; and the 987th AFA Battalion was short thirteen howitzers and thirty-six cargo trucks.[41]

The situation had not much improved by 1952. In mid-October, soon after completing the MTP, the 37th Infantry Division reached its highest operational readiness rating while still mainly an "Ohio" unit, a rating of "65% C." This meant that the 37th had reached 65 percent of its potential combat effectiveness as an organization, but that "its equipment status *does not* permit operational employment of unit without correction of major equipment deficiencies."[42] (emphasis in original)

The army's logistical difficulties also affected other items required to complete the ATPs. Many units entered federal service without all the manuals and forms required by their type of organization, and the army could not immediately fill all the resulting requests for publications. Not surprisingly, given the nation's lack of preparedness for war and the course of events in Korea, ammunition supply was also a concern. In the field artillery battalions at Lewis, Hood, and Carson, the firing batteries received a good deal of artillery ammunition to train with, but small-arms ammunition sometimes ran short.[43] The 45th Infantry Division's artillery ammunition often arrived only a day before the scheduled shoot, and on several occasions service practice firing had to be postponed because the ammunition did not arrive in time. Other ammunition shortfalls in the 45th reflected production problems and heavy consumption in Korea: 4.2-inch mortar shells, 57-mm and 75-mm recoilless rifle rounds, and 3.5-inch antitank rockets. The 179th Infantry's commander noted that the lack of ammunition for 3.5-inch rocket launchers "was detrimental to the training of those individuals who will have to use it in event of combat."[44]

Protection of the Postmobilization Training Period

Effective implementation of a postmobilization training plan requires that units be protected from disruptions and distractions. Unfortunately, many guard units mobilized in 1950 and 1951 encountered significant obstacles to effectively implementing their ATPs. Some of these obstacles, as mentioned above, were equipment and supply shortages, the rundown condition of training sites, unhelpful relationships with higher headquarters, and the sometimes poor quality of fillers sent to a unit. But the underlying reason for many of the problems units encountered was that the AFF's planning for postmobilization training shared the same assumptions that had shaped army mobilization planning: the next war would be World War III with the Soviets, with a total mobilization of America's resources and time to train reserve component units as the navy and air force carried the initial burden of the war. How much the actual circumstances of the war in Korea undermined these assumptions can be seen in the terrific manpower dilemmas that confronted the army during the war and how it dealt with those dilemmas.

Eighth Army's need for replacements in late 1950 so outstripped the available supply that some units received levies that could only be met by using guardsmen. In early December, less than a month after starting its MTP, the 28th Infantry Division received a levy for 193 enlisted men qualified in engineer, field artillery, survey, and general duty MOSs for units deploying to Korea. Only guardsmen met the levy's requirements, so the division had to use them, although the 28th did not fully meet the levy, providing 144 men.[45] Even after operations in Korea had settled into fixed positions, the demands of the rotation system and the army's manpower ceilings affected postmobilization training for the guard divisions mobilized in early 1952. In May, the 37th Infantry Division received a levy for overseas service that was soon followed by others. Although small in number and counterbalanced by the arrival of some replacements, these levies were damaging since to fill them the 37th had to give up a number of key personnel and specialists. Newly commissioned officers and draftees could not readily replace the skills and experience lost in the levies. These levies also affected training by disrupting unit cohesion and lowering morale, especially among guardsmen who now had good reason to fear that "Go With Those You Know" was just a hollow slogan. The AFF inspectors visiting the 37th in July to observe infantry battalion ATTs noted that the division's morale "needs improvement." They found a "lackadaisical attitude" among both officers and enlisted men, which the AFF team blamed on the effects of levies for overseas service and rumors that the division would be converted from a tactical to a training unit.[46]

During the winter and spring of 1951 a manpower crisis gripped the army, a result of heavy casualties in Korea coupled with the limited resources available under a partial national mobilization. The army's training system could not keep pace with the demand for new soldiers, so it turned to units conducting postmobilization training. One response was to send units more enlisted fillers than they needed to reach full TO&E authorizations. The units were to give these untrained draftees and enlistees basic training, then the men would be transferred from the unit, with Korea as the next duty station for most.[47]

In December, 1950, the 163d MP Battalion received thirty new untrained recruits and 101 arrived at the 171st MP Battalion. Each battalion set up separate recruit detachments to conduct basic training for the new men, further thinning each unit's available resources. Also in December, New York's 715th AAA Gun Battalion received an additional group of enlisted fillers. To avoid burdening the battalion, the 209th AAA Group established a provisional training battery for these fillers and other black troops sent to Camp Stewart. By January, 1951, the 171st MP Battalion was at 116 percent of its authorized enlisted strength, but because of the small number of black officers in all components of the army, the 171st had only 76 percent of its authorized officer strength. The segregated army, hard-pressed to find facilities to train its increasing numbers of new African American enlisted men, sent 151 of them to the 171st in February, forcing the battalion to start another recruit training cycle in addition to its collective training. In March, all three MP battalions felt the effects of Eighth Army's casualties, as each was levied for enlisted men, taken from among the fillers received in 1950: the 163d sent 167 men overseas, the 168th transferred 212 enlisted men to the 101st Airborne Division (at that time a training unit), and the 171st sent 100 men to the Far East Command (FECOM). In return, all three battalions received further shipments of untrained enlisted men. During March, troop trains delivered 253 men to the 163d, 275 to the 168th, and 121 to the 171st. This forced the battalions to set up new recruit detachments that siphoned off trained officers and NCOs from ATP training. By the end of March, the 171st had four provisional training companies in operation.[48]

The confluence of the army's racial segregation policies and the manpower crisis was a heavy burden on African American guard units conducting their ATPs. In early 1951, the 272d FA Battalion received a stream of untrained fillers at irregular intervals. By May, the battalion had 1,038 enlisted men assigned, 171 percent of its authorized strength. The battalion had to run a series of basic training detachments while simultaneously trying to conduct collective training according to the ATP, and when the fillers graduated from basic training they then had to be integrated into unit training. The battalion commander understatedly told an AFF inspector that the "excessive numbers of untrained fillers" was "hampering unit training." The 171st MP Battalion's enlisted strength peaked in June—the month it took the battalion ATT—at 174 percent when the 272d FA Battalion, preparing to leave for Germany, dumped 275 excess enlisted men into it. The battalion's officer strength never kept pace, dipping as low as 53 percent available for duty in June. Causing further difficulties was the fact that many of the enlisted men the 171st received were unfit for the demands of military police work. They had been sent to the battalion simply because it was the one of the few black units available to take them.[49]

White units also found themselves adjuncts of the army's training system. Camp Stewart received thousands of untrained enlisted recruits in early 1951, fresh from reception centers. To avoid disrupting the gun battalions' ATPs, each AAA group headquarters formed provisional training units, although battalions had to provide the cadre to staff them. Once the new fillers completed their individual training, they were distributed among the battalions and integrated into the units' collective training, swelling the enlisted strength of some battalions beyond their TO&E authorizations and causing problems in training and supervision for the available qualified officers and NCOs. The 746th AAA Gun Battalion at Fort Lewis, for example, received shipments of 450 and 550 recruits in February, 1951. The men were attached to the battalion for only basic training.[50]

The army also turned to mobilized guard infantry divisions, levying thousands of their enlisted fillers for overseas service. In January, 1951, the 45th Infantry Division was ordered to provide 650 of its enlisted fillers for "immediate overseas service." A month later, the 28th Infantry Division was levied for 3,000 of its enlisted fillers for duty in FECOM. The division in turn levied its subordinate units, though not in equal amounts since units had received their fillers at different times and not all the men had completed the fourteen weeks of basic training required by army regulations for overseas service. The 112th Infantry lost 1,649 enlisted men, but only 120 were taken from the 109th Infantry. The division commander recalled that it "was a sad day to see the draftees leave us for the Korean War, only after an inadequate fourteen weeks of military training with us." (The army required that soldiers used to meet levies for overseas service complete a minimum of fourteen weeks training after it was alleged early in the war that untrained or poorly trained men had been committed to combat.) To replace these losses, the 28th received 3,000 untrained recruits. Depending on how many fillers they had lost, the division's subordinate units organized provisional basic training battalions or companies, thus diverting qualified officers and NCOs from unit ATP training. In March another round of levies came down, followed by the assignment of more untrained recruits and new provisional training units for the replacements for the men shipped overseas. By April, the 28th's infantry regiments were operating several provisional training battalions at different stages of basic training, the Division Artillery had two battalions, and the tank, engineer, and medical battalions were each operating a training company.[51]

The 45th Infantry Division received 4,006 recruits between 4 January and 7 February 1951, and parceled out a thousand men to each infantry regiment. Each regiment created a training battalion to conduct the fourteen weeks of basic training for the recruits. The division artillery received the final thousand and established its own training battalion of four batteries, each battery linked to and staffed by one of the four field artillery battalions. The division boasted that the new men were "receiving excellent training," but it came at a significant cost. The 158th FA Battalion had to provide one officer and forty-two NCOs, and the 179th Infantry staffed its provisional training battalion with fourteen officers and thirty-two NCOs taken from other units in the regiment. The 179th's commander noted that this requirement, together with attendance at service schools, left the 179th's officers and NCOs "spread very thinly, placing a severe burden on those remaining." A little help in dealing with these problems came in early January with the arrival of six first lieutenants and forty-four second lieutenants transferred from the 5th Armored Division (a training formation), but an AFF inspection team visiting in March noted that while the training in the provisional battalions was well prepared, it suffered from a shortage of qualified instructors and supervision by the infantry regiments and division artillery.[52]

Developments in the theater of operations also affected units' post-mobilization training, interrupting it or cutting it short. On 24 February, Fourth Army alerted the 45th Infantry Division that it would be sailing the next month for Japan, which had been stripped of ground combat units for use in Korea. The division stopped unit training the day after receiving the alert notification to concentrate on preparing for the move to Japan. It would not be combat ready when it arrived in Japan as the infantry regiments were just finishing the platoon level of unit training and the field artillery had not yet finished the service practice firings prescribed by the ATPs.[53] The 45th faced many problems in preparing for embarkation in little more than a month, beginning with the effort to get clear and helpful guidance from higher headquarters. "The receipt of the complete movement order answered many pertinent questions but gave rise to many additional ones," forcing the division's staff to remain "constantly in telephone communication with their counterparts at 4th Army or the Department of the Army."[54] The 145th AAA Battalion had to be recalled from Fort Bliss. Showdown inspections had to be held and requisitions to fill shortages had to be submitted. Arrangements had to be made for clearing Camp Polk. Preparation for Overseas Movement (POM) tasks required by army regulations for troops moving overseas had to be accomplished. Training on skills required to move the division, such as rail loading, packing and crating, and preparing all the shipping paperwork, had to be organized and conducted. Then the Thunderbirds had to put all this new knowledge to use in packing up the division. Information on Japan and its people had to be disseminated throughout the division so that all could be "indoctrinated with the necessity of a friendly treatment and consideration toward the Japanese people."[55]

Some Thunderbirds would not meet the Japanese people because the POM review unmasked a number of underage enlistees, some soldiers applied for and received discharges on grounds of hardship or dependency, and others failed the POM physical or could not get their medical profiles upgraded to meet POM standards—most notably the 279th Infantry's commander. The division's major headache in trying to prepare for the move was what to do with the four thousand recruits received in January and February. Nowhere near completing basic training, they could not go overseas until they had completed it. Nor could they be sent to another training center: the lack of slack in the army's training system was the reason they had been sent to the 45th. The answer was to create the 45th Division Training Regiment. This headquarters, augmented with a personnel section and a medical detachment, took control of the four provisional training battalions. The regiment would complete the recruits' training, after which the cadre and those men required by the 45th would join the division in Japan. Men who were excess to the 45th's needs would be sent to other units. At its peak, the regiment had 137 officers, eight warrant officers, and 1,242 enlisted men to take care of the 4,006 fillers. After a tremendous flurry of activity, the division held a farewell parade on 26 March and its last unit left Polk on the thirtieth, sailing from New Orleans the next day. After arriving in Japan, the division would have to resume MTP training at the point it had left off in February.[56]

The press of events in late 1950 led to the postmobilization training of some guard units being cut short. Since the war's start, FECOM had pressed for shipping the field artillery battalions tabbed for service in Korea to the theater as soon as possible, even if they had not finished their ATP training, arguing that they could complete the program in Japan. The army staff preferred that the battalions remain in the ZI until completing the ATP, but after China intervened in the war, the nine battalions were ordered to Korea.[57] None of the battalions were ready for combat. In five battalions at Hood and Carson, five of the fifteen firing batteries failed their initial ATT, and only in the 936th FA Battalion did any of the batteries achieve a passing score exceeding 80 percent. While some of the battalions were able to conduct battalion level collective training, none had taken the battalion ATT before receiving the alert order for deployment. In the five battalions visited by an AFF inspector in January, 1951, operational readiness ratings were rather low for units preparing to deploy to a combat zone—ranging from 50 percent for the howitzer-poor 176th AFA Battalion to 72 percent for the 196th FA Battalion, which was rich in World War II field artillery veterans. The 300th AFA Battalion, which had been gutted by the Fort Lewis personnel section, also left for Korea with a rating of 50 percent. Despite these low ratings, once units received the alert order for deployment, training ceased as they prepared equipment for movement, conducted the POM training required by army regulations, and did a thorough review of soldiers' medical and administrative records. The guard field artillery battalions arrived in Korea between 2 and 17 February, where Eighth Army ordered that they undergo training and testing supervised by their respective corps artillery headquarters before entering combat. Since Eighth Army was slowly moving north again and the Chinese were gathering strength for a spring offensive, there was time available for this training.[58]

The Effectiveness of Postmobilization Training

There are several ways to measure the effectiveness of postmobilization training. One is to look at scores on Army Training Tests taken by units at the conclusion of the company/battery and battalion phases of the postmobilization training. The range of scores was extensive, reflecting the quality of cadre units brought into federal service, equipment shortages, and, most importantly, the burden of training recruits excess to the unit's needs during the ATP. The 163d MP Battalion's battalion-level ATT was delayed for almost two months as it struggled to both provide basic training and conduct collective training, but the delay proved beneficial as it scored 84.4 percent, earning a rating of excellent. The 171st did not receive a delay, taking its battalion ATT on 7–8 June, 1951, and failing—which came as no surprise given the problems the battalion encountered at Camp McCoy. Later that month, in accordance with an AFF inspection team's recommendation, the 171st moved from McCoy to Fort Custer, where it retook the ATT and earned a satisfactory rating with a 77.7 percent score.

The 272d FA Battalion's performance on ATTs reflected the many internal and external impediments affecting it. After completing the ATP in April, 1951, the battalion took its ATTs in May. Two of three firing batteries failed ATT 6-1, and the battalion scored zero points on ATT 6-2-1.[59] Five days later, the battalion commander left to attend the Field Artillery Officer Advanced Course and the battalion operations officer—a 1948 graduate of the Associate Officer Basic Course—assumed temporary command. The battalion began a program of remedial training, which worked to some degree at the battery level. Retested on 12 June, the two batteries that failed ATT 6-1 in May passed it with scores of 71.0 percent and 71.6 percent. However, the 272d still could not function effectively as a battalion: a retest of ATT 6-2-1 on 9 June resulted in a score of just 29 percent. Taking ATT 6-5 on 11 June, the battalion scored 59 percent. After the battalion commander and operations officer were relieved, their replacements put the battalion through "intensive" training under the new commander's "immediate and close supervision and planning." In addition to unit training, twice weekly officer and NCO courses of instruction were conducted after duty hours. This training was designed to be only a band-aid, allowing the unit to make the minimum scores required to release a unit for overseas service. The VI Corps Artillery administered battalion and battery ATTs in August, but tested only technical field artillery skills. It did not test the battalion on the tactical portion of the ATTs. The 272d scored 75.25 percent, 75.2 percent, and 63.4 percent on the ATTs and AFF released it for overseas service.[60]

Iowa's 194th FA Battalion, another towed 155-mm howitzer outfit at McCoy, faced problems similar to those encountered by the 272d, but not to the same extent. It also received excess enlisted men, but its enlisted strength rose only to 125 percent of its authorized TO&E strength. The 194th likewise suffered from the cold weather, from the loss to training of officers and NCOs sent to service schools, and from a shortage of vehicles. The 194th's key advantage was that it had ties to a field artillery unit in the 1940 troop list and possessed a nucleus of experienced field artillerymen around which it had built the postwar battalion. The 194th did pass its ATTs, though not spectacularly, with scores ranging from 75.9 percent to 80.8 percent.[61]

In the 28th Infantry Division, the effects of levies and backfills noticeably manifested themselves when units began higher-echelon collective training. Without a solid foundation of individual and small-unit training, and with many inexperienced officers and NCOs, performance suffered in a number of units during the spring of 1951. In both the 109th FA and the 229th FA Battalions, one firing battery failed the ATT conducted during March, while the performance of the battalions' other batteries revealed many deficiencies. When the four field artillery battalions took ATT 6-2 in April, two battalions failed and one just barely passed. The 103d Medical Battalion failed its ATT in early June. Most infantry battalions passed their ATTs in late spring and early summer, but with only "satisfactory" ratings, probably in part because the division skipped the company-level ATTs in an effort to keep to the MTP's timetable. Watching an infantry battalion ATT in late June, an AFF inspector saw many tactical and staff errors, complained of a lack of aggressive spirit in the troops, and noted that the unit had trained at the battalion level for only two weeks before taking the test. Watching infantry units during field training in early July, another AFF inspector remarked upon the "poor" discipline of soldiers, the low morale of infantrymen, and the lack of realism in the training conducted. The inspector found major fault with most of the NCOs he encountered, calling them "timid and lacking in initiative."[62]

Another way to gauge postmobilization training is to check unit performance during major maneuvers soon after completion of the training program. Before leaving for Germany, the 28th and 43d Infantry Divisions would participate in Exercise Southern Pine, a two-week maneuver scheduled for August in North Carolina. Southern Pine's stated purpose was to provide post-graduate training for the two divisions, numerous non-divisional units, and elements of the air force's Tactical Air Command. (Southern Pine's scenario began with the 82d Airborne Division conducting a delaying action, followed by an attack by the 28th and 43d, then a defense by the corps, and concluded with the 28th and 43d resuming the attack to link up with the 82d, which had been dropped behind "Aggressor" lines.) However, there was concern at AFF headquarters that the guard divisions were not ready for deployment. The exercise thus provided an excellent opportunity to examine the ability of the 28th and 43d to function as divisions for an extended period under simulated combat conditions. The exercise was also used to test the newly formed VII Corps staff, also slated for deployment to Germany, and its commander, General Burress.[63]

The 28th came out of Exercise Southern Pine with mixed reviews. The 110th Infantry's operations officer thought the exercise "rigorous and very useful." General Strickler believed that Southern Pine "proved to be very valuable to us and gave me personally a grand opportunity to operate and observe the units of my organization in the field." Colonel H. D. McHugh, who took command of the 109th Infantry just before Southern Pine, wrote that the exercise had "brought to light many minor, but few major deficiencies in training and procedure" and that "much progress" was made over the course of the two weeks in correcting these problems. The 112th Infantry thought the exercise provided much "valuable experience" and disclosed that the regiment's "most glaring need was for more small unit training."[64]

Army Field Forces observers watching the 28th at Southern Pine agreed that the division's greatest deficiency was at battalion level and lower. While individual soldiers were generally proficient at their skills, units had difficulty with small-unit tactics and coordinating infantry and artillery operations, and demonstrated a "general lack of emphasis on security measures." On the positive side, the 28th displayed "an excellent level of discipline and showed good control during the exercise." The 28th also demonstrated that it could learn quickly: "Command and staff functioning improved as the maneuver progressed. Aggressiveness increased and most of the major units were well handled during the latter phases." The AFF observers believed that many of the problems revealed by the maneuver were the result of the massive levies imposed on the division.[65]

Also observing operations was Lt. Gen. John R. Hodge, the Third Army commander and director of Southern Pine. He reported that soldiers in the 28th "proved to be better than they looked on initial contact," and that the division "learned a lot from the maneuver." Hodge evaluated Strickler as "an intent, sincere commander," but "if anything, he may over-command in the sense that he does quite a lot himself." Like the AFF observers, Hodge also believed that the division's major problem was the need for more training at the small-unit level. He added that junior officers and NCOs needed "more training in leadership." Overall, Hodge believed that the 28th and the 43d were "basically in far better shape than were the divisions I saw in any of the 1941 maneuvers, either National Guard or Regular" and that both divisions were "reasonably ready to go to Europe." Hodge believed that "many of the minor deficiencies exhibited will be corrected after their first contact in battle and I know of no way of correcting these faults without battle experience."[66]

General Clark urged Fifth Army's commander to make "every effort to further improve the combat effectiveness of the 28th Division in the short time remaining" before it sailed for Germany, with an emphasis on small-unit training from battalion downward. In early September, Strickler wrote to Fifth Army's commander that "refresher work and training is being instituted to correct deficiencies." And that is exactly what the 28th did during the first two weeks of that month, building on the progress made during Southern Pine. The 103d Medical Battalion passed its ATT retest on 20 September, and two days later its new Regular Army commander replaced most of his staff officers, company commanders, and first sergeants. Army Field Forces's final inspection in mid-September found morale in the division "good" and rated the 28th's operational readiness at 75 percent, estimating that the division needed eight more weeks of unit tactical training. For most of the 28th's units, all but the most perfunctory training ceased after the second week of September as the division began preparing for the move to Germany.[67]

Postmobilization training for almost all Army National Guard units during the Korean War did not go according to plan. The ATPs themselves were sound, but assumptions used for army mobilization planning—that the next war would be World War III—were overturned by the actual conditions of the Korean War. All guard units entered federal service significantly short of their full TO&E authorization and temporarily lost the services of many cadre personnel while they attended schools. Many units suffered from poor external support and some discovered they had cadre unequal to the task. A few units had their ATP training interrupted or cut short by the course of events in Korea. However, the major source of disruptions to postmobilization training was the army's efforts to improvise solutions to problems created by overturned planning assumptions. The effects of these disruptions, most notably levies on units and making them adjuncts to the replacement training system, greatly hindered completion of ATP training, the building of units' collective skills, and the seasoning of inexperienced junior leaders. Performance on ATTs and Exercise Southern Pine revealed some effects of these disruptions, but the best way to gauge the effectiveness of postmobilization training is to examine how a unit performs its assigned mission. The next four chapters will follow units to duty in Korea, Germany, and the Zone of the Interior, and to the end of their federal service.

CHAPTER 4

In the Land of the Morning Calm

The army deployed forty-one nondivisional National Guard units to Korea: eleven field artillery battalions, one field artillery observation battalion, two antiaircraft artillery battalions, one antiaircraft artillery group headquarters, six combat engineer battalions, three engineer bridge companies, one engineer group headquarters, six truck companies, two truck battalion headquarters, three ordnance maintenance companies, two ordnance battalion headquarters, one signal battalion, one medical collecting company, and one quartermaster group headquarters.[1] Most nondivisional units arrived between January and March, 1951, deployed to make up the shortfall created when the General Reserve could not fulfill all of Eighth Army's requests. Other nondivisional units arrived later in 1951 and in 1952 to enhance Eighth Army's capabilities in certain areas, such as fire support and air defense.

It is not surprising—although it was disappointing to many senior guardsmen—that the army guard's battlefield participation during the Korean War did not match its contributions during World War II. Early in the war the army had lacked the resources to prepare and deploy mobilized guard units in time to affect the course of events before the Chinese intervened. President Truman's decision not to fully mobilize for the Korean War, and the decision after China's intervention to limit the war to restoring the prewar status quo meant that mobilizing the guard on the same scale as during 1940–41 and deploying it to Korea could not have been supported and would not have made a significant difference in achieving American war aims after the spring of 1951.

Overall, despite their handicaps and the many obstacles they faced during postmobilization training, the guard nondivisional units sent to Korea fulfilled their role as the army's first-line reserve force and greatly enhanced Eighth Army's firepower, engineer capabilities, and logistical system.

Transportation Companies

The first guard units to arrive in Korea were transportation truck companies and transportation truck battalion headquarters detachments deployed in late 1950 to reinforce Eighth Army's increasingly creaky logistical support system. Two of these were Alabama's 107th Transportation Truck Company and the District of Columbia's 715th Transportation Truck Company. Both entered federal service in August, 1950, and arrived in Korea in January, 1951.[2]

Both companies at mobilization were better off in personnel than in equipment. The 107th, thanks to recruiting after the alert notice, entered active duty at its full TO&E strength of four officers, one warrant officer, and 127 enlisted men; the 715th had three officers, one warrant officer, and ninety-five enlisted men upon induction. Neither company commander had been a transportation officer during World War II. The two lieutenants in the 715th were both enlisted World War II veterans, and of the three lieutenants in the 107th, two had been enlisted men during World War II and the third, an Alabama guardsman in 1940, was a warrant officer when the war ended. Both companies were short of two-and-a-half-ton trucks: of the required 56 trucks, the 107th had 17 and the 715th had 20.[3]

Both companies, through no fault of their own, had little constructive training between they time they were inducted and their departure for Korea. The 107th went to Fort Bliss, where it supported the recruit training center and spent much of its time practicing for and performing in parades honoring the outgoing and incoming post commanding generals. Training was cut short on 15 November, when the company received its alert for overseas service and had to focus its attention on POM required tasks. The 715th's experience at Fort Eustis was similar.[4]

The 107th moved to San Francisco and the 715th to Seattle, where they boarded transports and arrived at Pusan on 7 January and 5 January, respectively. After recovering their vehicles on the docks, both companies were quickly put to work and their inexperienced drivers began intensive on-the-job training. The 107th drove 250 miles over "very poor Korean roads" in hard winter weather to Ch'ungju. There the company began hauling cargo from the railhead to the 2d Infantry Division's supply dumps, demonstrating "their quality by fulfilling every commitment in a commendable manner" despite operating around the clock over poor roads in "extremely cold weather" without adequate cold weather equipment. In late February, the 107th left the 2d Infantry Division's sector, and until the end of March spent most of its time supporting the 1st Marine Division. The 715th initially hauled ammunition to different 2d Logistical Command depots. In February, it moved forward to support the 1st Marine Division, then in March was placed in general support of IX Corps. The demands placed on the 715th, the conditions under which it operated, and its performance were similar to those of the 107th.[5]

Their intensive on-the-job training from January to March provided the drivers with invaluable experience for the greatest trial the two companies would face while still National Guard in character: the Chinese spring offensives of April and May, 1951. During April, the 107th remained attached to the marines, putting 89,202 miles on their vehicles. The 715th hauled supplies forward from railheads to various X Corps units. In May, the 107th spent most of its time moving troops: Koreans, the 7th Infantry Division, and, in its most important operation, helping to shift the 3d Infantry Division from its reserve position in western Korea across the peninsula to help reinforce X Corps, the main target in the Chinese May offensive. In the X Corps sector, the 715th recorded "a big increase in the tonnage and passengers hauled" as it supported the corps' operations. A platoon, supporting one of X Corps's typical ad hoc combat task forces, was ambushed, but suffered no casualties.[6]

From this high point, operations for both companies settled into more routine rear-echelon trucking missions, usually bringing supplies forward from railheads and Eighth Army supply dumps, although the pace of missions naturally ebbed and flowed with the pace of combat. Both companies, however, often had to commit most or all of their available trucks to missions because they were caught in a vicious circle. They had come to Korea with rebuilt World War II–vintage trucks that—with the poor roads of Korea, the heavy loads, and hard use they received—soon began to break down. The pace of operations during the first five months, combined with a shortage of spare parts, meant that broken trucks often spent a long time in maintenance, forcing the companies to use whatever trucks were available to meet commitments every day, thus wearing them out faster. The 107th, for example, had to suspend operations for much of July while working to bring its fleet back into service. In June, the 715th noted that to "keep a representative number of vehicles on the road the unit Maintenance Officer and his Section had to work feverishly day and night."[7]

Beginning in the summer of 1951, the two companies began to experience personnel turnover as reservists were sent home for discharge from active duty and some guardsmen were transferred to other units in Korea. The 107th lost two guard lieutenants in the autumn of 1951 when one transferred to a field artillery battalion and one transferred to another truck company. The 715th's commander was transferred in August, 1951, to the staff of a driver training school at Taegu. Most of the enlisted replacements received from the Zone of the Interior had not been given driver training, forcing the companies to send the new men to an Eighth Army driver's school. This turnover was used by Eighth Army to begin desegregating both companies as part of Far East Command's racial integration program, starting in November with the white 107th and in March, 1952, with the black 715th. Both companies reported no problems with integration.[8]

Although both companies remained in Korea until the end of the war, early in 1952 guardsmen began returning to the ZI under the Far East Command's rotation plan, and by the spring of 1952 they had lost their guard character. The two companies, despite short-circuited postmobilization training and weary trucks, had performed successfully under very demanding conditions.[9]

King of Battle: Nondivisional Field Artillery Battalions

When the Korean War began, Eighth Army did not have the corps artillery headquarters, field artillery group headquarters, or separate field artillery battalions that doctrine called for in a field army. The lack of this capability in Eighth Army affected its combat effectiveness in a number of ways. Indirect fire support was crucial to American tactical doctrine, and became even more important in Korea to compensate for the uneven quality of American infantry early in the war and the numerical superiority enemy infantry often enjoyed in engagements. The large losses the enemy inflicted on field artillery units in the first six months of the war made corps artillery reinforcing fires even more important. Corps artillery also was needed to support Republic of Korea (ROK) divisions, units that had very little organic artillery. These considerations made obtaining sufficient battalions and headquarters elements to create corps artilleries one of FECOM's high-priority requests for reinforcements. In July, 1950, it requested fifteen, then twenty-five nondivisional field artillery battalions for Eighth Army.[10]

Unfortunately for Eighth Army, the same budgetary limits that had helped strip it of nondivisional field artillery units had also greatly curtailed the number of artillery units available to use in creating the required corps artillery organizations. The General Reserve contained only seven battalions of the usual corps artillery weapons (8-inch howitzers, 155-mm howitzers, and 155-mm guns), plus four 105-mm howitzer battalions. Three 155-mm howitzer battalions, the 8-inch howitzer battalion, a self-propelled 105-mm howitzer battalion, an observation battalion, and a field artillery group headquarters deployed to Korea. Getting these units up to strength, along with supplying personnel for additional 105-mm howitzer batteries and replacing casualties, drained the level of trained field artillerymen in the ZI to extremely low levels.[11]

The army thus turned to the National Guard, both to build up the Eighth Army's corps artillery organizations and to rebuild the General Reserve.[12] During August and September, 1950, the army ordered into federal service thirteen howitzer battalions and four gun battalions, five field artillery group headquarters, and four observation battalions. These orders mobilized 57 percent of the guard's nondivisional field artillery battalions and 42 percent of guard field artillery group headquarters. In 1951, after the Chinese intervention prompted commanders in Korea to call for more artillery, the army would order an additional seven howitzer battalions and one gun battalion to active duty.[13]

Of the guard artillery units mobilized, eleven eventually served in Korea: five self-propelled 105-mm howitzer battalions, two self-propelled 155-mm gun battalions, three towed 155-mm howitzer battalions, and one observation battalion. These field artillery units varied in proficiency and degree of readiness upon mobilization, but all shared the characteristics of the army guard in 1950. These characteristics were especially troubling for field artillery units given the highly technical nature of fire direction tasks and gun crew drill, and the complexities of planning and coordinating fire support. As a result, many guard artillery commanders focused much of their training time during drills and summer camp on the first two tasks. Nondivisional outfits usually had little opportunity to train on the third task. A sergeant in the 936th FA Battalion recalled of his battery: "we could shoot. The rest of it, the perimeter defense stuff, the Army stuff, we didn't know nothing, no one did, but we could shoot."[14]

The army concentrated most nondivisional field artillery units mobilized in August and September, 1950 at four training sites: Camps McCoy and Carson, and Forts Hood and Lewis. Nine of the guard battalions at Hood, Carson, and Lewis were selected for deployment to Korea. However, with the confusion between Inchon and the Chinese intervention over what reinforcements Eighth Army needed, these battalions did not receive their warning orders until late December or early January. The problems that existed in all guard units before mobilization, combined with the many obstacles encountered at training sites, were not conducive to quickly establishing combat readiness. While some of the battalions did conduct battalion-level collective training, none had taken their battalion ATT before being alerted for deployment. Despite their low readiness ratings, in January, 1951, the nine battalions were even more urgently needed in Korea. By the time they finally reached Pusan in February, Eighth Army had retreated back into South Korea and the Chinese had taken Seoul.[15]

Upon disembarking, the battalions encountered the usual problems of units deploying by ship into a combat zone's rear echelon: waiting for their equipment to be unloaded (or to arrive on a different ship), familiarizing themselves with an unfamiliar country, and dealing with all the red tape and administrative confusion then enshrouding Pusan. The 204th FA Battalion received an especially quick course on life in the rear echelon and how the war had ravaged Korea. One of the battalion's trucks was stolen and soon after it set up its bivouac site a few miles from Pusan, a group of prostitutes and other camp followers moved in nearby. The battalion sent a detail to run off their new neighbors and burn down their camp. The 213th AFA Battalion had to maintain a "constant and thorough vigil" for its equipment, which had been loaded on several ships. As they waited for their gear to arrive, be unloaded, and prepared for use, battalions conducted individual training in the cold, muddy tent cities around the port city.[16] Aware that the battalions had not completed postmobilization training and already receiving criticism back home for the performance of poorly prepared units, Eighth Army, concerned about squandering this valuable new asset, ordered that all newly arrived guard and reserve field artillery battalions undergo training and testing supervised by corps artillery headquarters.[17]

Each guard battalion sent groups of men forward to observe corps artillery battalions in operation. Once all their equipment arrived, most battalions began a training program that lasted for three to four weeks. These programs used a building block approach to collective training, starting with sections, then batteries, and finally working together as a battalion. Battalions conducted this training under the supervision of staff officers from corps artillery headquarters. The program culminated with a battalion ATT, as modified by corps to reflect combat conditions in Korea, such as the need for more emphasis on high-angle fire and on perimeter defense. It was, the 204th FA Battalion commander recalled, "a very strenuous training program." The training after arriving in Korea, the 955th's commander believed, had made the unit "a good battalion, indeed ready to add its weight to the UN Forces."[18]

Imminent entry into combat not only motivated good training, it also led some commanders to make significant personnel changes in an effort to get the best available persons into key positions. In the 955th FA Battalion, all three firing battery commanders were sacked and replaced by battalion staff officers. Four days later, two Regular Army majors, both veterans of combat service in Korea, replaced the battalion's executive and operations officers. On 8 March, the battalion commander was transferred to the 2d Logistical Command and replaced by a lieutenant colonel from Eighth Army's artillery headquarters. Eight days later, the three sacked battery commanders were transferred to three different division artillery units and later that month the two redundant majors were finally transferred out of the battalion.[19]

Less drastic but still troubling personnel problems afflicted some of the units that had trained at Fort Lewis. The 213th AFA Battalion had an "informal" visit from the IX Corps inspector general, checking on complaints from nonguard enlisted men who had been assigned shortly before the unit sailed even though they did not have MOSs needed by the battalion. The battalion commander's answer was to retrain these fillers as artillerymen. A number of infantry fillers assigned to the 300th AFA Battalion just before it sailed deserted when they arrived in Korea and headed north for the front line after hearing stories that they would be taken in without questions by infantry units. The 300th's unhappy infantrymen were quickly rounded up and returned to the battalion, in part because they had made their way north in vehicles they had stolen from the unit.[20]

Not surprisingly, given the difficulties it had faced at Fort Lewis and its lack of a field artillery heritage to draw on, the 300th had a very difficult training period after arriving in Korea. While its firing batteries passed their ATTs, the unit failed its battalion ATT in the presence of the I Corps Artillery commander. The I Corps Artillery immediately dispatched a team of officers to provide remedial training for the battalion's officers in all phases of field artillery operations, and for the enlisted men in the two most technical artillery specialties: fire direction and survey. At the same time, a team from the Eighth Army inspector general's office descended upon the unit's administration, maintenance and supply personnel. On 9 May, two weeks after failing, the 300th AFA Battalion retook the battalion test and passed with a score of 84 percent.[21]

Beginning in late March, all the guard field artillery battalions, save the 300th, moved forward to the battlefield, some remaining with the corps that had supervised their training, others moved by Eighth Army to a different corps. The first guard battalion to fire in combat was the 936th FA Battalion, which provided reinforcing fires for the 3d Infantry Division on 30 March.[22] The 937th FA Battalion's arrival on the battlefield attracted special attention because it was the first self-propelled 155-mm gun battalion in Korea. Wishing to exploit the surprise effect of this weapon's range and power, which the Chinese had not yet faced, Eighth Army ordered the battalion to conduct an artillery raid against Chinese staging areas near Chorwon, nearly fifteen miles from the American front line. The 937th created a composite battery that drew sections from each firing battery and practiced the mission. On the night of 7–8 April, escorted by elements of the 25th Infantry Division, the composite battery moved forward to its firing point and in thirty minutes sent 120 rounds 25,715 yards to the north, where they impacted among some very surprised Chinese.[23]

Meanwhile, Eighth Army mounted Operation Dauntless, a slow, careful advance north to secure good defensible terrain just above the 38th parallel. Operation Dauntless provided eight of the battalions an opportunity for a gradual introduction to combat service. The 955th FA Battalion fired a total of 6,811 rounds between 9 and 22 April. The daily high was 1,068 on 12–13 April. The battalion moved twice during that period, and one of its firing batteries moved a third time. The 204th FA Battalion, which supported the 3d Infantry Division in the I Corps sector, also fired missions for a British brigade. The 213th AFA Battalion, assigned to IX Corps, supported the 6th ROK Division and the 1st Marine Division between 7 and 22 April, but did not fire its first rounds in combat until the twenty-second. Also assigned to IX Corps, the 987th AFA Battalion supported the 1st Marine Division from 15 to 21 April, firing mainly harassment and interdiction missions.[24]

As the eight guard battalions acquired more experience, Eighth Army prepared for the Chinese offensive it expected to begin later in April. Lieutenant General James A. Van Fleet, the Eighth Army commander, believed the Chinese would make Seoul a key objective during their offensive. Determined that the South Korean capital would not fall a third time, Van Fleet concentrated combat power in I Corps, which defended the approaches to the city with three American divisions, a ROK division, a British brigade, a Turkish brigade, and a corps artillery that included five guard battalions: the 955th FA, the 176th AFA, the 936th FA, the 937th FA, and the 204th FA.[25]

The Chinese attacked on 22 April, a large-scale offensive weighted against I Corps that was launched with the hope of inflicting such a severe defeat on UN forces that it would end the war. Eighth Army's plan to defeat this offensive combined gradual withdrawals to prevent the enemy from overrunning and destroying UN units with a hurricane of firepower designed to shatter advancing Chinese units. Once the Chinese had been sufficiently weakened, Eighth Army would counterattack to destroy the remaining enemy forces. The newly arrived guard battalions would play an important role in that effort while receiving a combat test more demanding than any ATT. For most of the battalions, the period 22–29 April was one of numerous fire missions and frequent moves, sometimes just ahead of the advancing Chinese.

In hard-pressed I Corps, the five guard battalions usually received missions to reinforce the fires of division artilleries, or even direct support battalions in RCTs. The 204th FA Battalion, with its long-range 155-mm guns, supported the 3d Infantry Division from 22–27 April, then returned to I Corps control after firing 10,215 rounds. The 955th FA Battalion's 155-mm howitzers, reinforcing the 24th Division Artillery, fired 2,774 rounds in three days and displaced five times between 22 and 30 April. The 176th AFA, 936th FA, and 937th FA Battalions were in the 25th Infantry Division's sector. These three battalions provided a significant part of the firepower the 25th used to break up Chinese attacks and helped plug the hole created when the Chinese broke through the Turkish brigade. Despite the tremendous amount of steel expended against them, the massed Chinese pressed I Corps backward toward Seoul as expected. However, the advance came at a terrible cost to the Chinese, as American firepower killed or wounded thousands of enemy infantrymen. By late April, these losses, and the difficulties the Chinese had sustaining large-scale offensives for an extended period, left the Chinese units opposite I Corps too weak to press forward any farther.[26]

While the Chinese attack in the IX Corps sector was their offensive's secondary effort, it caused more difficulties for the two guard battalions assigned to IX Corps than for the five battalions assigned to I Corps.[27] Both units, the 213th and 987th AFA Battalions, employed self-propelled 105-mm howitzers. The 105-mm howitzer had a shorter range than the 155-mm and 8-inch weapons normally used by corps artillery units, forcing the two battalions to move farther forward than normal for corps units and encouraging supported commanders to use these battalions for direct support of infantry units instead of in the general support role. During the April offensive, IX Corps, like I Corps, fought a generally decentralized artillery battle. The 987th's initial mission was reinforcing the 6th ROK Division. After that division collapsed, the battalion was assigned to general support of the 1st Marine Division, whose artillery commander often gave the battalion a mission reinforcing one of the 11th Marines's direct support battalions. Then, on 30 April, the 987th returned to reinforcing the 6th ROK Division.

On 22 April, the 213th AFA Battalion was in general support of the 1st Marine Division. The next day, IX Corps moved it to fire in direct support of the 6th ROK Division's crumbling regiments. On the twenty-fourth, IX Corps again moved the 213th, this time to reinforce the the British 27th Commonwealth Brigade's direct support battalion—a mission it performed until 28 April, although on the twenty-fifth most of the battalion's fire missions were again in support of the 6th ROK Division. On the twenty-eighth, the battalion shifted to general support of the 24th Infantry Division.

The 213th and 987th AFA Battalions not only found themselves firing reinforcing missions, their M7 lightly armored, open-topped howitzer carriages led some supported commanders to use the M7s in rearguard operations. The 987th covered one withdrawal by marine units on 24 April while the 213th performed the same mission twice for the 27th Commonwealth Brigade and once for the 24th Infantry Division. The 213th's battery assigned this mission on 24 April withdrew under small-arms and mortar fire while the battery performing the mission on 27 April had its perimeter probed by Chinese patrols. The battalion commander found this "excessive in-as-much as in all cases the unit to which Battalion was attached had organic light artillery."[28]

The need for fire support to shore up the 6th ROK Division led IX Corps to place the 987th AFA Battalion in an untenable position. Sent down a ragged mountain road that kept crumbling under the weight of the battalion's tracked vehicles on 22 April, only half the howitzers had managed to occupy firing positions when the Chinese attack began. Warned by its liaison officer that the ROK division was disintegrating, the 987th attempted to withdraw, but the road collapsed when the first M7 tried to make its way out. With routed Koreans running through their positions and the Chinese moving onto surrounding high ground, the Americans disabled the nine howitzers, abandoned the wheeled vehicles, and moved on foot back down the road to link up with the battalion's remaining nine howitzers. An attempt the next morning to recover the abandoned vehicles was ambushed by Chinese infantry and led to the battalion's only combat fatality during the offensive. The Chinese also turned back marine efforts later in the day to reach the vehicles. Meanwhile, the 987th's liaison team and forward observers struggled to reach safety amidst the rout of the 6th ROK Division. Two forward observers, originally listed as missing in action, were discovered later in the month to have been wounded and evacuated through marine channels. The action on 22–23 April cost the battalion a total of one killed and four wounded.[29]

Their use as direct support battalions, mainly with nonarmy units, created problems for the 213th and 987th AFA Battalions as their TO&E did not provide enough men and equipment to field the proper number of liaison and forward observer parties required for direct support missions. This forced both battalions to strip men and equipment from the firing batteries to provide the necessary parties.[30] Both battalions during many critical moments in April had to work extra hard at fire support coordination because IX Corps had them supporting units with different doctrine, procedures, and skill levels: U.S. Marines, the British, and the South Koreans. Supporting the Koreans proved especially difficult. The language difference was a major source of friction; infantry-artillery coordination was not a well-developed skill in most ROK units by that stage of the war; and American units supporting ROK divisions feared that the South Koreans would not hold against the enemy, leaving American gunners vulnerable to envelopment by the Chinese.[31]

While Eighth Army was unable to mount the crushing counterattack it had planned, UN forces had won a major victory against their enemy. For the seven guard battalions in I and IX Corps, it had been a memorable introduction to intense combat.[32] Despite a number of close calls for battalions in both corps, only the 987th AFA Battalion, stuck at the end of a mountain road as a ROK division collapsed around it, suffered significant equipment losses. None of the battalions had significant personnel losses. Thus, by the end of April, eight of the nine guard field artillery battalions in Korea had been introduced to combat in such a way that they gained extensive experience without having to pay an exorbitant price for it. Even in the 987th, which lost a third of its vehicles and half its howitzers, the operations officer believed that by the end of the month the battalion's combat efficiency had "improved noticeably."[33]

During the first two weeks of May, the eight guard battalions absorbed the lessons of the previous month and trained on problem areas as needed. They fired many fewer missions than during the last week of April and were joined on the battlefield by the 300th AFA Battalion. Now certified as combat ready, the 300th was assigned to X Corps, which promptly split it up, attaching one battery to the 1st Marine Division and the remainder of the battalion to the 2d Infantry Division. Meanwhile, Eighth Army picked up indications that the Chinese were massing for another major offensive, which General Van Fleet believed would once again target Seoul as the main objective. The preponderance of Eighth Army's combat power, including the corps artillery units, therefore remained concentrated in I and IX Corps.[34]

During the first week of May, the 987th AFA Battalion was issued equipment to replace what it had lost while supporting the 6th ROK Division. Because there were no M7s available, all of A Battery and half of B Battery were issued towed 105-mm howitzers to replace the nine M7s abandoned the previous month. At the same time, the battalion commander made major changes in officer assignments: the three firing battery commanders were relieved, replaced by three battalion staff officers, and five lieutenants swapped positions. Two of the relieved battery commanders in the 987th were ORC officers, and the third was a guard captain who had been an Army Air Forces navigator in World War II. Two of the new battery commanders had been enlisted field artillerymen during the war and were commissioned in 1945. The third had been an infantry officer during the war. The 955th FA Battalion commander also made some changes during this period, relieving one howitzer chief and busting him to private for using an 8-inch howitzer powder charge. When fired, the more powerful charge badly damaged the 155-mm howitzer and slightly wounded three men in the section. The 955th's commander also engaged in some officer swapping: seven officers changed positions, but only one firing battery command changed hands.[35]

The battalions assigned to I and IX Corps prepared themselves for the expected Chinese offensive, but the enemy had other plans; on 16 May, an estimated fifteen Chinese and five North Korean divisions assaulted X Corps and the two ROK corps on its right flank. This development did not come as a surprise to X Corps, which had predicted the Chinese course of action. The 1st Marine Division and the 2d Infantry Division had stockpiled large amounts of ammunition and developed extensive fire support plans, and X Corps had placed the 196th FA Battalion in general support of the 2d Infantry Division. But X Corps's plans for defense were unhinged by the collapse of its two ROK divisions and the ROK corps to its right, creating a hole through which the Chinese advanced, threatening to envelop and destroy the 2d Infantry Division.

In response, the 2d Division Artillery and X Corps Artillery provided another demonstration of why field artillery was the greatest killer on the battlefield. The 300th AFA Battalion's A and C Batteries fired 6,100 rounds during the first forty-eight hours of the attack, while the 196th FA Battalion expended 2,650 155-mm rounds during the first twenty-four hours. Eighth Army also reinforced the X Corps Artillery with a composite artillery task force built on the 937th FA Battalion: the 937th, less one of its firing batteries, plus a battery of 8-inch howitzers from the 17th FA Battalion. In the 300th AFA Battalion, ammunition trucks backed up directly behind M7s and remained there until the howitzers fired off the trucks' loads. Battalions fired these amounts as they displaced up to five times a day in response to the changing tactical situation. The still sometimes shallow level of field artillery skill in the 300th AFA Battalion revealed itself during this period. To speed up its rate of fire, the 300th fired its missions without computing the optimum charge. Instead, to simplify procedures for howitzer crews and fire direction personnel who had only recently passed their remedial ATT, missions were fired with the maximum charge, despite the tremendous wear that significantly shortened tube life. When one battery had to relay the battery at night for a new direction of fire, the battery leaders suddenly realized they had never before performed such a procedure. Luckily, one soldier with World War II experience was able to relay the battery and it uneasily continued to fire missions until dawn, when the new lay could be verified by the officers.[36]

The 300th AFA Battalion found that units in X Corps were just as prone to regard the M7 as more than an indirect fire weapon as those in I and IX Corps. On 18 May, the 2d Infantry Division used one battery of M7s to support, with both indirect and direct fire, an attempt to break a roadblock preventing the 23d Infantry's withdrawal. The most flagrant use of the M7 as an assault gun took place during X Corps's counterattack once the Chinese offensive stalled. On 25 May, X Corps assigned the 300th to reinforce the fires of a task force composed of the 187th Airborne RCT and the 72d Tank Battalion. The task force was to counterattack north across the Soyang River to seize a key road junction at Kansong in hopes of cutting off the retreat of Chinese and North Korean units that had survived the hurricane of steel X Corps had used to help defeat their attacks.

Under intense pressure from the X Corps commander, Lt. Gen. Edward M. Almond, to advance quickly, on 26 May the task force's advance guard moved forward with the 300th's A Battery in the lead, acting more as assault guns than field artillery. On the twenty-seventh, the advance guard, supported by A Battery's lightly armored, open-topped M7s using direct fire, took most of the intermediate objective of Inje. The battery was preceded into the town by only three tanks and a small group of infantry. Meanwhile, the task force's main body struggled along poor roads to catch up, and the 300th's remaining tracked vehicles and overloaded ammunition trucks had an especially hard time.

Luck ran out on 28 May. Pushing north from Inje, A Battery encountered heavy enemy resistance as it advanced along a narrow mountain road. Three thousand yards north of town, the battery and its accompanying infantry were stopped by a roadblock, then pinned down by small arms and mortars for four hours—until the task force ordered them to withdraw, a tricky operation on such a road. With the 300th's other two batteries firing suppression missions, A Battery was able to turn around and disengage. The day's action cost the battery two killed and twenty-three wounded, including its executive officer, who was shot dead as he directed howitzers turning around on the road.[37]

Meanwhile, I and IX Corps's guard battalions had been supporting their corps' attacks toward the 38th parallel, which were designed to take pressure off X Corps and block the withdrawal of surviving enemy forces. During much of this action, the corps assigned their guard units general support reinforcing missions, often tasking battalions to support an American division and a ROK division at the same time. The IX Corps Artillery also created several ad hoc artillery task forces during this action, most notably from 27 to 29 May, when it created one to provide general support to the 24th Division Artillery and a ROK division. Corps ordered the 987th AFA Battalion to attach its remaining M7s to the 955th FA Battalion. In return, IX Corps added to the 987th's nine towed 105-mm howitzers a battery of towed 155-mm howitzers from the 955th and a battery of 155-mm guns from the 937th.[38]

Also supporting the 24th Division Artillery for much of this time was the 213th AFA Battalion. Again, the mobility of self-propelled 105-mm howitzers led supported commanders to use this unit in a direct support role. Ordered on 22 May to reinforce the 52d FA Battalion, which was in direct support of the 21st Infantry, the 213th was then ordered by the 52d FA to move forward of the 52d and join the 21st Infantry. On occasion, the 21st Infantry used the M7s more as assault guns than as field artillery, and on the twenty-seventh the 213th's Headquarters and A Batteries did the same, counterattacking a Chinese force assaulting the perimeters of the 213th and the 21st Infantry's command post.[39]

After the defeat of the Chinese offensives in April and May, 1951, the war changed from one of large-scale movement to a war of posts, and the guard battalions entered a period of transition. The first major change for all the battalions was the release from active duty of the enlisted reservists who had joined them shortly after mobilization, and in June the first groups of these men began leaving Korea. By the end of the year, few of these men were left in the battalions. The question of what order these Enlisted Reserve Corps (ERC) fillers within a battalion would leave under the phase-out program was a potential source of great friction. To forestall this, the 955th FA Battalion established its own internal point system to determine the order in which its ERC personnel would leave for home.[40]

Their departure created problems, as many filled key technical specialties and NCO leadership positions. Included in the first group of ERC fillers (nineteen NCOs and six other enlisted men) to leave the 300th AFA Battalion in June were the battalion operations and personnel sergeants, the Service Battery first sergeant, a chief of firing battery, a battery motor sergeant, a communications specialist, and some mechanics and cooks.[41] The loss of the ERC personnel foreshadowed even further personnel turbulence. Eighth Army in late spring began its Rotation of Combat Personnel

(RCP) program, and by December those guardsmen, reserve officers, and regulars who had come to Korea in February with the battalions would become eligible for rotation back to the ZI. In any case, guardsmen would have to begin returning home in the spring of 1952 as the expiration of their federal service neared.[42]

The problem of losing personnel was exacerbated by the inadequate number of qualified men the army could find to ship to Korea as replacements, leaving the battalions facing the prospect of a serious deficit in skilled manpower by summer 1952. Replacements came from a mixed pool. Some were men already serving in Korea or Japan, mainly regulars, but with a seasoning of reservists and guardsmen. Most of the Regular Army officers arriving as replacements were field grade officers, usually sent to replace guard battalion commanders as the latter departed for the ZI, as in the 204th FA, 213th AFA, 300th AFA, and 987th AFA Battalions. The reverse took place in the 955th, whose Regular Army battalion commander was replaced by a guard lieutenant colonel stripped from a unit in the ZI.[43]

More common were guardsmen levied from units sent to Europe or kept in the ZI. This source often provided officers and enlisted men with little or no experience in field artillery, or experience on a weapon different from the one used by the unit they joined in Korea. The 987th AFA Battalion noted that a "great number" of the replacements it received in 1951 either had field artillery experience on some other type of weapon or did not have a field artillery MOS. The merger of the field and coast artillery into a single artillery branch after World War II affected the usefulness of replacement officers. For example, most field artillery units in Korea received officers stripped from mobilized guard AAA battalions and reserve officers whose only experience was in AAA. Few Regular artillery officers, let alone guard and reserve officers, had become proficient in both types of artillery since the merger of the two branches. Wilfrid Boettiger, a World War II guard AAA officer who joined the ORC after the war, volunteered for active duty in 1950. After attending the AAA Officer Advanced Course, he was assigned in August, 1951, to the 64th FA Battalion, whose commander greeted Boettiger with "Another Goddamn antiaircraft officer." The 987th AFA Battalion, receiving one such officer from a Virginia AAA unit in the ZI, made him the billeting officer, then noted in its command report that the "assignment of such an officer to a combat unit is an injustice to the officer and the unit."[44]

Draftee replacements were often either basic training graduates shipped to Korea without any training in a specific MOS or soldiers awarded an MOS after incomplete training for service in Korea. The battalions did receive a large number of reserve officers during 1952, both freshly commissioned lieutenants and battery and field grade officers on extended active duty status. This group's training and experience varied greatly, from trained but inexperienced lieutenants to officers with significant World War II field artillery experience. In the 987th AFA Battalion by May, 1952, only one officer, a guardsmen who had agreed to an extended active duty tour, remained in the battalion among those who had arrived with it in February, 1951. The battalion's officers included two Regular Army officers, the battalion commander, and a second lieutenant. There were five guard captains and two guard lieutenants levied for service in Korea from units in the ZI. The battalion's remaining twenty-eight officers were reservists: both majors, eleven captains, eight first lieutenants, and seven second lieutenants. The replacement officers received by the 955th FA Battalion by the end of February, 1952, two months before the battalion completely lost its guard character, consisted of one guard first lieutenant, one Regular Army second lieutenant, and twenty-one reservists (three majors, six captains, nine first lieutenants, and three second lieutenants).[45]

The shortage of qualified replacements resulted in many who were eligible to return home having to spend extra time in Korea until either a qualified replacement arrived or one could be trained within the unit. While the start of rotation in the 987th AFA Battalion generated a "noticeable improvement" in the battalion's morale, the 955th FA Battalion noted a significant negative effect on the morale of those eligible to go home, but who had been retained because their replacements had not yet arrived. Officers were especially likely to be held until a qualified replacement arrived. When four new officers reached the 955th in February, 1952, the command report remarked that this "brightens the Officer rotation picture." The 955th noted in November, 1951 that "the men awaited eagerly for news of replacements so that they could be rotated." That month the battalion had 247 enlisted men eligible for rotation who could not leave for lack of a replacement. In November, the 213th AFA Battalion sent home 120 of 270 enlisted men eligible for rotation under the RCP; in December, it sent home two of twenty-six officers and 136 of 242 eligible enlisted men. The 987th AFA Battalion in November was able to rotate home 177 of its 280 RCP-eligible enlisted men thanks in large part to the trained—albeit on a different type of weapon—artillerymen it had received.[46]

Racial integration added to the battalions' personnel turbulence as the war of movement came to an end. In the summer of 1951, FECOM had no political inhibitions about integrating the corps artilleries' guard battalions, as it did with the 40th and 45th Infantry Divisions then training in Japan. During July and August, the 300th AFA Battalion received more than 80 black enlisted men, approximately 14 percent of the battalion's total strength. In August, the 213th and 987th AFA Battalions received their first black enlisted soldiers, 26 and 27 respectively, while the 204th FA Battalion received 26 black enlisted men. By October, black enlisted strength in the four guard battalions assigned to I Corps Artillery varied form 8 to 13 percent. By December, the 987th AFA Battalion had 99 black enlisted men, or 17 percent of the battalion's enlisted strength.[47]

Racial integration proceeded more or less smoothly. The 204th FA Battalion's commander recalled that integration did not create any problems in his unit. In others, such as the 300th and 987th AFA Battalions, commanders assigned the black troops they received fairly evenly among their batteries, and saw these soldiers, most of whom were recent basic training graduates, as a welcome source of manpower. However, integration created more concerns in the 955th FA Battalion, a New York City unit, that by early December was complaining to corps that it was getting "too many" black soldiers as replacements.[48]

As the battalions attempted to deal with this personnel turbulence, Eighth Army called on them to provide even greater amounts of firepower to offset the enemy's numerical superiority and to keep casualties down among the friendly infantrymen digging in atop the hills and ridgelines. As the enemy was also digging in and building up his indirect fire capability, the battalions now faced the additional problem of dealing with increasing amounts of counterbattery fire. As the opposing Main Lines of Resistance (MLR) began to congeal, the Chinese turned out to be better bunker builders than did the Americans. Their positions often withstood normal indirect fire from division artillery units, and as a result, division artillery headquarters would call upon the self-propelled 155-mm gun and towed 8-inch howitzer battalions in the corps artillery to send one or two sections forward to the MLR to snipe at enemy fortifications with direct fire.[49]

At the same time, Eighth Army also tasked the battalions to act as division artillery headquarters for ROK divisions and to assist in training ROK field artillery units as part of the American effort to expand and improve the ROK army. Often, a corps artillery headquarters would assign a battalion headquarters the additional mission of controlling a provisional field artillery group of one to three other battalions—sometimes American, sometimes ROK, and sometimes a mix from both nations. The 955th FA Battalion from January to mid-February, 1952, commanded a provisional group supporting the 9th ROK Division in I Corps. From mid-February to late March it continued to support the 9th ROK, but by then the 987th AFA Battalion controlled the provisional group. Usually these provisional groups acted as a ROK division's artillery until the ROK field artillerymen were judged capable of operating on their own. Controlling these provisional groups, supplying ROK units with forward observer and liaison parties, and training ROK field artillerymen placed a heavy burden on the available skilled manpower in the battalions, as none of those tasks had been planned for in the design of the battalions' TO&Es.[50]

Because the corps artillery organizations were dominated by guard units—nine of thirteen battalions in September, 1951—these guardsmen had the opportunity to work with men from different parts of the United States. Men from Wyoming's 300th AFA Battalion, working in a provisional group with New York City's 955th FA Battalion, remembered the latter as good soldiers, but claimed they were harder to understand than Koreans. Those guardsmen sent to help train Korean artillerymen remembered the units they worked with as enthusiastic and hard working, but inclined to dispense with sophisticated techniques of targeting and adjusting fire: "they liked to shoot and just keep firing until they hit the target; even if it took a hundred rounds."[51]

These demands on the battalions' resources intersected with the personnel turbulence between the early autumn of 1951 and the late spring of 1952 to generate pressures on the units, which, while not as dramatic as the battles of April and May, placed a great strain on them. Both battalions and corps artillery headquarters grew concerned during the autumn of 1951 over the erosion of skill within units. In November, I Corps Artillery ordered the 204th FA Battalion to fire a series of missions designed to test the battalion's gunnery skills. The results showed that the battalion's ability to quickly mass fires on a target had declined considerably because of the loss of experienced soldiers and their replacement by soldiers who were poorly trained or untrained in gunnery skills.[52] Each corps artillery and its battalions developed their own programs to maintain combat effectiveness. Corps artillery staffs gave short courses in the duties of key positions, such as battery executive officer, and mandated that battalions train on certain tasks. Battalions rotated junior officers among different positions, both to broaden their skills and to distribute equitably the hazards of forward observer duty. While battalions developed formal training programs that covered both collective and individual tasks, the problems with replacements meant that the emphasis was on the latter. Because the battalions were never placed in reserve during this period, the major form of training in individual skills for new soldiers was on-the-job training.[53]

By the end of the spring of 1952, the personnel crisis in guard units that had arrived in early 1951 had passed with the departure of the last original guard and reserve officers. The army decided to keep the units' colors in federal service until the end of the war, making them guard units on paper but no longer in character.

While none of these units were tested as severely as Regular Army units in the summer of 1950 or during the Chinese offensive that November, the units had arrived in Korea just in time to receive a thorough examination in various aspects of combat: defense, withdrawal, attack, and pursuit. Some performed better than others, but none failed. During the 1951 spring battles, these guard units provided Eighth Army with important engineer, transportation, and fire support resources that it had lacked during its previous battles in Korea. Although none of them were ready for deployment on M-Day, all proved to possess a strong base upon which could be created combat effective units. The use of reservists as fillers did much to speed the building of combat effective units.

The field artillery battalions had the greatest challenge. Crucial to their success—given that the orders for overseas movement cut short their ATP training—was the fact that each battalion did not immediately move forward to the battlefield after arriving in Korea. Instead, they had the opportunity to train under the supervision of officers experienced in the problems facing field artillery units in Korea, allowing the guard battalions to profit from the lessons learned at a significant cost by units that deployed in 1950. The battalions then had from several weeks to at least a few days to make the transition from training to actual combat during a period of relatively light battlefield activity. This combination of intensive training in theater and a gradual introduction to the battlefield did much to prepare the battalions for the shock of intense combat during the Chinese spring offensives.

CHAPTER 5

The Thunderbirds in Korea

Only two of the eight National Guard infantry divisions ordered into federal service deployed to Korea: California's 40th and Oklahoma's 45th, the Thunderbird Division. The 45th experienced many difficulties during its postmobilization training, including moving to Japan before completing its MTP. The Thunderbirds arrived in Korea from Japan after the war's large-scale movement phase ended, and although the 45th was not tested in combat to anywhere near the same degree as divisions deployed in 1950, it performed as well as Regular Army divisions during the roughly six months of its existence as a guard division in Korea.

The Pride of Oklahoma

In 1950, the Thunderbird of the 45th Infantry Division flew high and wide over Oklahoma. The division possessed one of the strongest links in the nation between a guard unit and its community, a link forged from several different sources. There existed in Oklahoma after 1945 what one junior officer described as "a very strong military mindset." This aspect of state culture combined with a strong sense of pride in the 45th Infantry Division as one of the state's great achievements. The 45th had earned a reputation as one of the best divisions of the World War II army, spearheading the invasions of Sicily, Italy, and southern France, and ending the war by capturing Munich. The 45th had produced, in Lt. Gen. Raymond

S. McLain, the most successful guard officer of the war and, in Sgt. Bill Mauldin, the greatest voice of the war for the enlisted soldier. The power of this reputation within the division and the state was maintained by veterans of the wartime 45th, who made up approximately 10 percent of the officers and 5 percent of the enlisted men in the postwar 45th. In the postwar reorganization of the guard, the NGB assigned Oklahoma only one other army guard unit, an engineer bridge company, in addition to the entire 45th. In 1948, the NGB reinforced the 45th's sense of being an elite force by selecting it as one of six guard divisions in a mobile strike force earmarked for early deployment after mobilization. Army Field Forces inspectors praised the 45th's training. The 45th enjoyed good relations with the Oklahoma legislature—three of its officers were members of the Oklahoma House of Representatives—and close ties with the Oklahoma press, especially Oklahoma City's *Daily Oklahoman* newspaper.[1]

The 45th Infantry Division in 1950 had a pool of combat experienced commanders at battalion level and above. The division commander was Maj. Gen. James C. Styron. Born in Texas in 1898, Styron attended high school in Oklahoma and graduated from West Point in 1918 with one of the war-shortened classes, but too late to see service in France. Commissioned into the coast artillery, Styron resigned his commission in 1920 and returned to Oklahoma to become a cotton broker. In 1922, Styron joined the 45th Division as a field artillery first lieutenant. By 1940, he was a lieutenant colonel, executive officer of the division's field artillery brigade, and a graduate of the National Guard officer courses at the Field Artillery School (1937) and the Command and General Staff School (1939).

During the 45th's World War II service, Styron was promoted to colonel, served as division chief of staff, became executive officer of the division artillery in 1942, and then went back to division chief of staff in 1943. In March, 1944, after serving through mobilization, training, the Sicily and Salerno campaigns, and several months at Anzio, Styron was evacuated from the beachhead because of illness. After recovering, he spent the rest of the war at the Field Artillery Replacement Training Center and on the War Department committee considering postwar policy for the National Guard. After a brief stint in the Pacific as a corps operations officer, Styron left active duty in February, 1946, with a Silver Star and a Legion of Merit. Back in Oklahoma, he accepted a commission as a brigadier general in the Oklahoma guard. That same year, Gov. Robert S. Kerr, on General McLain's recommendation, gave Styron command of the division, which led to his promotion to major general later in the year.[2]

Styron, with McLain's advice, selected men to fill the senior positions in the 45th with an emphasis first on service with the division in the war, and second on service overseas during the war. The assistant division commander was Brig. Gen. Ray W. Kenny, born in 1895 and commissioned into the field artillery from Officer Training Camp in 1917. He joined the guard in 1925 and commanded a field artillery battalion in the 45th during World War II. He returned to Oklahoma upon demobilization, where Governor Kerr made him the state adjutant general. The division artillery commander was Brig. Gen. Hal Muldrow, Jr. Born in 1905, Muldrow joined the 45th as a field artillery officer in 1929. Muldrow also commanded a field artillery battalion in the division during World War II.[3]

The division chief of staff was Col. Ross H. Routh. Born in Texas in 1907, Routh enlisted in the guard in 1930. Commissioned as an infantry officer in 1932, Routh changed branches in 1940 to become a finance officer. He spent the war with the 45th as its finance officer. Demobilized in 1946, by 1950 he was the U.S. Property and Disbursing Officer for Oklahoma, the NGB's supervisor of federal money and supplies sent to the state. Three of the four division assistant chiefs of staff were pre-1940 veterans of the 45th. All were infantry lieutenant colonels with an average age of forty.[4]

The three infantry regimental commanders, with an average age of forty-one, were all Oklahoma natives who had enlisted and then been commissioned in the guard. Colonel James O. Smith (180th Infantry) was commissioned in 1940 after eleven years of enlisted service. Described as a "very experienced combat officer" by one of his junior officers, he served with the 45th from mobilization in 1940 to V-E Day in 1945. Colonel Herbert G. Sitler (279th Infantry), commissioned in 1935 after four years of enlisted service, left the 45th after mobilization to serve as a battalion commander and executive officer of the 325th Glider Infantry Regiment. Both Smith and Sitler ended the war as lieutenant colonels. Colonel Frederick A. Daugherty (179th Infantry), commissioned in 1936 after two years of enlisted service, also left the 45th after mobilization in 1940, spending much of the war on the Sixth Army staff, and ended the war as a colonel. Daugherty and Smith both returned to Oklahoma in 1946, where they took command of their regiments and began organizing them. Sitler returned to the guard in 1949 and took command of the 279th.[5]

The nine infantry battalion commanders at mobilization in 1950 were all World War II veterans, although not all had served with the 45th. With an average age of thirty-seven, all but one of the commanders were native Oklahomans. Four had received their initial commissions in the Oklahoma guard, three in the reserve, and two during the war. All but one had served as enlisted men in the Oklahoma guard for periods ranging from two to eight years. During the war, one reached the rank of colonel, two became lieutenant colonels, and the rest were majors. All joined the postwar 45th in 1946 or 1947.[6] The four field artillery battalion commanders at mobilization had been battery commanders or artillery staff officers in the 45th in 1940. With an average age of forty-one, three of the four had been born in Oklahoma and all had served as enlisted guardsmen for periods ranging from one to eight years. All had attended battery officer training courses at the Field Artillery School during the war. Three of the four ended the war as captains and one as a major. All rejoined the 45th in 1946.[7] Only one of the four separate battalion commanders was a native Oklahoman, but three had been in the division when it was mobilized in 1940. After the war, two joined the division in 1946, and two did so in 1947. Of the four, whose average age was thirty-eight, only the 245th Tank Battalion's commander had graduated from an army service school in the branch in which he now commanded a battalion, and he had attended the associate basic course.[8]

Between reorganization in 1946 and mobilization in 1950, the 45th lived the life of a typical guard division, though with a greater sense of esprit and community backing than many. It suffered the same problems as other guard units, and when Army Field Forces selected the 45th in July, 1950, as one of the most ready guard divisions, *ready* was a relative term. The division was short major pieces of equipment, such as tanks, howitzers, and antiaircraft guns, and also of many of the smaller items required to run a division. In 1950, a full-strength infantry division needed 910 officers, 132 warrant officers, and 17,460 enlisted men. The reduced National Guard authorization called for 851 officers, 130 warrant officers, and 12,777 enlisted men. On 1 August the 45th reported 698 officers, 64 warrant officers, and 7,651 enlisted men. This total of 8,413 was 61 percent of the division's National Guard reduced authorization and 45 percent of its full-strength authorization. The 45th's commissioned officer strength was at 82 percent of its reduced National Guard authorization and 77 percent of its full strength authorization. For enlisted soldiers, the respective figures were 60 percent and 44 percent.[9]

Postmobilization Training

At midnight on 8 September 1950, the 45th Infantry Division Command Post opened at Camp Polk, Louisiana. By 11 September, the division had completed the move from Oklahoma. Before arriving at Camp Polk, a significant change occurred in the 45th when General Kenny stepped down as assistant division commander to remain in Oklahoma as the adjutant general. Styron asked that Col. Robert L. Dulaney be assigned to the 45th to replace Kenny. Commanding an infantry regiment in Austria at the time, Dulaney was a 1923 West Point graduate and Regular Army infantry officer who had served with the 45th in World War II. He arrived at Polk in late September and the next month regained the brigadier general's star he had briefly worn during the waning months of the war in Europe. The division chief of staff was transferred out of the 45th in November and replaced by Col. Preston J. C. Murphy, a former Thunderbird who had integrated into the Regular Army after World War II.[10]

There were also several changes among the separate battalion commanders. In August, General Styron promoted the 120th Medical Battalion's commander to division surgeon and replaced him with the 179th Infantry's medical company commander. Shortly after arriving at Polk, the 145th AAA Battalion's commander moved to command of the 160th FA Battalion, in which he had served during World War II and which his experience better suited him to command than the 145th AAA. Lieutenant Colonel J. S. Wilkes arrived in early October from Fort Meade, where he had commanded the 70th AAA Gun Battalion, and took over the 145th. Wilkes had been a guard cavalry officer in New York before World War II. His regiment converted to antiaircraft artillery before mobilization in early 1941, and Wilkes integrated into the Regular Army as an AAA officer after the war. Shortly after this change, another guardsman turned Regular Army officer, Lt. Col. J. M. Throckmorton, joined the division. A guard cavalry first sergeant from Pennsylvania who was commissioned during the 1940 mobilization, Throckmorton took command of the 245th Tank Battalion.[11]

Although thousands of men from the rest of the nation joined the 45th at Polk, the Thunderbirds remained the pride of Oklahoma. During the Christmas season, Kerr's department store in Oklahoma City advertised a $1 plastic helmet. Painted olive drab, the helmet sported "the famous red 'n white 45th Division insignia!" The ad boasted: "kids! here's a real THUNDERBIRD helmet like a GI's." From September to December, 1950, the Oklahoma press offered extensive coverage of the 45th, fed by a steady stream of stories from the division's public information office. In December, WKY radio began broadcasting "Following the 45th," a program transcribed at Polk and flown back to Oklahoma City for transmission. The new medium of television also joined in: WKY-TV sent a crew to Polk in September to film reports broadcast later in the month.[12]

Communities kept in touch with their Thunderbirds at Polk, although not without some unexpected difficulties. Many World War II Thunderbirds and their families out of habit used the 45th's wartime Army Post Office address. Unfortunately, after 1945 the army had reassigned that address to the Far East Command, so for several months after mobilization many letters from Oklahoma traveled across the Pacific before finally arriving at Polk. Friends and family members traveled to Polk to visit their Thunderbirds, some bearing gifts. Battery C, 160th FA Battalion, received a semitrailer load of furniture from its hometown of Haskell after some soldiers' mothers visited and found a bare battery day room. A delegation from Chickasha went to Polk in December bearing gifts for its hometown battery. The seeming closeness between Camp Polk and Oklahoma tempted traffic in the other direction, as Thunderbirds attempted to drive home and then back to Louisiana on thirty-six-hour weekend passes.[13] The Christmas season brought a large flow of traffic between Louisiana and Oklahoma. General Styron authorized seventy-two-hour passes, with half the division getting one for Christmas and the other half getting one for New Year's. The Oklahoma Air National Guard dispatched several transport aircraft to ferry Thunderbirds home and back to Camp Polk, as well as to carry Christmas mail to the division. The holiday airlift expanded when private planes and the planes of several oil companies joined the ferry operations.[14]

The desire of soldiers to return home during the holidays was sharpened by the news from Korea. The 45th had left for Polk under the cloud of summer disasters and desperate battles along the Pusan perimeter, with mounting Sooner casualty lists. The clouds lifted with the shattering of North Korean forces following the Inchon landing and the pursuit deep into North Korea. Statements by senior Defense Department officials in late October painted a bright future for the Thunderbirds. Secretary of Defense George C. Marshall announced that involuntarily recalled guardsmen and reservists would be released as soon as they had finished their training and there were sufficient draftees and volunteers trained to take their places on active duty. Three days later, Secretary of the Army Frank Pace said that he hoped to begin releasing guardsmen in the summer of 1951 and that the army no longer planned to send guard units overseas. When the Chinese launched their stunning offensive in late November, however, uncertainty once again settled over the division's future after it completed its MTP.[15]

The infusion of men from the rest of the nation made Sooners a minority of Thunderbirds by the end of 1950, but the links between the 45th and Oklahoma remained strong, and stories about the 45th continued to appear regularly in Oklahoma newspapers. The 45th's military government officer, Lt. Col. Roy P. Stewart, was also the *Daily Oklahoman*'s senior writer, and he returned to the state in late January, 1951, to address the Oklahoma Press Association convention. General Styron also returned to the state for a brief visit, telling fellow Oklahomans in early February that the division would finish its MTP training in June, but that plans for the 45th after that were "indefinite."[16]

Interlude in Japan

The 45th, like other guard units, encountered significant problems in conducting postmobilization training: insufficient qualified cadre, equipment shortages, inadequate facilities, personnel levies, and an excess of untrained recruits. The greatest disruption to the MTP came in February, 1951, when the 45th and 40th Infantry Divisions received orders for movement to Japan. The 45th stopped unit training on 25 February to concentrate on preparing for its move, knowing that it would not be combat ready when it reached its destination. The movement order came as the infantry regiments were finishing platoon-level unit training and the field artillery batteries had not finished the service practice firings prescribed by their ATPs. Some Oklahomans protested the decision to send the 45th overseas on the grounds that the division had not had "sufficient combat training." However, this effort faded when Thunderbirds home on leave spoke out against the protest.[17]

Reactions in Oklahoma fell into several categories. One was a feeling of resignation. Congressman Tom Steed said that given the current situation in the Far East, "I don't know how it can be avoided." Another was anger, especially among the families of World War II veterans, who believed it unjust to call on those soldiers to serve overseas for a second time.

Closely related to anger was fear that the 45th would be committed to combat in Korea before it could finish its MTP training. Governor Johnston Murray offered reassurance, based on a telephone call from Army Secretary Pace, that the 45th would be kept in Japan unless there was an "emergency" requiring its use in Korea.[18]

Given the belief of many Oklahomans that theirs was an elite division with a proud past, it was no surprise that another reaction to the news was pride that the Thunderbirds once again led the way. The *Daily Oklahoman* quickly pointed this out in an article headlined "Division Adds Another to Long List of Firsts." The paper's editorial, "Oklahoma's Own," added: "[A]ll Oklahomans have reason for pride in the fact that Oklahoma is one of the handful of states whose organized militia was ready for activation when the first call to the colors came. . . . [T]his is a great tribute indeed to the patriotism and fighting spirit of the lads of Oklahoma."[19]

General Styron, not surprisingly, endorsed that view: "We have a natural feeling of pride that the department of the army has chosen us as one of the first civilian component divisions to be sent overseas in this emergency." Roy Stewart, in a March *Daily Oklahoman* article, favorably compared the 1951 division with its 1941 counterpart, marveling at how the present-day division was "better led due to experience, better trained due to new methods and new training aids, better informed as to national purposes and international conditions, better equipped, better supplied and better able to add its bit to the bitterly earned tradition of Oklahoma's own divisional unit."[20]

Not all of his subordinates, however, shared General Styron's pride at the honor accorded the Thunderbirds. Some had pinned their hopes on rumors that the division would be sent to Germany as part of NATO's military buildup. Others were concerned that Japan was only a way station on the road to combat duty in Korea, particularly after remarks in mid-March by Senator Kerr that this was possible. Some World War II veterans were uneasy about becoming "rear echelon" troopers in Japan while American troops were hard pressed nearby in Korea. But the dominant emotion came to be resignation, for as General Styron stated in announcing the news, the division was "under army orders, and will go wherever it is assigned."[21]

As was the case in other guard units alerted for overseas movement, not all the Thunderbirds would be going to Japan. The POM review uncovered a few underage guardsmen, and other guardsmen could not meet the physical requirements for overseas service. The most notable loss was Colonel Sitler, who gave up command of the 279th Infantry because of ill health. The regiment received a new colonel on 22 March, Col. Frank R. Maerdian, a Regular Army officer and commander of an infantry regiment in the closing days of World War II. He joined the 279th from the University of Oregon, where he had commanded the army ROTC program.[22]

The division held a farewell parade at Camp Polk on 26 March. Governor Murray, Adjutant General Kenny, Maj. Gen. W. S. Key, and "Congressional and local dignitaries" traveled from Oklahoma to watch the 45th pass in review. Governor Murray expressed his pride in the division, but many families watching the parade under an overcast sky shared the sentiments of a young woman newly married to a departing soldier: "They look so handsome and strong. God knows when we'll see them again." Following the parade, "a stream of cars, many of them bearing Oklahoma tags, started pouring onto the gray highway and the grayer afternoon."[23]

The last unit of the 45th left Polk on 30 March and sailed from New Orleans the next day. Units found considerable confusion at the port, creating a good deal of friction and misunderstandings. The greatest casualty of confusion was equipment for use in training during the voyage; it was loaded into ships' cargo holds instead of being kept accessible and could not be used, destroying the elaborate training schedules created for the trip.[24] The *Daily Oklahoman* kept its readers informed of the 45th's move by sending one of its reporters along with the division. During the voyage a new wave of concern arose in Oklahoma over the use of the 45th. Once again, Oklahoma politicians produced pledges from the Department of the Army that the division would not be broken up and that Thunderbirds would not be stripped from it and used as individual replacements for units in Korea.[25]

The ships carrying the division arrived at Hokkaido, Japan's northernmost island, between 25 and 30 April. Sent to Hokkaido to guard against the possibility of a Soviet invasion, the 45th found only enough permanent quarters to house a third of its personnel. The rest of the Thunderbirds moved into several tent cities hurriedly organized by the division's advance party using Japanese labor, and completed with the assistance of the division's engineer battalion. Once established in Hokkaido, the 45th had two missions. The first was to prepare to defend the island against a Soviet invasion, a threat that appeared unlikely to materialize. However, the division drew up plans for defense, scouted positions, and kept watch on nearby Soviet-controlled Sakhalin Island.[26]

The more important mission was completing the MTP. The division's infantry regiments restarted their unit-training phase with platoon problems in mid-May and company level training in the final week of May. The division's artillerymen began shooting service practice missions in the latter part of May—missions that showed "the loss of skill through disuse was evident." The 145th AAA Battalion, bolstered by the issue of twenty-two self-propelled multiple machine-gun weapons from depots in Japan, turned in its obsolete weapons and picked up where it had left off at Fort Bliss in February. Only the 245th Tank Battalion, still very short of its authorized tank strength, lagged behind, forced by the shortage to conduct infantry instead of armor training.[27]

Between mid-May and 1 September, the division completed the MTP, thanks in large part to its finally being able to settle down and concentrate on training without having to worry about thousands of overstrength fillers, levies to provide replacements for other units, filling school quotas, or moving halfway across the world. Nevertheless, the division's greatest problem while in Japan continued to be personnel turbulence. Unlike earlier in the year, however, the problem during this period arose from a number of sources separately small in numbers, but which cumulatively had a sizable impact on the division's training and day-to-day operations. Early in this period, cadre and fillers of the 45th Division Training Regiment began arriving from Camp Polk, and the division disbanded it in July. Along with the Training Regiment, those soldiers in service schools when the 45th left Polk began returning to their units, and both these groups had to be integrated into the level of collective training their units had achieved during their absence. Soldiers returning to the 45th from army schools sometimes had to run the gauntlet of an army replacement system that treated soldiers as interchangeable parts. One night, while waiting at Camp Drake outside of Tokyo for transportation to Hokkaido after graduating from medical training at Fort Sam Houston, Texas, M.Sgt. Charles Brown and twenty-four other members of the 180th Infantry's Medical Company were informed they would be leaving for Korea the next morning. Brown called division headquarters to alert the personnel office of the attempted theft. The next day, the group's orders were revoked and it continued on to Hokkaido.[28]

In July, the 10th Ranger Company rejoined the 45th after completing its training at Fort Benning, Georgia, but its life was cut short when the army decided to disband divisional Ranger companies. Its time in Japan saw considerable friction between the airborne company and the rest of the "leg" division, which General Styron found "silly" given that all involved were "wearing the Thunderbird." When the company disbanded in September, its members had the choice of transferring to the 187th Airborne RCT or returning to their original 45th unit. Those guardsmen returning to their units found the "Go With Those You Know" slogan a reality. Ex-Ranger Allan Turner "was glad to see old buddies from my home town of Norman, Oklahoma . . . it was like a homecoming under difficult circumstances."[29]

There was a small but constant loss of manpower for a variety of reasons. A steady trickle of officers and men returned to the ZI for discharges of various sorts, mostly on grounds of hardship, dependency, and expiration of guard enlistment. While not lost to the army, the 45th every month lost a small number of enlisted men to Officer Candidate School (OCS) in the ZI because army policy was not to return OCS graduates to their units. Ironically, a significant number of men accepted for OCS from FECOM units, including the 45th, used this loophole to get out of Far East service. These men would report to OCS and then resign from the school shortly thereafter. For example, nineteen of the fifty-three Thunderbirds sent to Field Artillery OCS between February and December, 1951, resigned. The army put an end to this scam in March, 1952, by requiring that soldiers suspected of leaving OCS for that reason be shipped back to their unit. The *Daily Oklahoman*, in a 25 January 1952 editorial reflecting the growing war weariness in America, found the OCS scam raised "questions truly disturbing." However, if "some soldiers are in a mood to trifle with their responsibilities it may be because they feel they were trifled with first. Invariably in the past this country's soldiers have conducted themselves honestly and bravely, but always before they knew they were fighting for keeps."[30]

These drains on manpower steadily increased the longer the division stayed in Japan. In October, as the division moved into its post-MTP training cycle, losses increased from a new source: providing replacements for other units in Japan and to Eighth Army in Korea. As the 45th ranked behind Eighth Army in priority for replacements from the ZI, it never made up those losses, even after it began to receive soldiers rotating from units in Korea. At the end of August, the division had 872 officers, 109 warrant officers, and 17,199 enlisted men, and by the end of October it had 827 officers, 111 warrant officers, and 16,535 enlisted men. The shortages especially affected artillery units and the 700th Ordnance Company, which were so understrength in officers that it significantly impaired their effectiveness.[31]

Another problem facing the division during its stay in Japan was a shortage of several important types of equipment and supplies. The most critical was in the long-suffering 245th Tank Battalion, which only in July received enough tanks to switch from infantry to armor training. With understatement, the 245th's commander described August, the battalion's first full month with enough tanks on hand, as "most certainly a progressive period for this Battalion." The 45th also suffered from a shortage of some types of artillery ammunition, some types of communications equipment, and a wide variety of repair parts. The 158th FA Battalion was forced to deal with an interesting problem for field artillerymen: its battalion Fire Direction Center (FDC) did not have a fire direction set, having turned in its previous one as unserviceable before leaving Polk. It received a replacement in July, but the device contained coordinate squares (used to plot fire missions) graduated in scales that the army had stopped using years ago. Not surprisingly, the battalion's FDC "failed miserably" its practice ATT on 30 July.[32]

Despite these problems, the 45th made steady progress in completing the MTP. In June, the division finished the company- and battalion-level portions of the MTP. In July, regimental combat team training began, and XVI Corps, of which the Thunderbirds were a part, tested the infantry, AAA, and medical battalions. August saw division-level field training exercises and XVI Corps tests of the RCTs, the artillery battalions, and the engineer battalion. The training and ATTs were bringing units together, both in competency and esprit. Battalion and regimental commanders all commented on how the challenges and hard work of unit training kept morale in their units at "high" to "very high" levels. Units scored well on the ATTs administered by XVI Corps. On 1 September 1951, General Styron looked back on the previous year and wrote: "the organization has come a long way in its training and development into a combat ready division. It has accomplished much and has been a source of pride to its commander."[33]

The 45th also continued to remain a source of pride in Oklahoma, and the division worked hard to maintain its ties with the state, sending home a steady stream of stories, photographs, and recorded radio and television programs. In Washington, Roy Stewart—forced from federal service when he failed the POM physical—kept watch over the 45th as the *Daily Oklahoman*'s Washington bureau chief. Raymond McLain, then serving as comptroller of the army, visited the division in Japan and reported back to Oklahoma that it was "in fine shape" and that the XVI Corps's commander had told McLain that it was "the best trained division he has ever seen." Congressman John Jarman also dropped in on the 45th, finding morale "high" and the division "ready for anything" in mid-November.[34]

The 45th may have been ready for anything, but it saw several significant command changes while in Japan. The AAA and engineer battalions both received new commanders in September.[35] However, it was the ever-turbulent 279th Infantry that again saw the greatest changes. In July, the 1st Battalion received its third commander since mobilization. Then, in November, the regiment lost its second commander and second executive officer since mobilization. Colonel Maerdian, at his request, was transferred to Eighth Army headquarters and Colonel Murphy, the former guardsman turned regular, moved from division chief of staff to command of the 279th.[36]

While Thunderbirds and Oklahomans felt a great deal of pride in the division's achievements since mobilization, the burning question after completing MTP training in August was what the army would do with it. The division had only one more year of federal service left, and the war in Korea had apparently reached a stalemate, with peace talks under way. Moreover, neither the Chinese nor the Americans appeared willing to mount and bear the costs of the offensive campaign required to sweep its opponent off the Korean peninsula. At the end of November, 1951, United Nations forces thus found themselves conducting an "active defense." This policy focused on digging in to hold the current trace of UN positions, small attacks designed either to occupy better outpost positions or to deny such to the enemy, constant patrolling in front of the UN lines, and the liberal use of American firepower—especially field artillery.[37]

The summer and autumn of 1951 saw increasing speculation over what the 45th would do in its second and final year of federal service. Thunderbirds and their families exhaled with relief in July when the army announced that President Truman's recent executive order extending enlistments for one year would not apply to guardsmen. The division established good relations with Japanese civilians on Hokkaido, and some wives of 45th soldiers, hoping that the division would finish its federal service as benevolent occupiers, wondered if they would be allowed to join their husbands after FECOM removed its ban on military dependents in Japan.[38] In August, however, Thunderbirds and their families began receiving mixed signals concerning the division's fate. From Washington, Roy Stewart warned readers that the 45th was most likely going to Korea and that "friends and families of the division might as well get ready for it." But in early November, Raymond McLain reported to Oklahomans that Gen. Matthew B. Ridgway, MacArthur's replacement as FECOM commander, had recently told him that the 45th would go to Korea only if it could be replaced in Japan by another division.[39]

War in the Land of the Morning Calm

In late November word arrived that General Ridgway had found a division to replace the 45th in Japan: the 1st Cavalry Division, which despite its name was an infantry division that had been fighting in Korea since July, 1950. Unknown to Thunderbirds and their families, the army chief of staff, General Collins, had forced this decision on the FECOM commander. Ridgway did not want the 40th and 45th Infantry Divisions in Korea, preferring to leave the two guard divisions in Japan and strip them of trained personnel to use as individual replacements for the troop rotation program in Korea. General Collins rejected Ridgway's plan based on the belief that not to use the 40th and 45th in Korea would poison the army's relations with the guard's many supporters in Congress, inflame traditional Regular Army–guard tensions, and imply that the MTP was a failure. Collins added that leaving the divisions on occupation duty in Japan would disappoint their soldiers, who he thought expected and deserved to serve in Korea. On 18 November, FECOM alerted Eighth Army that the Thunderbirds would not be disappointed and that the 45th would move to Korea in December and take over the 1st Cavalry's positions.[40]

General Styron took the news of the alert "with justifiable pride. . . . [T]he division has trained hard and the results appear to be excellent. Morale is high and it is believed that the officers and men will acquit themselves well in their new assignment. The men feel the compliment of being the first National Guard Division to receive a combat mission in the present world crisis."[41] Not all Thunderbirds viewed their deployment to Korea as quite the compliment seen by General Styron. The *Daily Oklaho-*

man found the alert "got a reception as cold as the weather in this snow-blanketed headquarters," a reception made chillier by the fact that many men had just moved out of tents into new brick barracks. A reporter's tour of division units found "only glum comments from men who had felt sure they were ticketed to remain in Japan until they were transferred back home."[42]

Back in Oklahoma, Congressman Jarman reported that the 45th took the news "in good stride." Roy Stewart told his readers the 45th would be replacing combat-weary troops to give them a chance to rest in Japan, and that the unit would be committed to Korea as a division, not broken up and its components spread across the peninsula. He also reassured Oklahomans that the 45th's "command channels are filled by men experienced and tried in battle, to whom the division means more than just an army unit." As a proud Thunderbird and veteran of the 1940 mobilization, Stewart could not pass up the opportunity to remind readers that the 45th had defeated the 1st Cavalry Division during the 1941 Louisiana maneuvers. The *Daily Oklahoman* published an editorial cartoon showing a fresh Thunderbird moving forward into smoke, passing a tired, scruffy infantryman moving to the rear. The Thunderbird is patting the veteran on the shoulder and telling him, "You need a rest—I'll take over!" However, the 1st Cavalry was not as weary as press reports painted it. Few of the soldiers who had landed in Korea with the division in July, 1950, remained. Most had been lost to death, wounds, capture, or rotation back to the ZI.[43]

The plan for the exchange called for the 45th to leave all of its vehicles and large crew-served weapons in Japan for the 1st Cavalry, which would leave its equipment in Korea for the 45th. Advance parties and liaison teams left Japan for Korea in late November to coordinate the move with the 1st Cavalry and its higher headquarters, I Corps. In Japan, the 45th once again went through an administrative review, weeding out those soldiers medically unfit for combat duty and those whose enlistments would expire by March, 1952. Other losses during November included 166 enlisted men returned to the ZI for various types of discharges, 209 enlisted men transferred out of the division, and 11 officers transferred to other units in Japan because they were sole survivors and could not serve in combat. In return, 126 officers, 18 warrant officers and 946 enlisted men were transferred into the division. The result of these movements was that by the end of the month the 45th had 911 officers, 124 warrant officers, and 16,715 enlisted men. Meanwhile, the 179th and the 279th RCTs ran battalion combat team exercises, and the 180th RCT stood down from training to begin preparation for the move to Korea.[44]

The first Thunderbird unit to arrive in Korea was the 189th FA Battalion, landed at Inchon on 1 December. By the fifth, the battalion had moved into the 1st Cavalry Division's sector and, under I Corps control, was firing missions in support of the 8th Cavalry Regiment. The remainder of the 45th crossed over to Korea in increments throughout the month, with the last element, the 145th AAA Battalion, arriving at Inchon on 29 December. The 180th Infantry relieved the 8th Cavalry on 16 December and the 179th Infantry occupied positions of the 3d Infantry Division's 65th Infantry on 27 December, after I Corps took advantage of the relief to adjust divisional boundaries. The 45th Infantry Division headquarters assumed responsibility for its sector of Line Jamestown, I Corps's section of the Eighth Army front, on 23 December.[45]

While the 1st Cavalry Division's troops may not have been as battle-weary as reported, the division's equipment was. Every unit in the 45th commented on how their counterpart's equipment was, as the 245th Tank put it, "in the main, badly in need of general rehabilitation and repair." Also in need of extensive work were the positions turned over by the 1st Cavalry to the 45th. Bunkers on the MLR often were weakly built and poorly sited. Roads, bridges, airstrips, and rear-area positions all varied greatly in the quality of their construction. Once it arrived in the 45th's sector, the 120th Engineer Battalion immediately began a program of constructing and upgrading facilities behind the MLR. Another relic of the 1st Cavalry's messy housekeeping was the presence within the division's sector of a number of unmarked American minefields, a "menace" to the 45th that caused some of the division's first casualties in December.[46]

Another legacy from the 1st Cavalry was the thousands of its troopers transferred to the 45th to bring it up to full strength as the divisions swapped positions. Despite the November transfers, the division was still short 59 officers, 40 warrant officers, and 1,239 enlisted men on 1 December. The 36 officers and 2,411 enlisted men transferred from the 1st Cavalry Division all had less than twenty points of Constructive Military Service (CMS) in Korea, and thus were not yet eligible for rotation out of the country. Many of these soldiers had valuable experience, but the 45th's records do not discuss this aspect of the transfer. Some 1st Cavalry troopers initially resented being assigned to a "rinky-dink National Guard unit," and others were upset that they had been kept in Korea, but there is no available evidence that these frictions had a major effect on the 45th's operations.[47]

The Thunderbird Returns to Combat

The 45th's combat experience did not differ significantly from the experiences of other American divisions in Korea at the time. The war had settled into a pattern of patrols between the opposing lines, raiding Chinese positions, and defending against Chinese raids—with both sides trading large amounts of mortar and artillery fire. The 45th's sector of the UN line was in the Chorwon corridor, a relatively open area for Korea and a major avenue for attacks aimed at Seoul. The division put two regiments on line and held its third in reserve, then rotated the regiments on and off the line. The division artillery supported the regiments on the line and fired interdiction missions beyond the Chinese MLR.

While the war lacked the sweep and movement of its earlier phase, it still held a considerable degree of discomfort and danger, as the 45th quickly discovered. During December, the Thunderbirds were introduced to the rugged Korean terrain and the intensely cold Korean winter. Although the division conducted no raids during the month, patrols and indirect fire killed six, wounded twenty-six, and left one man missing in action. One of the wounded was Col. James Smith's son, a twenty-year-old sergeant first class serving in his father's 180th Infantry.[48]

The 45th's senior commanders and staff believed the division was "in excellent condition" and "well prepared" for combat when it entered the line in December. As General Styron correctly pointed out at a 6 January 1952 commanders' conference, the 45th arrived "in better shape than any other American Division" that preceded it to Korea.[49] Genearl McLain, while not the most impartial of observers when it came to the 45th, told General Van Fleet he would "find them a darn good outfit," and praised the division's senior leaders. The Eighth Army's commander wrote back that the I Corps commander was "overjoyed with, not only having the 45th Division in his Corps, but with also the exceptionally high degree of competence and combat effectiveness which it is currently displaying." Van Fleet's first visit to the 45th left him "immensely impressed." His only concern was the division's "over-eagerness for battle."[50]

However eager the Thunderbirds might have been, the combat envisaged in the ATTs differed sharply from what the 45th encountered in Korea. With a potential air threat that never materialized, the 145th AAA Battalion found its impressive firepower directed against ground targets. With static battle lines, the 45th Reconnaissance Company found itself detailed to act as an early warning system on the division's right flank, in case the 9th ROK Division collapsed during a Chinese offensive. Men of the 45th Recon also found themselves running patrols with the infantry regiments. The 245th Tank Battalion initially found itself placed in reserve in the 9th ROK Division's sector to help bolster the ROK position, as ROK divisions did not have tanks. The battalion's tanks were used as glorified mobile pillboxes by the 45th, supporting infantry raids and sniping at Chinese fortifications.[51]

Like the nondivisional field artillery battalions that arrived in 1951, Thunderbird gunners found they needed more training on firing high-angle missions. They also experienced great difficultly acquiring and destroying targets because the Chinese were masters at building and camouflaging field fortifications. Chinese mortars and artillery also were hard to locate, both because of Chinese skill at deception and because of weaknesses in American counterfire efforts. This became an increasingly serious problem: in March, the Chinese fired 2,096 rounds into the 45th's sector, and the number increased to 14,264 rounds in May. When the 45th's observers did detect targets, the strength of the Chinese positions often defeated the division's 105-mm and 155-mm howitzers. Occasionally, I Corps sent an 8-inch howitzer section to the 45th for temporary duty. When that occurred, the division artillery headquarters would move this much more accurate and powerful weapon into forward positions to snipe at Chinese positions with direct fire. The demands of covering patrols, supporting MLR outposts attacked by the Chinese, and firing harassment missions beyond the Chinese MLR kept the division's artillery busy firing many missions and expending thousands of rounds a month. An old artilleryman, General Styron instructed his regimental commanders: "We can't fight these Commies hand to hand and we don't want that. We want to keep them away from us and tear them apart with our fire power."[52]

The 45th's infantry regiments also had to make adjustments, starting with the improvement of defensive positions inherited from the 1st Cavalry. Building extensive field fortifications had not been a large part of the Thunderbirds' training and this showed in the division's early efforts.

At a 6 February commanders' conference, Styron chastised the regimental commanders, warning them: "we don't know what our people are going to do if they are fired upon. If they are in good strong positions, they will fight and we will save a lot of lives. These bunkers are still not good." Two weeks later, Styron told his senior commanders that "some of these bunkers we are building are not worth a damn," and noted that "we know how hard it is to get these Chinese out of their positions and that is because they are so well dug in."[53]

Styron believed much of the responsibility for this weakness was "a question of supervision. We would all do a lot better if we would put the heat down on these junior officers." In February, Styron created a Division Defense Board to examine the current condition of MLR positions and develop suggestions for improvements. The board published its findings and suggestions in March, but the Thunderbirds showed little desire to emulate their enemy's diligence in this matter. Up until he rotated home in May, Styron had to continually stress the need for improving positions and the need to hold NCOs and company grade officers responsible for this work.[54]

Another infantry task the regiments were not fully prepared for was patrolling. Patrolling was the main form of infantry combat for the 45th, whether it was to locate and destroy Chinese positions, take prisoners, or ambush Chinese patrols. Concerned over the possibility of a Chinese offensive in the spring and the deleterious effects of static battle lines on his infantry, Styron on 22 January told his senior commanders:

> This patrolling is the finest training I have yet seen. You have to get these patrols out. This patrolling can be considered or compared to life insurance; some day, it is going to pay off. I want this explained to the men; I want it carried down to them; let them know that we are doing it for their own protection. The only way we can play safe is to prepare for the enemy if they do hit. It just doesn't make sense unless we do this with that in view. We must be ready for them.
>
> Patrols and raids are ways of keeping our people ready. I want that explained to them.[55]

In early January, Styron told his regimental commanders: "I want a contact every day to see where the enemy is. Don't let these people edge in on us. These patrols should go out until they draw small arms fire."[56]

The experience of the 179th Infantry during January suggests that the division's infantrymen only partially met their commanding general's guidance. The 179th spent the entire month on the MLR in the division's left sector with all three battalions on line. It ran numerous patrols, both day and night, between the opposing lines and into Chinese positions. However, Chinese skill at camouflage and their excellent fire discipline, coupled with the Americans' combat inexperience, gave them the initiative most times. During January, the Chinese initiated contact eighteen times with the twenty-one 179th Infantry patrols that saw action, although the Americans usually were the ones to break contact—often with the assistance of mortar or artillery covering fire. These patrols cost the regiment 5 dead and 23 wounded. The 179th's MLR positions detected and fired upon one Chinese patrol. The regiment called fire missions on groups of Chinese soldiers observed during the day from American positions. In return, the Chinese harassed the 179th's sector with intermittent artillery and mortar fire. The regiment also mounted two raids during January. The objective of both was to destroy Chinese bunkers. The first found empty bunkers, and the second, conducted by a reinforced company, encountered significant Chinese resistance that killed 3 Thunderbirds and wounded 27. Patrolling and raiding accounted for 54 percent of the regiment's total battle casualties of 9 dead and 98 wounded during the month.[57]

The 180th and 279th Infantry regiments reported similar experiences. After eight days of planning, reconnaissance, and coordination, shortly after dawn on 24 January a reinforced rifle company from the 279th Infantry hit Chinese fortifications on "Old Baldy." This was a steep knob on Hill 290, a large T-shaped hill that dominated the Chinese MLR opposite the 45th. Crossing the line of departure fifteen minutes late, one assault platoon crept to within a hundred yards of the bunker line before the Chinese opened fire. The platoon attempted to continue onto the objective, but "intense fire" forced it to withdraw under cover of supporting American fire after an almost forty-minute firefight. Seeing this, the company commander ordered another platoon to attack. This platoon made it to the objective supported by heavy American covering fire and destroyed two bunkers before withdrawing with "heavy" casualties. Total losses for the 279th in this operation were 4 dead, 23 wounded, and 3 missing. The 180th Infantry raided a hill from which the Chinese fired on American patrols. The Chinese "bitterly opposed" the raid with small-arms fire, grenades, and mortars. Unable to close with the enemy positions and destroy them, the patrol withdrew, although Thunderbird artillery later attacked the Chinese positions unmasked during the raid. The cost to the 180th was 5 dead and 27 wounded. Raids during the month cost the 45th a total of 12 dead, 77 wounded and 3 missing—59 percent of the division's total battle casualties for January.[58]

Adapting to Combat in the Land of the Morning Calm

Throughout the period January to May, the 45th rated itself as having "excellent" combat efficiency and morale. The division command reports credited this condition "to the increased confidence and skill of the individual soldier and his leaders." The division did not define "excellent." Perhaps the best measure of the Thunderbirds' skill is the question of how they adapted to the conditions they faced in early 1952. Certainly the 45th was better prepared, both in training and in personnel stability, than army divisions sent to Korea in 1950. However, the tactical situation the 45th faced, while not much resembling the one used to develop ATTs, was much less demanding than the situations other divisions had experienced during the first year of the war.[59]

Reviewing his regiment's experiences at the end of January, Colonel Daugherty commented on the strength of the Chinese positions, particularly their imperviousness to most weapons available to the 179th. As for his troops, their combat inexperience showed when they went to ground when caught in the open by Chinese indirect fire during raids, instead of pressing forward into Chinese positions that would provide them with cover from the fire. Soldiers needed more training on patrolling, especially at night. Daugherty believed raids needed at least five days planning to ensure full coordination between the raiders and all the supporting elements, especially artillery.[60] While pleased with the performance of his infantrymen during the Old Baldy raid, the 279th Infantry's Colonel Murphy found fault with the measures taken to coordinate supporting fires. Overall, however, Murphy believed his troops were "too dependent" on fire support and that "more forceful leadership," particularly at the platoon level, was needed.[61] General Styron agreed with these evaluations, particularly the lack of detailed planning and preparation for patrols and the quality of junior leadership in the infantry. In early February, he told senior commanders that "we know where the enemy is, and if these patrols are organized, we will get contact. These patrols go out and don't get contact."[62]

These difficulties attracted often very detailed attention from echelons above division. The I Corps commander, Lt. Gen. John W. O'Daniel, made several visits in late January to discuss the results of that month's raids and how to improve the performance of Thunderbird infantrymen. The 45th was not alone in this; the static nature of the front lines tempted higher echelons to closely monitor the work of subordinates. A 2d Infantry Division raid in January that went badly wrong was formally investigated by corps headquarters.[63]

The 45th took several steps to improve its ability to "get contact" and improve the effectiveness of its raids. Division headquarters became much more involved in the planning and preparation of patrols and raids. Regiments' plans for each day's patrols had to be forwarded to division no later than noon of the preceding day for review and approval by the assistant division commander.[64]

Infantry regiments conducted extensive training with an emphasis on patrolling when in division reserve. In early February, each of the 179th Infantry's rifle companies conducted sixteen hours of training on patrolling, sixteen hours on weapons, and eight hours on small-unit tactics during the regiment's two weeks in reserve. Realizing that one way to lower casualties was to use the cloak of night, the regiment spent one-third of its training time in darkness. Also given attention was the problem of attacking fortified positions. The regiment spent sixteen hours on this subject, with an emphasis on actions once assault groups were within fifty yards of their objective. In all training, "practical work by the individual was stressed and lecture type classes were kept to a minimum." While in reserve, battalions selected possible targets to raid during their next period on the line, planning and rehearsing the raids while in reserve. Artillery battalions taught infantry officers and sergeants how to call for and adjust indirect fire. Two soldiers from each rifle platoon were trained as snipers. The 179th, concerned about its junior leaders' abilities, conducted weekly schools for officers and NCOs. The Thunderbirds were not the only division with such concerns. In January, for example, the 2d Infantry Division established schools for its infantry squad leaders and platoon sergeants.[65]

The 45th, like other divisions, also turned to a less doctrinal response to the problem posed by raids: the 179th and the 279th Infantries created "Raider" groups to undertake operations "requiring training or ability beyond that of a normal rifle squad." Volunteers accepted for this group were relieved of all duties with their parent unit, and trained and operated as a group directly controlled by the battalion or regimental commander. Each Raider group was built around a nucleus of men from the disbanded 10th Ranger Company, who ran the group through a training program based on their Ranger training.[66]

The Raider program paid off during the latter part of February and in March. The 179th Infantry spent ten days during February and all of March on the MLR. During that time, most of the regiment's patrols still did not make contact with the enemy. However, of the regiment's twenty-two patrol contacts, ten were by Raider patrols, some of which aggressively engaged much larger Chinese patrols. The 279th Infantry's largest patrol contact during March also was initiated by a Raider patrol. Colonel Murphy of the 279th believed the problem in his regiment was that regular infantry patrols still were not aggressive enough, which he blamed on a lack of aggressiveness among the regiment's junior leaders.[67]

The 45th mounted three major raids on Chinese positions during February. The first, by the 279th Infantry, was a night raid by a reinforced platoon against Chinese positions on Hill 290, preceded by a two-hour artillery preparation designed to isolate the objective and fifty rounds of direct fire into the Chinese positions from an 8-inch howitzer. After tripping a Chinese mine, the platoon reached the objective, where it spent fifty-five minutes before withdrawing. The platoon killed five Chinese and destroyed one bunker, at a cost of four dead and twelve wounded.

The second raid, also a night operation by the 279th, did not reach its objective as the reinforced platoon had to engage two separate Chinese patrols in heavy firefights that cost it one dead and three wounded. While the second raid did not reach its objective, "planning for this raid and execution of plans were considered to be an improvement over the previous raid." The third raid used two platoons from the 180th Infantry's tank company to shoot up Chinese bunkers and trenches at a cost of one tank destroyed by mortar fire, two disabled by mines, and 9 soldiers wounded. These raids accounted for 5 of the 6 dead and 24 of the 36 wounded suffered by the division in February. Orders from higher headquarters prohibited further major raids, with their potential for high casualties, from March to May, by which time most guardsmen had left the division.[68]

While the 45th could not mount raids after February, the Chinese found other ways to inflict casualties on the Thunderbirds until the phase-out of almost all guardsmen in early June. As Chinese activity grew, so did the

45th's casualty list. There were 72 battle casualties in March, 104 in April, and 146 in May. Increasing numbers of artillery and mortar rounds hit the division's positions each month. The 279th Infantry's Colonel Murphy noted that this indirect fire led to an "increasing number of unnecessary casualties" because "in many instances, the basic principles of cover, concealment and dispersion were not being followed." The Chinese also began paying the 45th more visits. Patrols probed American positions and the Chinese attempted to win control of the space between the opposing MLRs by attacking American outposts.[69]

On 1 March, the Chinese raided a 179th Infantry outpost, killing 3 Thunderbirds and wounding 1; 1 man was listed as missing. On 22 March, the Chinese mounted a major raid on a key 45th outpost. Outpost Eerie sat on the southern end of Hill 290, the northern section of which had been the target of many patrols and several raids by the Thunderbirds. Two reinforced squads from the 179th Infantry manned the outpost. The Chinese attacked with a force estimated to be company sized, which breached the outpost's defensive wire and overran the position despite a hard fight by the twenty-six defenders. Before they could consolidate on the position, artillery airbursts drove the Chinese off the outpost. The relief force sent to Eerie found 8 dead, 5 wounded and 2 missing. The Americans collected their casualties, stripped the outpost of its equipment, and returned to the MLR. The fight for Outpost Eerie caused 21 percent of the 45th's casualties for March. The division did not reoccupy Eerie until June.[70]

The next major Chinese attack was on the night of 25–26 May, when a battalion-sized enemy force hit an outpost on Hill 200 manned by a reinforced platoon from Company F, 179th Infantry. The Chinese fired a brief, intense artillery preparation on the outpost. Then, under heavy covering fire directed at the outpost and American MLR positions, the Chinese assault force moved forward. A platoon breached the wire barriers on the outpost's western side, but American fire prevented them from penetrating further into the outpost. On the outpost's eastern side, a company breached the wire barriers and forced the Americans to abandon several bunkers. Forming a skirmish line using trenches and shell holes, the Americans stopped every subsequent Chinese attempt to overrun the outpost.

Almost an hour after the attack began the outpost commander fired a signal flare requesting reinforcements. The alert platoon from G Company left the MLR, but the Chinese directed heavy machine-gun fire on it. After calling for mortar fire to silence the Chinese weapons, the platoon moved forward again, but part of the Chinese company attacking the eastern end of Hill 200 turned away from the hill and attempted to encircle the relief platoon. The ensuing firefight prevented the platoon from reaching the outpost, but it diverted significant power from the Chinese effort to exploit their penetration on Hill 200.

The 179th Infantry's heavy weapons and the 160th and 189th FA Battalions attempted to suppress the Chinese weapons firing in support of the attack. The artillery and mortars fired illuminating rounds over the area, but the tide turned decisively with the arrival, approximately three and a half hours after the battle began, of an air force flare ship. The Chinese quickly broke off their attack once the aerial flares began lighting up the hill and large portions of the surrounding area, exposing the Chinese to accurate indirect fire. A two-platoon relief force from Company I reached the outpost without opposition. After more than four hours of combat the Chinese had been defeated, at a cost of seven dead Thunderbirds and fifty-four wounded.[71]

Combat Effectiveness in a Limited War

The 45th's efforts to improve its battlefield performance produced mixed results. The division accurately diagnosed its problems and prescribed good remedies, as seen in its training programs, the Defense Board, and the creation of the Raider groups. Patrolling did improve thanks to training and command supervision. Robert A. Howes, a 1951 West Point graduate, joined the 45th in March, 1952, as a forward observer in the 160th FA Battalion. The two enlisted men in his team, both guardsmen, impressed him with their skill. On his first patrol, supporting the 279th Infantry, Howes found himself taking Chinese fire from three sides. Favorably impressed by the reactions and skill of the infantry he was accompanying, Howes called in large amounts of indirect fire, forcing the Chinese to break contact. The Chinese left behind twenty-two bodies and the patrol suffered one dead and six wounded.[72]

The fact that Raider units had a large percentage of the successful patrols suggests a significant difference in skill and motivation between them and non-Raider patrols. The 279th's Colonel Murphy found patrols like Lieutenant Howe's disquieting. Such patrol actions demonstrated to Murphy an excessive reliance on fire support, substituting it for aggressive leadership and infantry skills. Attempts in March to force patrols to be more aggressive by ordering them to remain out until they made contact with the Chinese were soon rescinded.[73]

Other American units had similar problems in maintaining an aggressive and effective patrolling effort. The Chinese also had difficulties with the skill of their infantry and motivating infantrymen to conduct aggressive patrols. One platoon leader in the attack on Hill 200 in May botched the reconnaissance of and approach march to the objective and a company participating in the same attack was assigned the mission as punishment for the "poor showing" of its patrols.[74]

The 179th Infantry's defense of Hill 200 in May did feature well-designed and built fortifications combined with a good defensive plan properly rehearsed and well executed. Yet even though the fortifications on Hill 200 played an important role in the defense of the outpost, they still were not on the same level as those built by the Chinese. Several Thunderbirds were killed or wounded when 155mm shells hit their bunkers. Most of the bunkers, when subjected to the stress of hits and near misses, showered their occupants with dirt, fouling weapons. This was a major reason why the Chinese were able to exploit their breach of the wire on the outpost's eastern edge. For several minutes the only machine gun covering the area was out of action as its crew disassembled, cleaned, and reassembled it. General Styron's continual complaints and increasing casualties from escalating Chinese indirect fire show that the Thunderbirds never came close to matching their opponent's skills in constructing field fortifications.[75]

A major problem for the 45th was that the war had stalemated by the time it arrived in Korea. This situation denied the division an opportunity to demonstrate its ability to meet all the varied challenges combat can pose, and thus live up to its World War II predecessor's standard. The stalemated war also eroded the sense of purpose among Thunderbirds and Oklahomans. For a division and a state that just seven years earlier had gloried in the 45th's linear progression from mobilization to V-E Day, the seemingly endless attrition in Korea was poor fuel indeed for generating support for the war.[76]

Another factor affecting the 45th's ability to demonstrate its full potential was that, unlike the World War II Thunderbirds, soldiers arriving in Korea in 1952 knew the calendar, not victory, would bring them home. Guardsmen looked forward to their return to the ZI for release from active duty, whereas others in the 45th counted the days until they accumulated sufficient CMS points for rotation. General Styron was well aware of this factor, believing it was "a very serious mistake that we let these men know when it is planned that they will be leaving." How much this knowledge affected the division's performance, particularly in patrolling, is impossible to quantify, but it surely colored some decisions made on cold nights out between the opposing MLRs. Waiting out Chinese artillery fire in a bunker with a friend late in May, William Craig recalled that it "was not lost on me or Kubala that we had only two weeks to go in-country." Watching the calendar also affected morale. In April and May, the division artillery noted there was "anxiety among draftees about discrimination" against them, since the guard phase-out program allowed some men to leave Korea several months before they would have earned sufficient CMS points for rotation. In May, the 279th Infantry noted that morale was "high" in part because sufficient replacements had arrived to allow those eligible for phase-out and rotation to leave for the ZI.[77]

The quality of leadership within a military organization always is a crucial factor in unit performance. General Styron and his senior leaders never had an opportunity to demonstrate their full potential in combat as tacticians, but the extent of that potential—as well as that of the 40th Infantry Division's senior leaders—did concern General Van Fleet, who earlier in the war had gained a negative impression of guard divisional leadership when, as commander of Second Army in the ZI, he was forced to investigate charges of favoritism and incompetence directed against General Cramer, commander of the mobilized 43d Infantry Division. Van Fleet concluded that to send the guard division commanders home before most of their men would damage unit morale, and that the 40th and 45th, as long as they had a significant percentage of guard personnel, would fight better under guard leaders than under unfamiliar Regular Army officers.[78]

General Styron was greatly concerned about the quality of the 45th's junior leadership, but he was never able to impose his will fully on the division's heterogeneous collection of junior leaders. In late January, he warned senior leaders against an "apparent laxity throughout the Division." Styron believed this was created in large part by the attitude of junior leaders, and on an almost monthly basis chastised his senior commanders for not holding junior leaders to higher standards of performance in building fortifications and running patrols. The commanding general often complained about a distressing lack of military courtesy throughout his division. In April, he reminded senior leaders that in "relations between officers and enlisted men, it is not that an officer thinks he is any better than an enlisted man, but we all realize that close association, drinking together, playing cards together, and calling them by the first name, causes the officer to lose his discipline over the men."[79]

General Styron's discontent had several sources. Many junior officers in the 45th had little experience in their duties, or even as officers before the division entered combat. Many guard junior officers had been commissioned from the ranks in August, 1950, or they had no experience in their duties prior to mobilization beyond weekly drills and a few two-week summer camps. In December, 1951, the month it became the first Thunderbird regiment to arrive in Korea, the 180th Infantry had 20 officers with August, 1950, commissions in the Oklahoma guard. Only 11 of the 34 guard officers in the regiment who were commissioned during World War II were initially commissioned in the infantry. In January, 1952, the 189th FA Battalion had only 2 guard officers with commissions dating from August, 1950, but of the 13 who had received commissions during or shortly after World War II, only 5 had served in the field artillery. Particularly in units that had not shuffled officers among subordinate elements, the long, boring watching and waiting could allow hometown associations to wear down the type of military discipline Styron believed his officers should enforce.[80]

Many junior officers sent to the 45th as fillers or replacements were either 1950 or 1951 ROTC graduates ordered to active duty after commissioning, or OCS graduates. One of the most affected units was the 189th FA Battalion. By January, 1952, officers from these sources filled 11 of its 32 battery officer slots, and 2 slots were vacant. In the 180th Infantry, by December 1951, 27 percent of its company grade officers were not from the Oklahoma guard.[81] Those lieutenants usually had little experience before joining the division beyond their training and perhaps a short period spent training draftees in the ZI. The 45th, like other units in Korea, also received a number of reserve officers ordered to active duty and guardsmen stripped from other mobilized units and sent to the Far East as individual replacements. These officers often had much more experience than did ROTC and OCS lieutenants, but their abilities and motivation, particularly reservists recalled involuntarily, varied considerably.[82]

After arriving in Korea, the division began receiving replacement officers who reflected the blend of experienced reserve and inexperienced ROTC and OCS officers the army was using to keep units overseas up to strength. There was a light sprinkling of Regular Army officers, and the army continued stripping officers from mobilized guard units, a source that provided a mix of experienced and inexperienced officers. Lieutenant Howes noted in his diary that while processing in at the 45th Replacement Company in March, 1952, "there was quite a discussion about me, the one Regular Army man against all the other reservists national guardsmen and draftees. The Catholic Chaplain got quite a kick out of the discussion in fact he egged it on." From March to June, 1952, the 189th FA Battalion received thirty officer replacements. Two were Thunderbirds transferred into the 189th from elsewhere in the 45th, 5 were guardsmen stripped from other mobilized units and sent to Korea as individual replacements, 2 were 1951 college graduates given Regular Army commissions, and one was the new battalion commander, a Regular Army lieutenant colonel. The remaining 20 officers were reservists or ROTC and OCS graduates. The 179th Infantry received 50 new officers from January to May 1952. Three were guardsmen stripped from the 31st and 47th Infantry Divisions—mobilized in early 1951—and there were 2 lieutenants, 1 captain, and 1 major from the Regular Army. The remaining 43, mostly lieutenants and captains, were reserve, ROTC, or OCS officers.[83]

The uneven levels of maturity, skill, experience, and motivation among junior officers also characterized the 45th's noncommissioned officer leadership. Few NCOs were regulars, or reservists and guardsmen with World War II experience relevant to their current position. Some of the 45th's guard NCOs inducted with the division in 1950 left during 1951 when their guard enlistments (and the president's one-year enlistment extension) expired. By the time the division arrived in Korea, many of its NCOs were guardsmen and 1950 draftees promoted after little active service and sometimes graduation from a leadership school in the ZI. John Blount, an ROTC graduate who joined the 45th in 1951 as a rifle platoon leader, remembered that these NCOs "were very young and barely trained. The shortage of career NCOs was a serious consideration."[84]

After integrating the 1st Cavalry Division troopers acquired during the December swap, the 45th depended on normal army channels to provide enlisted replacements for casualties, guardsmen and 1950 draftees scheduled for phase-out, and for former 1st Cavalry soldiers who had accumulated enough CMS points to qualify for rotation. The 45th, like the nondivisional artillery battalions, was not pleased by the replacements provided. The division's January command report complained that the "quality of replacements is considerably lower than that previously experienced by the division." In one artillery battery, the average AGCT score fell from 104 to 77. In addition to problems with human raw material, the division was dissatisfied with the numbers of replacements received, the distribution of MOSs among the replacements, and the training the soldiers had received in the ZI. In April, the 279th Infantry received 41 school-trained cooks, but it needed only 16. The excess 25 were assigned to other positions in the regiment, no doubt at a significant cost to their morale and to their unit's efficiency as they had to learn their new duties on-the-job.[85]

Concern over the quality of replacements extended beyond current combat operations. By the end of June, almost all the 45th's guardsmen were eligible to return to the ZI, and by early autumn all the 1950 fillers also would be leaving active duty. If this massive personnel turbulence was to be prevented from gutting the 45th's combat effectiveness, then the Thunderbirds would have to devise their own solutions to the problem. In February, the division established a School of Standards to train replacements in certain skills they lacked. The school included classes in intelligence and signal skills, artillery and mortar fire direction, and medical, chemical, and food service operations. The school also ran a leadership course for junior NCOs. The cadre was drawn from division units, and unit commanders complained this was a "serious problem," diverting qualified manpower away from their units. General Styron agreed this levy was a burden on units, but argued that units were "more than compensated for" it by the benefits of receiving school-trained replacements.[86]

A group of cooks and bakers was the first class graduated from the School of Standards. An "informal investigation showed that Battalion and Company Commanders were highly pleased with the improvement in mess operations" when these soldiers rejoined their units. By the end of April, 388 soldiers had graduated from the school and 346 were enrolled. By the end of June, with increasing rotation and the completion of the phase-out of enlisted guardsmen, 1,491 replacement soldiers had graduated from courses at the School of Standards.[87]

The school's success inspired other efforts within the 45th to improve the replacements' skills. The division established an Infantry Replacement Training Center for riflemen and hospital returnees that featured a weeklong course focused on the problems of combat in Korea. In late April, the division artillery established its own replacement school with forty hours of instruction. Graduates then underwent "closely supervised" on-the-job training in their units. During May, 296 soldiers went through this school. Also in May, the division established a twenty-four hour orientation course for all replacement officers to provide them with "information peculiar to the local situation for an intelligent approach to their assigned duties."[88]

The division's efforts paid off in early June when General Styron's successor ordered an attack to seize a new outpost line that would provide more depth to the American position and deny the Chinese some key terrain. By that time, the last enlisted guardsmen were preparing for rotation home and only a handful of guard officers remained in the division. The attack achieved its objectives and then the 45th hung on to them against heavy Chinese counterattacks and shelling until the 2d Infantry Division relieved it in mid-July.[89]

In the end, the 45th accomplished the mission assigned it in Korea, although that mission lacked the sweep and drama of the Thunderbirds' role in destroying Nazi Germany. The division adapted to the conditions of a static battlefield, though not to the degree desired by its senior leaders. However, this result is not a surprise given the combat conditions in Korea in 1952, the human resources available to the division, and the lack of an objective besides reaching their rotation dates to motivate soldiers. One guard master sergeant, a veteran of the 45th's European campaigns, told reporters on his return from Korea: "We've never seen a war quite like this one. It certainly is not like the last one."[90]

The End of the Oklahoma 45th in Korea

The Sooner state continued to keep a close eye on its division once the Thunderbirds entered combat. The 45th assisted by producing and sending home a steady stream of copy, photographs, and recordings for radio and television broadcast. Oklahomans did not receive a sugarcoated picture of Thunderbird life on the MLR. Newspaper stories portrayed the difficulties and dangers of a combat zone, most noticeably in a Sunday magazine article entitled "BY THE WAY, HIS LEGS ARE GONE." As Department of the Army telegrams arrived at homes with news of Thunderbird casualties, the reports were noted in newspaper articles.[91]

Nevertheless, the war did not intrude into the state's life in the same way as had World War II. By early 1952, Korea lacked the dramatic large-scale sweep of events experienced during 1950–51, and it never had the sense of national survival being at stake that had colored the Thunderbirds' previous war. The small number of guard casualties also dampened interest. When the 45th entered combat, less than half the division was composed of guardsmen, and many of them, because of rank and position, had little exposure to combat in Korea. The 179th Infantry between January and April lost no guardsmen killed in action and only two missing. The bulk of the regiment's casualties were draftees and Regular Army enlistees. The major combat events during the 45th's time as a guard unit in Korea, the battles for Outpost Eerie and Hill 200, did not receive special coverage in Oklahoma. Instead, much of the coverage centered on the question of when the division's guardsmen would return to Oklahoma and whether the army would return the division to state control at the end of their federal service.[92]

The life of the Oklahoma 45th in Korea was short. As the Chinese picked up the tempo of combat during April and May, the 45th's Oklahoma National Guard character dwindled at both the division's bottom and top. The division had begun planning for the guard's phase-out while in Japan, but shelved that effort when it received the order for movement to Korea. Once the 45th settled into position in Korea, planning resumed. Priority for return was given to World War II veterans, those who had dependency or hardship situations, and those who served in combat while in Korea. An additional consideration was whether a trained replacement was available. The first group of guardsmen, 55 officers and 144 enlisted men, left in late March. Several hundred more guardsmen departed in April. May saw the greatest outflow of guardsmen, about 2,600, with the final burst of about 1,300 enlisted men in June and a coda of about 140 officers in July.[93] In April, General Muldrow left for Okalahoma, and General Dulaney left to become commander of the neighboring 3rd Infantry Division. Then, in May, as the single largest group of guardsmen left for home, General Styron turned over command of the 45th to Maj. Gen. David L. Ruffner.[94]

The guard phase-out program was the major, but not the only source of personnel change in the 45th that diluted and then ended its Oklahoma character. While in Korea, the racially segregated 45th became racially integrated. The Department of the Army, fearing the political fallout in California and Oklahoma, had exempted the 40th and 45th from the initial round of racial integration instituted by General Ridgway after he became head of FECOM in April, 1951. By the end of October, the 45th had only one black enlisted soldier assigned.[95]

Preparing the division for Korean service gave FECOM the opportunity to begin integrating it. During November, 126 of the 946 enlisted replacements assigned to the 45th were black soldiers. However, the 45th did not allow any black 1st Cavalry troopers to transfer into the division during December, and the black replacements received in November left the division far from FECOM's goal of 12 percent "Class II" enlisted personnel in each division. Once in Korea, though, the 45th received more and more black soldiers. By March, 1952, the 45th had 10 officer, 2 warrant officer, and 444 enlisted black personnel. By June, when the last enlisted guardsmen left for the ZI, the 45th had 30 officers, 4 warrant officers, and 2,215 enlisted black personnel assigned.[96]

The pressure from higher headquarters to have 12 percent of combat units manned by black soldiers, and the large number of vacancies in combat units, led to some misuse of black soldiers' skills. The 279th Infantry complained that it received many black soldiers with noninfantry MOSs, particularly military policemen, as replacements. General Styron's policy was to spread the black soldiers throughout the division to avoid charges of segregation and to "equalize" integration among the division's units. Another motive for distributing black soldiers at the rate of one to a squad if possible was, as Styron put it, "we don't want to let them gang up." Integration provoked no immediate press attention back home in Oklahoma, and by all available accounts, generated no widespread friction affecting the 45th's effectiveness.[97]

Back in the Sooner State

Oklahoma press reports eagerly tracked the first group of guardsmen to be sent home from Korea in April. After their troopship docked in Seattle, officers took airliners direct to cities across the state, while enlisted Thunderbirds boarded troop trains for Fort Sill. On 14 April, Will Rogers Field in Oklahoma City "was the scene of the happy homecoming of the first of Oklahoma's famed 45th division to reach their native soil." Three days later, the troop train pulled into Fort Sill. "Men were on the ground and running to greet relatives before the train ever rolled to a stop." Similar scenes followed the return of each succeeding group of guardsmen. General Styron reached San Francisco in early June. He was separated from active duty at Fort Sill and was back in Hobart by the twenty-second. Styron discouraged any special welcome home for himself, preferring that he just be included in the general statewide homecoming celebrations planned for the 45th at the end of August.[98]

Most enlisted men, their guard enlistments expired, were separated from the military at Fort Sill. Officers and those with time remaining on their enlistments were placed in the inactive National Guard until the 45th could be reestablished as a National Guard of the United States (NGUS) division later in the year. The army, desiring to keep the lineage and esprit of guard divisions in federal service, did not return the units' colors when their guardsmen left active duty. Instead, there would be two Thunderbird divisions, an AUS one in Korea and an NGUS one in Oklahoma. The 45th Infantry Division (NGUS) would operate with a reduced personnel authorization, collecting sufficient cadre, especially Korea veterans, until the army returned its colors to Oklahoma. General Muldrow was promoted from commander of the 45th Division Artillery to commanding general of the 45th Infantry Division (NGUS).[99]

The formal end of the 45th's Korean War service came on 25 September 1954 in Oklahoma City. On the reviewing stand at opening night of the Oklahoma State Fair—with the secretary of the army, retired Generals McLain, Key, and Styron, and a number of Thunderbirds who had remained on active duty behind him—Governor Murray returned to General Muldrow and five thousand Thunderbirds the "original battle flags and colors of Oklahoma's world-famed and storied 45th Infantry Division."[100]

Guard units missed the two most trying periods of the war for the United States, the retreat to and fighting around Pusan, and the surprise Chinese intervention in North Korea. It is highly unlikely that any guard combat units could have arrived in Korea before they actually did, given the course of events during the war's first six months, the Truman administration's desire to limit the resources committed to the war, the many problems the army faced in mobilizing for it, and the condition of guard units in 1950. Thus, the 45th Infantry Division arrived in Korea after the battle lines became static, so its abilities were never fully tested. Instead, the Thunderbirds adapted to conditions not foreseen by Army Field Forces training plans, and suffered from the same problems of manpower and motivation that affected other American divisions on the MLR. Although the 45th never reached the standards of performance its commander desired, the division did accomplish its assigned mission.

CHAPTER 6

Back to Europe

Alarmed by the course of the Cold War in 1949—particularly evidence that the Soviets now had atomic weapons and by the Communist victory in the Chinese Civil War—the Truman Administration in early 1950 had developed a plan for a massive military buildup. The tremendous cost of this plan, known as NSC 68, led President Truman to refrain from proposing it to Congress since he believed that without some major crisis to motivate it, Congress would never approve the plan. The crisis atmosphere caused by events in Korea, especially after the Chinese intervened in late 1950, became crucial in creating support for the military buildup called for by NSC 68. According to David Fautua, NSC 68 "helped the Army serve its own institutional agenda for the Cold War, thereby revitalizing more than just its overall force structure, but providing much of the intellectual rationale for more men, more weapons, and more money." A major part of that rationale rested on creation of a conventional defense for Western Europe, and the Korean War provided the political leverage needed to station a large ground combat force in Europe on a long-term basis.[1] As part of this military buildup in Europe, the army by the end of 1951 had deployed to Germany two infantry divisions, seven battalion or group headquarters, eight nondivisional battalions, and nine separate companies from among the Army National Guard units in federal service. Only in separate battalions did the number of guard units sent to Korea significantly exceed the number sent to Germany (nineteen to eight), a result of Eighth Army's prewar weakness in nondivisional field artillery and combat engineers and the heavy demands for those types of units in Korea.[2]

Although guard units sent to Germany suffered from the same problems during postmobilization training that afflicted units in Korea, many of the units sent to Germany suffered much larger levies for the Far East Command before moving overseas, and they had a lower priority for receiving reservists as fillers. Arriving in Germany, most units found the infrastructure to support Seventh Army's buildup inadequate: cramped barracks, often former German military *kasernes,* with buildings in poor shape and lacking in the troop welfare facilities Americans expected. Once in Germany, guard units, like the rest of Seventh Army, had a steady diet of alerts, inspections, field training, exercises, and Army Training Tests. Units sent to Seventh Army, like those assigned to Eighth Army, faced extensive personnel turbulence in 1952 as guardsmen, reservists, and 1950 draftees all left active duty during the year, and units in Germany were equally displeased with the quantity and quality of replacements they received from the ZI. Guard units sent to Germany never faced the ultimate test of their effectiveness by having to defend against a Soviet attack on NATO, and without such a test, one must rely on ATT scores and anecdotal evidence to evaluate their performance. Based on these, guard units sent to Seventh Army performed much like their regular and reserve counterparts.

37th Ordnance Battalion Headquarters Detachment

Organized in Cleveland in 1947, the 37th Ordnance Battalion Headquarters Detachment supervised several ordnance maintenance companies in Ohio. Between organization and mobilization in 1950, the 37th had a significant personnel turnover, including three battalion commanders. At mobilization, Lt. Col. Rudolph Maxa was in charge. Born in Ohio in 1917, Maxa had served three years as an enlisted man in the guard before World War II, but was not in the guard at the 1940 mobilization. Drafted in 1941, Maxa was commissioned in the Ordnance Corps and ended the war a major. He returned to the guard as an infantry major in 1947, and in 1949 returned to the Ordnance Corps and was promoted to lieutenant colonel in early August, 1950, after the 37th received its alert notice.[3] An ordnance battalion headquarters detachment's TO&E called for 10 officers, 2 warrant officers, and 35 enlisted men; the 37th entered federal service on 19 August 1950 with 6 officers, 1 warrant officer, and 11 enlisted men. On 30 August, the battalion arrived at Fort Knox, Kentucky, and on 7 September established its headquarters on post. The unit spent most of its time at Knox supervising a diverse group of existing and recently activated regular and mobilized reserve and guard maintenance and recovery companies.[4]

After being alerted and then stood down for deployment to FECOM, the 37th in late March, 1951, received an alert notice for movement to European Command (EUCOM). After turning its companies over to another battalion at Knox, the 37th packed and shipped its equipment and conducted the required POM training and administrative reviews. Leaving Knox at full strength, the battalion arrived in Germany on 23 May, where it joined Seventh Army and was attached to the 47th Ordnance Group. Accompanying the group commander to a conference with the Seventh Army ordnance officer on 24 May, Lieutenant Colonel Maxa received some rather unexpected and unpleasant news: Seventh Army had decided to use the 37th as an ammunition battalion—a mission for which the 37th had neither training nor experience. Many of the battalion headquarters officers and NCOs requested transfers to ordnance maintenance units when they learned of this mission. Seventh Army planned to move the battalion to the Münster Ammunition Depot, a former Luftwaffe ammunition depot that Seventh Army planned to use for storing its training ammunition. The Münster depot had only twelve usable ammunition bunkers; the Germans had destroyed the rest in 1945. The Americans had used the depot for ammunition storage from 1945 to 1949, and it had been closed since December, 1949. The depot required "considerable renovation and adaptation," a project contracted out to German companies and which proceeded at such a "slow" pace during 1951 that it remained unfinished at the end of the year.[5]

Nevertheless, the 37th moved to Münster in mid-July, where it took control of three ordnance ammunition companies. Two of these companies created considerable headaches for Maxa and his staff. The 443d and 450th Ordnance Ammunition Companies were both reserve units in which "the majority of officers and other key personnel were previously trained for other than ammunition work." Inactive reservists recalled to active duty and sent to the companies as individual fillers compromised a large percentage of the units' personnel. Many of these reservists did not understand why they had been recalled because of a war in Korea and then sent to Germany. Both companies suffered from chronic poor leadership. Most of the officers in the companies "were openly discontent with being in the service," and Maxa had to fire two company commanders in the 443d and one in the 450th. When the Department of the Army announced its inactive reservist phase-out program, "the problems of maintaining proper discipline, training, and efficiency became most difficult."[6]

The 37th's third subordinate unit was the 60th Ordnance Ammunition Company, activated on 1 July with a cadre of two white officers and twenty-two black enlisted men. The cadre was "excellent," and the company commander had extensive experience in ammunition work. While the black enlisted fillers shipped to the 60th were of generally good quality, all of them had received only basic training in the ZI. This required the company cadre to train most of the fillers in their MOSs, since the 60th received only eighteen slots at the EUCOM Ordnance School. The slow issue of equipment to the company after its activation added to its troubles.[7]

Poor living conditions and lack of recreational facilities compounded the problems facing the 37th and its companies. The 60th, stationed at the Rhine Ammunition Depot, began its life with "high morale," but this "deteriorated to an appreciable extent due to poor living conditions." The disgruntled reservists in the 450th spent more than a month living in tents in the middle of the Rhine Ordnance Depot, where they could observe that even a Polish labor unit had better facilities. The 443d and the 37th's headquarters detachment endured the slow pace of renovation at the Münster depot, where Maxa "spent a large part of his time and efforts on the matter of getting suitable buildings renovated or constructed for use of the units."[8]

The final blow to battalion readiness came as inactive reservists returned to the ZI for release from active duty. In the 443d, 193 of the enlisted men were inactive reserve fillers and the 450th had 112. When these men were released from active duty in late 1951, morale among the reservists who had entered active duty with the companies plunged even further. Another problem for the 450th was that it remained at Ludwigsburg without a mission or adequate training facilities for several months. Replacements from the ZI had no training in ammunition MOSs, and Maxa discovered "from the attitude, appearance, and conduct of these men it was all too obvious that considerable refresher basic training was necessary." Moreover, 167 of the replacements sent to the two companies had scored below 70 percent on the AGCT or had not completed the fifth grade.

The battalion noted that by the end of 1951, "operational readiness if it ever really had been obtained before, was now gone" in the 443d and 450th. The battalion quickly developed a basic training refresher program for the replacements. Because many replacements had AGCT scores so low that they could not get into EUCOM ordnance classes, the battalion adopted a five-week program developed by the 60th's commander to qualify men as ammunition supply specialists.[9]

The few guardsmen left in the 37th Ordnance Battalion headquarters as 1952 began continued to struggle with these problems. However, their remaining time in Germany was short, and in June, Maxa turned over command of the battalion, ending its last link with the Ohio National Guard. The 37th's experience in federal service had been a trying one, providing many examples of Murphy's Law in action both in the ZI and in Germany. Still, the battalion headquarters itself had performed well, a tribute to the high quality of the fillers it received after mobilization and to the guardsmen who brought the unit into federal service.[10]

272d Field Artillery Battalion

As described in chapter three, the 272d FA Battalion had a difficult time after entering federal service in 1950. Created after World War II from the 372d Infantry's Massachusetts battalion, the 272d encountered serious obstacles after arriving at Camp McCoy: unprepared cadre, significant enlisted overages, poor quality of fillers, inadequate supervision of the ATP by higher echelons, and what many in the battalion perceived as a hostile racial climate. These conditions led to the battalion failing its ATTs by significant margins. In late July, 1951, Fifth Army and Army Field Forces made two decisions concerning the unit. First, the battalion's deployment to Germany would be pushed back thirty days to allow for remedial training and retesting. Second, the battalion commander, Lt. Col. Karl B. Russell, and the operations officer, Maj. George G. Bingham, would be relieved, transferred out of the 272d, and replaced by two white officers. Russell's successor was Lt. Col. Cornelius A. Murphy, commander of the 97th FA Battalion at Camp Carson. Like the 272d, the 97th was a towed 155-mm howitzer battalion. Born in 1917 and a native of South Dakota, Murphy was a 1940 West Point graduate. During World War II he graduated from the Field Artillery Officer Basic and Advanced Courses, served in 1944–45 as operations officer of the XIII Corps Artillery, and ended the war a lieutenant colonel.[11] Murphy probably did not welcome the opportunity to give up command of the 97th in exchange for command of the 272d because the "lack of discipline, the training ineptitude and the administrative derelictions of the 272nd FA Bn were notorious in the Fifth Army Area, being common knowledge at Camp Carson."[12] Major E. J. Nyenhuis, a reserve officer on active duty serving as an ORC instructor in Minnesota, was chosen to succeed Bingham.

Murphy and Nyenhuis arrived at Camp McCoy on 6 August, and Murphy assumed command the next day. From 13 to 29 August Murphy put the battalion through what he described as "intensive" training under his "immediate and close supervision and planning." In addition to unit training, Murphy established twice weekly officer and NCO schools conducted after duty hours. The training was not designed to make the 272d a combat-ready unit; its purpose was to meet the minimum standards required for certification as ready for overseas service so that it could begin the move to Germany on 15 September. Between 24 and 28 August, the 272d took the three ATTs required of field artillery battalions, scoring 75.25 percent, 75.2 percent, and 63.4 percent. The tests did not cover the tactical portions of the ATTs, just the technical field artillery skills.[13]

From September to the end of November, the 272d packed its equipment, moved to Camp Kilmer, New Jersey, and sailed to Germany, where it joined the 35th Field Artillery Group, part of the VII Corps Artillery. During this period, the battalion became entangled in the racial politics of 1951 America, the result of Murphy's attempts to fix what he saw as the root cause of the 272d's problems: "unqualified officers and non-commissioned officers."[14] Examining his new battalion, Murphy concluded that for the 272d to become combat ready he would have to remove officers who were "mediocre" or "patently unsuitable." Unable to arrange their transfers out of the unit, Murphy initiated board of inquiry proceedings to determine the competency of five captains and six lieutenants in the battalion. At the same time, Murphy submitted a requisition for replacement officers that was filled by four captains and six lieutenants, all white, ordered to join the battalion at its port of embarkation.[15]

For the most part, officers referred to boards of inquiry were men with strong ties to the battalion and Lieutenant Colonel Russell. Two had been officers in the 372d Infantry in 1941 and four had been enlisted men in that regiment. Seven of the officers had been with the 272d since 1947, 3 were commissioned in 1949, and 1 enlisted in 1949 and was commissioned after the battalion was alerted in August, 1950. None saw action with an artillery unit in World War II, and only 1 graduated from the Field Artillery School before mobilization in 1950.[16] Two officers, both second lieutenants, requested relief from active duty in lieu of facing a board of inquiry. The other 9 went before boards of inquiry composed of officers stationed at McCoy. The boards recommended the commissions of 2 captains and 1 first lieutenant be terminated, that 1 first lieutenant and 1 second lieutenant be released from active duty, and that 3 captains and 1 second lieutenant be retained on active duty, but transferred out of the 272d. The post commander endorsed the boards' recommendations, and all but a second lieutenant were transferred out of the battalion. Murphy had a twelfth officer, 1st Lt. William Bingham, brother of the sacked operations officer, tried by special court-martial for "conduct detrimental to the battalion during ATT 6-5" and speeding and uniform violations. Although the court found Bingham guilty only on the uniform charge, the post commander transferred him without a board of inquiry to another unit at McCoy "because of his apparent dislike of the new battalion commander and a belief that he was agitating or would agitate against the new order."[17]

These actions quickly came to the attention of Collins George, the *Pittsburgh Courier* military affairs correspondent. The *Courier,* a leading African American newspaper, saw the Korean War, as it had World War II, as a way to advance the cause of civil rights in America. Since the start of the war, George and the *Courier* had argued that it was long past time to fully implement President Truman's 1948 executive order directing the racial integration of the military. George had already toured a number of military installations in the ZI earlier in 1951, checking on the treatment of black servicemen and the status of racial integration in all the services. After visiting Camp McCoy in May, 1951, he reported that "there is the most wanton, flagrant and shocking disregard of the President's executive order calling for full integration. Bald, open, old-fashioned racial segregation is the rule at McCoy." This situation, George claimed, was the result of the actions and attitudes of the post commander, Col. Peter C. Bullard. Bullard was gone by the time Murphy took over the 272d, however, and his successor, Brig. Gen. Frederick Brown, approved the results of the boards of inquiry.[18]

In a 6 October page one story, George described Murphy's actions and the boards of inquiry as "one of the most vicious bits of racial maneuvering this correspondent has ever seen." The article portrayed Murphy as a racist out to purge qualified, proven, dedicated black officers from the 272d and replace them with white officers of unknown quality. George quoted Murphy as saying his only objective was to build an excellent battalion, that he had not specifically requested white officer replacements, and that he would have welcomed "competent colored artillery officers." However, George reported, it "would be difficult to find any of the men or officers in the outfit who believe his denial of racial bias."[19]

The *Courier* sent a telegram to Secretary of the Army Pace demanding "full and immediate inquiry by an impartial and interracial board into the conditions surrounding the removal of colored officers of the 272nd Field Artillery Battalion."[20] The *Courier* recommended that, in the absence of racial integration, a full set of qualified black field artillery officers, including a battalion commander, be assigned to the 272d and that the battalion be reassigned to another post.[21] The publicity generated by this story brought the 272d to the attention of Massachusetts governor Paul Dever and Rep. John F. Kennedy. Both called for a delay in shipping the battalion and an investigation of the officer transfers. Instead, Secretary Pace ordered Fifth Army to review the McCoy Board's findings. Fifth Army reversed them in the cases of three captains and a second lieutenant, and ordered them to rejoin the 272d at the port of embarkation. Collins George was not satisfied, charging "Army Whitewashes Brass Charges At Camp McCoy." George wrote that Fifth Army had not investigated the "racial maneuvering" behind the boards, nor had it looked at the case of the Bingham brothers. Colonel Murphy, according to George, had staged a racist purge designed to recreate "the old world war type of outfit in which the enlisted men and junior officers are Negro, but the top command consists of whites using the outfit as a stepping stone to further their military careers."[22]

Nor was Murphy satisfied with Fifth Army's review. Having been "vilified by the negro press with no opportunity to defend himself," he charged that George was getting "information, much of it false or half-truths" from officers sent before the boards. Murphy argued that he had "acted on the assumption that units and individuals, not professionally qualified, should either be removed from the services or retained in the US until qualified" and that the removal of the boarded officers and the arrival of the ten white officers who were "far superior to their predecessors" had done much to improve efficiency and morale in the battalion. Finally, Murphy claimed, "the enlisted men as well as the non-affected officers of the battalion, were well aware of the previous officers inadequacies and welcomed the action taken." Murphy also lodged a "vehement protest" with a Department of the Army staff officer over returning the four officers to the 272d, but was told the army secretary had directed the action. Murphy added that he believed the only answer to preventing such controversies was to disband black units and racially integrate all units.[23]

Upon arriving in Germany, the 272d was stationed with another black field artillery battalion at a *kaserne* that was too small and lacked recreational facilities. The 272d quickly unpacked and then moved to the Grafenwöhr training area for three weeks of training focused on the battery level. The training was "invaluable," but the battalion's very poor maintenance discipline resulted in new vehicles "becoming junk rapidly. Reconditioned howitzers and prime movers were becoming unfit for service."[24] The 272d did not impress its new higher headquarters, the 35th Field Artillery Group. Colonel W. A. Enemark, the group commander, wrote that the battalion in late 1951 was "unsatisfactory tactically and technically. With few exceptions, the officers and enlisted men lack initiative and a willingness to learn." He further observed that "this battalion is not now or will be satisfactory within foreseeable future." The 35th, in its annual command report, noted that in the 272d "loyalty to the commander is lacking, esprit de corps is non existent, and field activity and firing have shown them to be disorganized, lacking an understanding of tactically sound procedures, and erratic in firing their primary weapon." Colonel Enemark sympathized with Murphy's position: His indorsement to Murphy's "Chronology" noted that the "retention within a unit of officers against whom Board of Inquiry action has been taken is extremely undesirable. Normally the individuals are dissatisfied with and resentful of the commander who initiated the action. Through their disaffection they tend to poison the minds of their contemporaries and their subordinates. In addition, the confidence of their subordinates in them is destroyed as a result of the inquiry and they can seldom, if ever, regain their stature in the unit."[25]

Faced with these unpromising conditions, in January, 1952, the 272d began its final months as a guard battalion in federal service. The battalion started a "program of basic education" for its large number of poorly educated enlisted men, and the 35th FA Group headquarters administered artillery proficiency tests to all of the battalion's officers. Lieutenant Colonel Murphy again attempted to remove officers he considered unfit, based on the results of these proficiency tests. Although these efforts failed,

Murphy did get the battalion's guard executive officer replaced in early January by a white reservist, and a number of other black officers requested and received transfers to other units in Germany. The battalion also returned to Grafenwöhr for two weeks of training that culminated in the firing batteries taking ATT 6-1. Two barely passed with scores of 70 and 70.25 percent; the third failed, but passed its retest with 73.9 percent.[26]

By January, the battalion's discipline and morale had collapsed. Among the serious incidents during this period were refusals to obey orders, the loss of classified signal material, an allegation of rape by a German woman, and allegations of homosexual activity. Compounding these incidents was the fact that "some officers in the battalion could not be trusted to conduct an investigation." The German woman could not identify her attacker among the soldiers of the 272d and the 599th FA Battalions at the *kaserne*, and intense criticism from the German press finally subsided after the 35th FA Group commander convinced reporters that the guilty soldiers had come from another army post. The homosexual activity investigation concluded with the discharge or release of eighteen men. Twenty-eight summary courts-martial, 11 special courts-martial, and 6 general courts-martial were held prior to racial integration of the battalion in April. The 272d's problems brought it to the attention of the VII Corps commander, who instructed the corps artillery commander to keep an eye on the battalion.[27]

By early 1952, following the successful example of FECOM, EUCOM moved to racially integrate its units. The command had begun small-scale integration efforts in 1951 when it received large numbers of black soldiers who were surplus to the needs of its segregated units. Many senior officers in Europe were against integration, but not Seventh Army's commander, who undoubtedly had units like the 272d in mind when he noted that as most of his black units were unsatisfactory, integration was vital to improving Seventh Army's combat effectiveness.[28] Lieutenant Colonel Murphy would not be present to see the 272d integrated; on 6 March he left the battalion for duty with the 36th FA Group. Collins George, in Europe checking on the status of EUCOM's racial integration program, wrote that the officer "who endangered the careers of a dozen or more Negro officers" had himself been relieved of command "after scarcely six months with the unit." Murphy's replacement was Lt. Col. John Blocker from the 18th FA Group. Blocker, born in Alabama in 1913, had been commissioned a reserve field artillery officer in 1936. He rose to the rank of colonel during World War II, and afterward integrated into the Regular Army as a lieutenant colonel. George reported that Blocker "seems to have made an excellent initial impression."[29]

The 272d stood down from training in early April to prepare for racial integration, which actually began on 27 March when a group of white officers transferred into the battalion from other units in Germany. Between 15 and 18 April a total of 262 black enlisted men, in four groups, were transferred from the 272d to four other field artillery battalions. Another 215 black enlisted men left the 272d on 19 April—all of them guardsmen heading back to the ZI for release from federal service. Finally, between 23 and 26 April, six groups of white enlisted men—totaling 410 men—transferred into the 272d from six different field artillery battalions, ending the racial integration process and the 272d's guard character.[30]

The battalion's performance after racial integration and the guard phase-out demonstrated that this was indeed a new 272d FA Battalion. After two weeks of reorganizing batteries and doing "much needed maintenance of vehicles and other material," the battalion on 12 May began a special training program. Because most of the new soldiers were already trained in their individual skills, the program focused on refreshing those skills and building teamwork. In July, the firing batteries took ATT 6-1. Two passed with scores of 91.7 and 89.7 percent; the third failed, but when retested scored 81.1 percent. In August, the battalion took ATT 6-2 and scored 87.85 percent, the highest score during 1952 of any towed 155-mm howitzer battalion in Europe. The 272d's 1952 command report noted that this turn around was the result of the integration program, "which allowed us to remove many of the undesirable persons from our unit and sent us new personnel in their places. With these new replacements and the best of our old personnel which we held over, we were able to build a new combat effective battalion." But the "new combat effective" 272d was not the National Guard 272d.[31]

The 194th FA Battalion, the 272d's neighbor at Camp McCoy, arrived in Germany in early September, 1951, but its equipment did not catch up until mid-December, a gap the 1951 command report noted could not be "utilized with any great degree of efficiency in training as a field artillery battalion." In January, 1952, the 194th moved to Grafenwöhr for field training and to practice ATT 6-1. In early April, the firing batteries took ATT 6-1, scoring 93.5 percent, 87 percent, and 86.26 percent. Also in April, guardsmen began to return to the ZI and the 194th transferred sixty-nine enlisted men to the 272d under the racial integration program. Black enlisted men who transferred into the battalion, including sixty-two from the 272d, did not impress the 194th's officers and NCOs; the 194th's 1952 command report noted: "the first effects of the racial integration program were felt as our court martial rate started to increase." By the end of June, the 194th's guard commander and most of his fellow Iowa guardsmen had returned to the ZI. This was about 35 percent of the 194th's January, 1952, strength, which was not completely replaced until the end of August. Despite this personnel turbulence, the 194th took its battalion ATT at the end of June and scored 74.6 percent. Late in 1952 the 194th lost the 1950 draftees who had joined the battalion at McCoy, and by the end of the year it had suffered a 90 percent personnel turnover. This forced the 194th to begin a modified version of the ATP in October, designed to rebuild the battalion's collective skill level.[32]

The 272d FA Battalion failed to become combat ready while it remained a racially segregated guard unit. There were many factors involved in that failure: poor guard officer and NCO leadership, a poorly managed transition of the battalion from infantry to field artillery, the decision to station the 272d at Camp McCoy, the quality and quantity of enlisted fillers sent to the battalion, racism within the army, the manner of Lieutenant Colonel Russell's and Major Bingham's relief, Lieutenant Colonel Murphy's command methods, the power of the press, state politicians' interest in their mobilized guard constituents, and the poor conditions of its *kaserne* in Germany.

The few comments Murphy made in official correspondence shed little light on his opinion of African Americans. There are hints in the two main documents he wrote, especially the battalion's 1951 command report, that he subscribed to the belief of many white officers that blacks would make good enlisted soldiers only if they were assigned to less-complex MOSs, and that black officers could not successfully perform command and staff functions at the battalion level. "[T]he military command of negroes by negroes has failed in this battalion," wrote Murphy. "Integration is recommended." Moreover, he contended, "as was the case during World War II, the bulk of the technical work in negro battalions must be accomplished by commissioned personnel. They must be superior officers in order that the unit may be satisfactory." It is unknown whether Murphy, while assigned to the XIII Corps Artillery during World War II observed or heard about the nine black nondivisional field artillery battalions that saw service during the campaigns in Europe. It is also not known if Murphy had read War Department Pamphlet 20-6, *Command of Negro Troops*, first published in February, 1944. But whatever the problems created by a white West Pointer taking command of a troubled black guard battalion, it is clear that Murphy's assumption of command did not trigger the 272d's slide into combat ineffectiveness. The battalion was broken by the summer of 1951, and some changes had to be made in order to salvage its second year of federal service. While it is counterfactual to suppose that Lieutenant Colonel Blocker could have done better than Murphy from August, 1951, to March, 1952, it does appear that Murphy's motivation to command the 272d was low, as he gave up a good battalion for command of what he considered a disaster area. In addition, Murphy's approach to the 272d's problems appears to have lacked any sensitivity for the battalion's entwined heritage as a black guard unit. In the end, what the story of the 272d Field Artillery Battalion's federal service demonstrates above all is the eternal military truth: good units are based on good troops, good training, and good leadership.

28th Infantry Division

The 28th Infantry Division was very much the gem of the Pennsylvania National Guard. It had seen some of the hardest service of any guard division during the two world wars. In World War I the 28th earned the nickname "Iron Division" after spending 102 days on the line at a cost of 2,874 dead and 11,265 wounded. Mobilized in early 1941, the division suffered a number of growing pains in its second war. Its guard commander, Maj. Gen. Edward Martin, left federal service in early 1942 to make a successful run for the governor's office in Pennsylvania. His Regular Army replacement was subsequently fired and replaced by Maj. Gen. Omar Bradley, who, like Lieutenant Colonel Murphy of the 272d FA, had to give up command of a successful unit to fix a broken one. However, General Bradley succeeded and was rewarded with a promotion after eight months in command. As commander of the First Army, Bradley fired his Regular Army replacement during the Normandy campaign, the 28th's first combat operation, and the division's new commander was killed in action the same day he took command. The 28th's next commander, Maj. Gen. Norman D. Cota, would last for the rest of the war and command the division during its two greatest trials. In November, 1944, the division was devastated in the "dark and bloody ground" of the Hürtgen Forest. In

December, as it tried to rebuild from that ordeal, the 28th was struck by the full force of the German Ardennes counteroffensive and, after fighting a hard and extremely confused delaying action against a full German panzer corps, was rendered combat ineffective in a week. After being reconstituted, the 28th went back into the line for the final push into Germany. Casualties for its nine months of combat were 2,483 dead and 9,609 wounded. As a unit from the "Keystone State," the 28th wore a red keystone symbol as its division patch; after the Hürtgen and Bulge battles, the division had a new nickname: the "Bloody Bucket."[33]

When the division returned to state control, Governor Martin gave the job of rebuilding the 28th to Maj. Gen. Edward Stackpole, a longtime Pennsylvania guardsman. Martin selected Brig. Gen. Daniel B. Strickler to be Stackpole's assistant. General Stackpole retired in June, 1947, and Strickler was promoted to major general and given command of the division. Born in Pennsylvania in 1897, Strickler was one of the most combat experienced division commanders in the postwar guard and had a long association with the Bloody Bucket. He enlisted in the local guard company in 1916, served on the Mexican border, and in April, 1917, was elected to serve as a second lieutenant in his company. He saw action in all of the 28th's battles in France, commanded a machine-gun company, and was wounded. He became a lawyer between the wars and was actively involved in state Republican Party activities. However, he did not return to the 28th. Instead he joined the ORC, and by 1935 was a colonel. In 1941, convinced the Regular Army would not allow senior reserve officers to serve with troops, Strickler visited his fellow Pennsylvanian Republican, General Martin, and convinced Martin to take him on as a lieutenant colonel and infantry battalion commander in the 28th. After arranging for his reduction in rank, Strickler rejoined the 28th. He commanded a battalion of the 109th Infantry in combat from July to September, 1944. When General Cota fired the 109th Infantry's commander, Strickler took over briefly until being displaced by a regular officer. Sent to the 110th Infantry as executive officer, he took charge of the regiment in the Bulge when its commander was captured and rallied the fragmented unit to fight a tough delaying action against the Germans. In recognition of his outstanding performance in the Battle of the Bulge, Strickler received a Silver Star, a Legion of Merit, permanent command of the 110th Infantry, and his colonel's eagles in late December. He commanded the regiment until the end of the war. With his impressive war record and long involvement in state politics, it was no surprise that in 1946 he would be appointed the 28th's assistant division commander and that he would run for and be elected lieutenant governor.[34]

Strickler's assistant division commander in 1950 was Brig. Gen. T. L. Hoban, a state judge. Born in Pennsylvania in 1893, Hoban was commissioned a National Army infantry lieutenant in 1917. After the war, he became a guard infantry lieutenant, and by 1939 was executive officer of the 109th Infantry and a lieutenant colonel—the rank he held throughout World War II. After returning to Pennsylvania, Hoban was promoted to colonel and given the task of organizing the 109th Infantry. When Strickler moved up to division command, Hoban replaced him. The acting division artillery commander at mobilization was Col. W. W. Gilmore. Born in Pennsylvania in 1905, Gilmore was commissioned as a guard field artillery lieutenant in 1931. At mobilization in 1941, Gilmore was a captain in the 108th Field Artillery, and was a lieutenant colonel at the war's end. Returning to the 28th in 1947, Gilmore was promoted to colonel and became division artillery executive officer. The division chief of staff was Col. J. G. Mackey. Born in Pennsylvania in 1899, he was commissioned as a guard infantry lieutenant in 1930 after spending a year in the ranks. A captain at mobilization in 1940, he ended the war a lieutenant colonel. Mackey returned to 28th in 1947 as an adjutant general lieutenant colonel. He moved back to the infantry the next year and was promoted to colonel and made chief of staff. His four assistant chiefs of staff, with an average age of thirty-eight, were all native Pennsylvanians. Three had been guard lieutenants at mobilization in 1941 and ended the war as lieutenant colonels; the fourth had been a reserve lieutenant and ended the war a captain.[35]

The division's three regimental commanders, with an average age of forty-six, were Cols. F. R. Evans (109th Infantry) and H. K. Fluck (110th Infantry), and Lt. Col. A. J. Dreibelbies (112th Infantry). The first two were native Pennsylvanians and Dreibelbies was from Ohio. All three had served as both enlisted men and officers in their regiments before mobilization in 1941. Evans ended the war as a major, helped organize the postwar 109th as a lieutenant colonel, and succeeded Hoban as regimental commander. Dreibelbies ended the war a lieutenant colonel and remained on extended active duty as a reserve officer until May, 1950. After returning to the state in early June, 1950, he received a commission as a guard lieutenant colonel and command of the 112th Infantry. Fluck transferred out of the 28th and ended the war as a lieutenant colonel and infantry battalion commander in another division. Upon returning to the 110th Infantry in 1946, he helped organize it as executive officer and took command of the regiment in 1948.[36]

The nine infantry battalion commanders, with an average age of thirty-nine, were of typical backgrounds: 4 had been officers in the 28th in 1941, 1 had been an officer in the Connecticut guard, 1 had been a reserve officer, and 3 had been drafted and commissioned during the war. Five ended the war as captains and the remaining 4 ended the war as a lieutenant, a major, a lieutenant colonel, and a colonel. Three joined the 28th in 1946, and 2 each in 1947, 1948, and 1949. Of the four field artillery battalion commanders, whose average age was thirty-five, 2 had been guard officers in 1941, 1 a reserve officer, and 1 was commissioned as a marine corps officer during the war. Two ended the war as majors and 2 as captains. One joined the 28th in 1946, and the other 3 in 1947. None of the four separate battalion commanders, with an average age of forty, had been guardsmen in 1941. Three had been reserve officers and 1 was commissioned during the war. The 3 reserve officers ended the war as lieutenant colonels, and the other as a major. Two joined the 28th in 1947, and 2 in 1949. Of the infantry battalion commanders, 3 attended the officer basic course during the war, 1 was sent to the battalion commander course, and 2 attended the associate officer advanced course in 1948. The three field artillery battalion commanders who served in the army in World War II all attended their branch officer basic course during the war. None of the separate battalion commanders had attended a service school in their branch. The commander of the 899th AAA Battalion had begun the war as a quartermaster officer, ended it an ordnance officer, and became an AAA officer in 1947 when he joined the guard.[37]

The 28th spent the years 1946–50 as most guard divisions did, trying to recruit up to its National Guard reduced TO&E strength authorization, coping with armory problems, and training as best it could given the constraints of time, personnel, and equipment. The National Guard Bureau selected the 28th, like the 45th in Oklahoma, as one of the priority guard divisions of the mobile strike force. Like the Thunderbirds, members of the Keystone division thought highly of their outfit, as did the state. And also like the 45th, the 28th made General Clark's July, 1950, short list of divisions most ready for mobilization. (A reporter quoted Clark as saying "it doesn't take much to figure out why the Twenty-eighth was called up.") When the army alerted it for mobilization in August, 1950, the 28th had just begun its summer training, which was cut short by a week to allow the division the full thirty days for induction preparation. After the traditional Governor's Day division review on 6 August, the 28th's units broke camp and headed back to their home stations.[38] On 5 September, the division entered federal service for its third war with only 726 officers, 134 warrant officers, and 8,856 enlisted men—52 percent of its authorized TO&E strength. After experiencing heavy losses of enlisted fillers and some guardsmen to levies, followed by their replacement by more fillers, the division completed its MTP training at Camp Atterbury, received word that it would be deployed to Germany as part of the NATO military buildup, and participated in Exercise Southern Pine, which highlighted the division's weaknesses in small-unit collective skills.[39]

The 28th had little time after Southern Pine to work on its weaknesses as all but the most perfunctory training ceased after the second week of September when the division began preparations for the move to Germany. Every Keystone soldier received two weeks leave. Overtaxed personnel sections handled the many administrative requirements for overseas movement, while other soldiers prepared vehicles and equipment for shipment. On 26 October, the 28th staged its final review at Camp Atterbury, with Gov. John S. Fine traveling from Pennsylvania to take the salute. In early November, the 28th took trains to East Coast ports. Most of the division left via Hampton Roads, Virginia, but about three thousand Keystoners paraded through Philadelphia on 12 November before a "silent and solemn throng" estimated at two hundred thousand, then boarded their troop transport at the navy yard.[40]

The division's units arrived in Germany during late November and early December, and the 28th established its headquarters in Goeppingen on 26 November. Once again under General Burress, their former corps commander in Indiana who now commanded VII Corps, the division spent the rest of the year settling into its new quarters—mainly renovated German *kasernes* spread out among six groupings in the Stuttgart area. Making up equipment shortages, running a modified form of the MTP, and personnel turbulence arising from the phase-out of guardsmen dominated the first seven months of 1952 for the division. The 28th, like the 45th and other mobilized guard divisions, had its colors retained in federal service after its guardsmen completed their active duty tours, although the 28th retained its guard character slightly longer than did the 45th.[41]

The Keystoners arrived in Germany still feeling the effects of the reduced equipment authorizations placed on units in the ZI. This was "a major obstacle" to combat readiness during the first half of 1952. In January, for example, a shortage of mounts and telescopes left none of the 155-mm howitzers and only 61 percent of the 105-mm howitzers operational. The division had none of its tanks and only 70 percent of its engineer equipment. European Command planned for the 28th to make up these shortfalls from stocks held in theater. The division's inventory improved each month, but only after the guard phase-out were most shortages finally filled. Like the 45th's tankers, the 628th Tank Battalion had a long wait for its key piece of equipment. The battalion did not reach full strength in tanks until April, but the M26s sent by EUCOM were old and in poor condition, which meant the unit had to perform extensive maintenance. Handicapped by a shortage of repair parts, the battalion had a high deadline rate. The 628th did not convert to the new M47 tank until after the guard phase-out. The 899th AAA Battalion was not so lucky; it was still armed with M15s in lieu of M19s at the end of 1952. The battalion commander noted that the M15, which had been "obsolete for several years, receives little confidence of the ones dependent upon its service." Because of these problems, the 28th instituted a special maintenance inspection program. This worked well, except that members of the division inspection teams often disagreed with the conclusions of VII Corps teams conducting a similar program. "This, of course, made it extremely difficult for the lower units to know exactly what sort of action to take in regard to the inspected equipment."[42]

In order to address the problems revealed during Southern Pine, the 28th conducted a modified version of the MTP featuring extensive field training from January to October, 1952. The program began with advanced individual and squad training, moved in March to the platoon and company level, then in May to the battalion and regiment level, and culminated with regimental combat team and division-level training from July to October. The division also ran command post exercises, opened NCO leadership schools, held a division field training exercise in March, gave Army Training Tests to its subordinate units, and endured numerous VII Corps inspections. Monthly practice alerts prepared the division to move from garrison to tactical field positions in case of a surprise Soviet attack.[43]

This training plan faced a number of obstacles. One was the shortage of equipment and repair parts. Another, primarily affecting the regimental and division artillery headquarters, was the "heavy drain" on time and personnel created by the administrative and housekeeping requirements created by running six separate garrisons.[44] A third obstacle was morale. Garrison and short-timer's attitudes grew within the division. Many soldiers "came to expect three-day passes regularly regardless of merit and morale, as a result, suffered during field problems when no passes were given." The venereal disease rate increased to five times what it had been at Camp Atterbury. The 229th FA Battalion noted an "attitude of indifference" among guardsmen during the early months of the year. Also affecting morale was a virtual freeze on promotions for both officers and enlisted men. Many guard officers who had entered federal service in a duty position calling for a rank higher than the one they held were not promoted while they were on active duty. This was a major reason why efforts to get guard officers to sign up for extended tours failed miserably in the 28th. The rank-position imbalance was exacerbated once the guard phase-out began. By late summer, many NCO positions in the 109th Infantry were being filled by privates first class.[45]

These attitudes came to a head during the 28th's Exercise Keystone, a five-day maneuver in March that pitted the bulk of the division against the 109th RCT. It was the first time the entire division had taken to the field since Southern Pine, and the "results indicated that the interval had been too great to maintain efficiency." At a special meeting halfway through the exercise, General Strickler told the 28th's senior leaders that the exercise "has thus far been deplorable and shockingly unsatisfactory from the conduct and performance of the troops and their leaders." Strickler was particularly upset given that most of the 28th's personnel had performed well during Southern Pine. This time, however, the "men displayed sloppiness, lack of interest, little enthusiasm, no realism, and discipline is far below normal." The fault, according to the division commander, was poor leadership. "Squad and platoon leadership had been the worst I have ever seen" and higher echelon commanders "seemed to be CP bound. All commanders must get out in the field." One possible source of poor leadership at platoon level was a shortage of second lieutenants. The division had lost "quite a few" of them when it moved to Germany because they had not yet attended their branch officer basic course, a requirement for overseas service. This left a number of platoons commanded by inexperienced guard NCOs.[46]

One answer to the problem was the creation of NCO academies in

March, with one each in the division artillery, the infantry regiments, and the separate battalions. Company and battery commanders selected soldiers to attend the academies, which were originally four and then six weeks long. The syllabus focused on general NCO skills: leadership, map reading, squad and platoon tactics, weapons, and drill and ceremony. The schools received extensive publicity within the division and a general officer always attended graduation ceremonies. The division's 1952 command report noted that the "success of the schools was evident in the continual improvement of the units in field operations."[47]

The NCO academies were also valuable in dealing with the 28th's greatest personnel problem of 1952: the phase-out of guardsmen and 1950 draftees. Planning began in February and the phase-out began in April with 1,188 enlisted men leaving for the ZI. In May, 103 officers, 15 warrant officers, and 1,148 enlisted men left, followed in June by 112 officers, 37 warrant officers, and 1,351 enlisted men. The last large group of guardsmen left in July: 59 officers, 4 warrant officers, and 1,066 enlisted men. These losses represented 27 percent of authorized enlisted and 29 percent of authorized officer strength. The guardsmen's departure had effects out of proportion to their numbers, for most of them, especially the enlisted men, held "specialist MOS's or positions requiring leadership abilities." The phase-out of 1950 draftees beginning in September only aggravated this problem, for among them were many men "who had accompanied the Division overseas and who were familiar with its problems." General Strickler decided to remain on extended active duty and commanded the 28th until November, 1952, when he was transferred to head the military assistance group in Italy. Strickler remained on active duty until September, 1957, serving on the Army Review Board Council and as FECOM's assistant chief of staff for civil and governmental affairs.[48]

Replacements for these losses came from three sources. The first was very short term: in order to cushion the loss of guardsmen in the spring and summer, in February and March Seventh Army transferred to the 28th about fifteen hundred enlisted men from other divisions who had autumn, 1952, discharge dates. The division easily integrated these already trained and experienced men.[49] The 28th also received a number of African Americans as part of EUCOM's racial integration program. Integration began in March, when a battalion's worth of black infantrymen arrived from Seventh Army's segregated armored infantry battalions. The division distributed them throughout the three infantry regiments so that no company contained more than 10 percent black enlisted men, the limit established by EUCOM. Further shipments arrived to integrate other units in the division, followed during the rest of the year by blacks arriving as replacements from the ZI. To balance these arrivals, units in the 28th sent groups of white enlisted men with the same distribution of MOSs and rank that they had received to Seventh Army's formerly segregated units. The division's 1952 command report stated that racial integration was "highly successful."[50] One tool used to manage racial integration was a policy that "no Race 2 NCO could be reduced in grade for inefficiency for a period of six months" after joining the 28th. The division noted the greatest problem with racial integration was that "immoral relationships between soldiers and German women (many of whom accompanied transferees from Berlin, Mannheim, and Nurnberg) increased with the beginning of the program." However, attempts to crack down on these relationships generated complaints of discrimination. While Strickler did not address this subject in his memoirs, at a division commanders' conference on 2 May he told senior subordinates to "treat integrated personnel fairly and make no distinctions."[51]

Command reports from subordinate units within the 28th vary in their evaluation of racial integration's effects. The division artillery headquarters noted that "small isolated incidents did occur immediately after the integration, but generally the program was successful and caused the minimum amount of friction." The 899th AAA Battalion found its black soldiers very valuable as the guard phase-out accelerated, for many of the new Keystoners were trained, qualified personnel. But the battalion also believed integration was partly responsible for a rise in misconduct after June, with the "graver incidents" committed by blacks. The 229th FA Battalion reported "only minor problems," but noted that because many black enlisted men had not attained a fifth grade education level before entering the service, they were often at "basic education" classes and thus unavailable for duty.[52] The 628th Tank Battalion and the 109th Infantry reported the greatest problems with integration. The 628th claimed it lost "too many" good white NCOs, and that the black NCOs it received in return "were not the answer." The battalion also complained there were few serious disciplinary incidents before integration, but afterward it experienced an increase, particularly in incidents involving knives. The 109th Infantry found "little evidence of interracial problems within the Regiment." Its difficulty with integration was that higher headquarters selected which white enlisted men to transfer out of the 109th, taking good soldiers, whereas segregated units were allowed to select the soldiers they would transfer, and sent the 109th many soldiers whose disciplinary records "indicated that they should long since have been kicked out."[53]

Like the 45th Infantry Division, the 28th's greatest problem with manpower quality was the replacements received from the ZI. These soldiers began to arrive in April, and most of the enlisted replacements had received only basic training in the ZI. Moreover, many were of a lower caliber than the troops who accompanied the division to Germany. The division artillery headquarters reported that "practically all" its enlisted replacements had not attended advanced individual training in field artillery MOSs, and that about 25 percent of its officer replacements were AAA officers who had no field artillery experience or training. Units had to conduct training on field artillery skills while in the field doing collective training or even taking ATTs. Ninety percent of the enlisted replacements sent to the 103d Engineer Battalion had not attended advanced individual training, and some officer replacements also lacked training in engineer skills. The 899th AAA Battalion found many of its replacements had records showing them as qualified, but the soldiers actually knew nothing about their MOS. Their former unit in the ZI had simply awarded the MOS to them before they shipped out to Europe so the unit could meet its levy quotas. Some replacements arrived at the 899th AAA with six months or less active service remaining. A partial exception to these trends was the 628th Tank Battalion, which reported that until November its enlisted replacements generally had training in armor MOSs. After November, however, its replacement stream was like those of other division units.[54]

Unlike the 45th in Korea, the 28th in Germany did not establish a division-level school to train replacements from the ZI. Instead, the 28th used on-the-job training for officers and enlisted men assigned to positions for which they had neither training nor experience. Seventh Army and EUCOM had a network of schools for technical specialties such as ordnance and signal, but these schools were not as useful as they could have been. On 12 January 1952, EUCOM changed its school policy, directing that "quotas for schools would be assigned on a mandatory basis even though spaces for a particular school had not been requested by a unit." These quotas "became increasingly hard to fill" as more and more men in the division fell below the minimum requirement of six months remaining in EUCOM after graduation, and many of the replacements fell below the minimum AGCT scores required to attend the schools. At the end of 1952, the 28th began setting up a program aimed at shoring up critically short MOSs in the division: enlisted men qualified in the MOS would teach their skills, using the resources of post education centers, but during off-duty hours.[55]

With all this personnel turbulence, the division artillery found that the "required state of combat readiness was maintained, but only with great difficulty." However, in early 1953, Colonel McHugh wrote that if his 109th Infantry should "be tried by combat, it would be found ready," and the 112th Infantry's commander rated his regiment's operational readiness as "good." The results of battalion ATTs appeared to support these comments. All nine infantry battalions passed their ATTs, which were administered by VII Corps between July and September. Field artillery battalions passed their ATTs in the early autumn, as did the four separate battalions. These ATTs, however, did not always accurately reflect trends within the division. Most units took their ATTs just before or as 1950 draftees and the enlisted men transferred into the 28th from other Seventh Army units in early 1952 began to return to the ZI. When these men departed, to be followed shortly thereafter by the enlisted men who joined the 28th at Atterbury in early 1951, units would once again have to rebuild teamwork and unit cohesion, and would face an increasing erosion of individual skill levels as their officers and enlisted men consisted more and more of replacements from the ZI who often were ill-suited for the positions to which they were assigned.

While battalions passed the ATTs, most did not achieve the high scores one would expect of units standing guard on the frontier of what some historians argue was the army's highest strategic priority of the period, the defense of Western Europe. Five of the nine infantry battalions and the 899th AAA Battalion only scored "Satisfactory," and the 628th Tank and 103d Engineers earned ratings of "Very Satisfactory." The 899th AAA's commander wrote that although "this score may be considered low, it was gratifying to pass the test considering the tremendous personnel turnover experienced the previous five months." The 229th FA Battalion clearly displayed the effects of this personnel turbulence. It earned an "Excellent" rating on the first part of its ATT in September, but this score depended on the "relatively few well trained" personnel in the battalion. Their departure showed in the second part of the ATT held the next month, when the battalion scored only "Satisfactory."[56] Only the 103d Medical Battalion earned a "Superior" rating. General Strickler was well aware of the problems facing his battalions. He wrote Colonel Fluck to congratulate him on all the 110th Infantry's battalions passing their ATTs: "I know the difficulties which have made it quite a job to get your battalions through but they have made the grade." One of Fluck's battalion commanders recalled that the night before the battalion began its ATT, it received a "couple hundred replacements." His battalion earned a "Satisfactory" rating.[57]

Back home, the Pennsylvania National Guard organized an NGUS division in 1953 to form the cadre needed to rebuild the 28th once the army returned its colors to the state. Governor Fine appointed Maj. Gen. Charles C. Curtis, back in the state after his 51st AAA Brigade left federal service in mid-1952, as division commander. Because Curtis was an AAA officer and sixty years old, Lt. Gen. F. A. Weber, Pennsylvania's adjutant general, moved to get a younger infantry officer as Curtis's assistant and most likely replacement. In October, 1952, Weber offered the position to Colonel Fluck, who had gone on extended active duty so that he could remain in command of the 110th Infantry. Fluck wanted the position, but was concerned the army would not release him. The adjutant general wrote Fluck not to worry: "I am having some influential friends check with the officials in the Pentagon, concerning your release and I have been informed there should be no trouble in securing it for you." Colonel Fluck returned to Pennsylvania, was promoted to brigadier general, and soon succeeded Curtis as division commander. On 22 August 1954, at the Governor's Day review during the division's first postwar summer training, the army returned the 28th's colors to the Commonwealth of Pennsylvania. General Fluck accepted the colors from Governor Fine, officially ending the Keystone Division's Korean War service.[58]

For the 28th Infantry Division, its third war was an unconsummated war. After training hard, the Keystoners found themselves back in Germany, where their greatest opponent turned out to be personnel turbulence generated by the army's desperate manpower dilemmas.

Sent to Europe as part of the NATO military buildup for the "long pull" of the Cold War, most guard units performed their symbolic role well, representing America's commitment to the new alliance. Although most guard units in Europe were much better prepared for combat than were guard units in 1942 or regular units in 1950, their combat effectiveness in 1952 and early 1953 remains questionable.

CHAPTER 7

Lost in the Zone of the Interior

Most Army National Guard units mobilized during the Korean War did not deploy overseas—instead they remained in the Zone of the Interior.[1] These units spent their federal service in limbo, most losing their guard character and drifting without a realistic operational mission after completing postmobilization training. Units remained in the ZI for two reasons. Many were antiaircraft artillery units, mobilized as part of the rush to create an effective air defense for the continental United States. Other units remained in the ZI to rebuild the army's General Reserve in case the communists challenged the United States elsewhere in the world.

Both AAA units and units assigned to the General Reserve fell victim to the army's desperate need for expedient sources of trained manpower. This need for manpower overseas led the army in 1951 and 1952 to strip most units left in the ZI—regular and mobilized guard and reserve—of trained officers and enlisted men, then use these units as supplements to its training facilities. With the introduction of a rotation program in Korea in mid-1951, these units also became holding areas for soldiers who returned to the ZI with only a few months of active service remaining before discharge. This process was especially painful for guard units. Personnel levies for overseas service mocked the guard's "Go With Those You Know" slogan, stirred up old suspicions about the regulars' attitude toward the guard, and were the source of the greatest anger and bitterness among guardsmen, their families, and guard supporters during the Korean War.

Not surprisingly, the stripping of trained manpower destroyed unit combat readiness, and the ensuing personnel turbulence created by using the units as adjuncts to the training system and holding areas for short-timers prevented the reestablishment of combat readiness in most units. The army carried this policy to its extreme with the two guard divisions, Ohio's 37th and Illinois's 44th, mobilized during 1952: after completing the MTP, these divisions were stripped of almost all their trained manpower, refilled with an odd assortment of replacements to create a new cadre, placed on a reduced table of organization, and officially assigned the training of individual replacements as their primary mission.

Policing the Zone of the Interior

The army ordered the 163d, 168th and 171st MP Battalions to active duty in 1950.[2] Although none of these battalions were part of the 1940 National Guard troop list, all had links to the pre–World War II guard. The 171st's commander, Lt. Col. S. F. Blackwell, a forty-eight-year-old native of the District of Columbia, was the longest serving guardsmen of the three battalion commanders, commissioned in 1927 into the 372d Infantry Regiment after six years as an enlisted guardsman. The 163d's Lt. Col. G. O. Weber, thirty-eight, served eleven years as an enlisted guardsman and was commissioned an infantry first lieutenant upon mobilization in 1941. Both Weber and Blackwell ended the war as lieutenant colonels. The 168th's Lt. Col. J. L. O'Connell, thirty-six, served less than a year as an enlisted guardsman before being mobilized in 1941. Commissioned a military police second lieutenant in 1943, he ended the war a captain.[3]

The officers Blackwell, Weber, and O'Connell commanded reflected the typical profile of guard units. The battalions' enlisted strength had the profile of a typical guard unit in regard to age and experience, and all three were significantly under their full TO&E authorization when alerted for mobilization: the 163d was at 50 percent, the 168th was at 43 percent, and the 171st was at 41 percent. Each battalion went to a different training site: the 163d to Fort Custer, Michigan; the 168th to Fort Meade, Maryland; and the 171st to Camp McCoy, Wisconsin.[4] Early in 1951, the guard identity of each battalion began to erode as levies for overseas service claimed some guardsmen and others either received hardship discharges or went home when their enlistments expired. Replacing these guardsmen were recruits, recalled reservists, and newly commissioned lieutenants who in turn were lost to levies or transfers and their positions filled by the same mix of personnel. As 1951 neared its end, men returning from Korea or Europe with only a few months of active duty remaining began joining the battalions. With little to motivate them, these men usually contributed little to their new units before discharge. Indeed, short-timers often harmed units. Lieutenant Colonel Blackwell reported that "many men holding T/O&E positions have been deprived of promotion because of Korean rotatees and other personnel have been transferred in grade into the battalion."[5]

Despite the many obstacles hindering postmobilization training efforts, the battalions completed their ATPs during the summer of 1951. Personnel turbulence delayed the 163d's ATT until 20–22 August, but the battalion scored 84.4 percent, earning a rating of excellent. The 171st took its ATT on 7–8 June and failed—hardly a surprise given the problems the battalion encountered at Camp McCoy. Later that month, in accordance with an AFF inspection team's recommendation, the 171st moved from McCoy to Fort Custer. There it retook the ATT, earning a rating of satisfactory with a 77.7 percent score. The 168th did not take an ATT in 1951. Instead, it participated in Exercise Southern Pine, which the battalion commander believed provided excellent training and gave unit morale a big boost, as the troops had "a chance to practice some of the things they had learned in the classroom."[6]

After completing the ATP, the three battalions settled into a routine they would follow until returning to state control in July, 1952. The battalions would try to perform tactical training to maintain combat readiness while burdened with three significant impediments to training. The first was that by early 1952 it became clear the battalions would not be deployed into harm's way. This removed a major motivation to focus on combat readiness and encouraged the growth of a garrison mentality, which was further exacerbated by orders to provide administrative military police support, including post policing, stockade guards, convoy escorts, courtesy patrols on trains, and security detachments at key facilities.[7]

The third impediment was the army's continued use of these battalions to support operations in Korea and Europe. Personnel levies stripped them of trained officers and enlisted men, tearing down the level of collective expertise and erasing the units' guard character. The 171st was the only battalion to keep a guard officer as commander. Fillers arrived to take the place of the men who were levied, but they often were of little use in establishing and maintaining combat readiness. Many were short-timers from Korea and Europe, and a significant percentage of these men did not even hold military police MOSs, which further complicated training. Other fillers had just graduated from basic training or were newly commissioned officers. Often before they could be integrated into the unit they were levied for overseas service or sent to service schools and then overseas. The pressure on the MP battalions was constant. Between January and June, 1952, the 163d lost 29 officers and 264 enlisted men to levies, 6 officers and 107 enlisted men were discharged, and the battalion received 11 officer and 354 enlisted fillers. While at Exercise Long Horn, 1952's multidivisional exercise, overseas levies, discharges, and the early release of guardsmen took 7 officers and 105 enlisted men from the 163d, which, the battalion remarked, "reflected in numbers approximately the same losses the organization might have suffered in combat without replacements."[8]

These battalions spent their last ten to eleven months on active duty trapped by these demands on their time and manpower. While many individual guard military policemen did receive an operational mission, courtesy of levies for overseas service, as units these three MP battalions found policing the Zone of the Interior during a period of limited mobilization a very unsatisfying mission.

Waiting for the Soviet Air Force

Believing that World War III, like its predecessor, would be a long struggle whose outcome depended in large part on effective industrial mobilization, American war plans called for unleashing the Strategic Air Command upon Soviet industry. Military planners, fearing the Soviet air force would retaliate, focused considerable attention on defending the continental United States against air attack. However, with declining defense budgets, many other pressing commitments, and without an easily identifiable Soviet bomber capability, the army devoted few Regular Army resources to air defense. Instead, it turned to the National Guard as the key component in dealing with this threat, creating many AAA units in the new troop list. By June, 1950, fifty 90-mm gun battalions, five 120-mm gun battalions, thirty-eight automatic weapons battalions, forty-one group headquarters, twelve brigade headquarters, twelve operations detachments, and twenty-five signal radar maintenance units (SRMU) had been organized. One group and one brigade headquarters, two operations detachments, four automatic weapons battalions, and fifteen SRMUs were on the troop list but had not yet been organized.[9]

Concerned that Korea might be the opening shot of World War III, the army ordered a significant mobilization of guard AAA units. By the end of September, 1950, seventeen 90-mm and four 120-mm AAA gun battalions, twenty-two SRMUs, nine operations detachments, and eight group and three brigade headquarters were in federal service. Of these units, fourteen 90-mm gun battalions, four group headquarters, and five operations detachments reported to Camp Stewart, Georgia, home of the Third Army AAA Training Center. These units were assigned to the 51st AAA Brigade, a Pennsylvania unit commanded by a veteran guard coast artillery officer, Brig. Gen. Charles Curtis. Born in 1893, an enlisted guardsman during the Mexican border crisis, and commissioned in the infantry during World War I, Curtis had been a guard coast artillery officer since 1922. Ordered to active duty as a colonel in 1940, he had commanded the 51st (then an AUS formation) in combat during the 1944–45 campaign in northwestern Europe. Returning home, he accepted a guard brigadier general's commission in 1946 and was appointed commander of Pennsylvania's AAA brigade. After "a short delay," the new brigade received the lineage of the wartime 51st AAA Brigade.[10]

The AAA units ordered to Stewart shared the same set of problems common to all guard units mobilized in 1950. While many of the units assigned to the 51st at Stewart had strong connections to the 1940 troop list, the level of AAA experience among officers varied considerably. Enlisted personnel strength and skill suffered from the same problems of turbulence and limited training that affected other types of guard units. Home station and annual summer training had provided little practice at the complex tasks of shooting aircraft out of the sky and coordinating air defenses. Units' AAA weapons and other equipment were often obsolete and worn out: M1 or M1A1 90-mm guns instead of the newer M2 models, M7 instead of M9 gun directors, and older models of other equipment such as power generators.[11]

After arriving at Stewart, the 51st AAA Brigade's units spent the remainder of the year settling into federal service and starting their ATPs. The brigade encountered all the typical problems that faced mobilized guard units and also had to deal with the Camp Stewart post staff, which AFF inspectors condemned for very poor support of the units stationed there. Units proceeded through the ATP at their own pace, moving with enthusiasm into the collective training phase, although personnel turbulence remained a problem in early 1951, when the AAA units were made adjuncts of the army's basic training system. Section crew drills, field training exercises, radar tracking practice, and service practice firings provided a sense of purpose and accomplishment, bringing units together and building esprit. Poor logistical support from the Stewart facilities and equipment shortages still created difficulties, but working in favor of units were the post's large size and good weather, along with the availability of aircraft at nearby Hunter Air Force Base for use in training. Additionally, visits by instructor teams from the AAA School at Fort Bliss were very helpful, especially in training officers. Despite the various problems, all units completed their ATPs by the early summer of 1951. The units then scattered across the eastern half of the United States to watch and wait for the Soviet air force. The areas defended included Chicago, Pittsburgh, upstate New York, New York City, Philadelphia, Boston, the upper Great Lakes, and the District of Columbia.[12]

These units joined a rapidly expanding air defense system as fears that the Chinese intervention in Korea was part of a plan to weaken American defenses had motivated a major air defense buildup in the ZI. The army, in three increments between January and May, 1951, tapped the guard for nineteen more 90-mm gun battalions, a 120-mm gun battalion, an automatic weapons battalion, three group headquarters, four operations detachments, and three SRMUs. Antiaircraft artillery units ordered to active duty in 1951 encountered the same problems that dogged units mobilized in 1950. By September, mobilized guard units made up a significant percentage of the Army Antiaircraft Command (ARAACOM): 60 percent of brigade and 50 percent of group headquarters, 60 percent of operations detachments, 52 percent of SRMUs, 31 percent of 120-mm gun battalions, and 75 percent of 90-mm gun battalions. The army's largest AAA commitment was New York City, with four 90-mm and two 120-mm gun battalions, then Washington, D.C., with two 120-mm and two 90-mm gun battalions, and the Hanford, Washington nuclear weapons production facility, with four 120-mm gun battalions.[13]

Behind those numbers, however, were significant weaknesses. Before June, 1950, little real work had been done to establish an effective air defense network in the ZI. Not until May had an ad hoc interservice committee selected areas in the country deemed critical enough to warrant AAA protection, and ARAACOM itself was not activated until July. Units leaving Fort Stewart often encountered a good deal of confusion and delay as the army scrambled to construct an AAA system in the ZI. Sometimes this worked to a unit's advantage. For example, the 51st AAA Brigade's headquarters enlisted men lived in a Chicago hotel. Group and brigade headquarters had to construct detailed AAA defense plans for the areas they were assigned to guard, a process hindered by shortages of equipment and the fact that AAA defense for major urban and industrial areas had not been a significant part of their training.[14]

Some AAA units set up housekeeping on established posts. Support from these installations varied. Often, AAA units were unwelcome interlopers, adding one more burden for post facilities already taxed by taking care of many units and usually not prepared to support an AAA unit's unique requirements. The 209th Group, when it arrived at Indiantown Gap, found the post "not equipped to cater to the problems of T/O&E AA units." However, "an aggressive program" by post officials, supported by Second Army, "very shortly" remedied the problem. Many posts did not have maneuver areas large enough for AAA units to conduct field training exercises (FTXs). The 209th Group made arrangements with the Pennsylvania Wildlife Commission to use a nearby state park for its gun battalions to conduct FTXs.[15]

Other units were sent to posts that had been closed or placed in caretaker status after World War II. Often these posts required a good deal of work to make them habitable, let alone suitable for emplacing AAA weapons. The 197th Group found all the kitchen equipment removed and heating equipment rendered inoperable at Fort Banks, Massachusetts. A "major task of area clean-up and improvement" was needed at Fort Hancock, New Jersey, only recently reopened when the 703d AAA Gun Battalion arrived. Such posts posed another problem in that they lacked the required stockpiles of forms, manuals, and office supplies. The 703d had to beg nearby posts to give it forms and individuals had to buy office supplies with their own money. A major problem for the 703d was that the battalion "has been unable to draw a single paper clip since its arrival at Fort Hancock and paper clip snitching is prevalent in the battalion headquarters."[16]

Gun battalions' new home stations often were not near the areas they had to defend, forcing them to establish remote operating sites through which they rotated firing batteries. The 736th AAA Gun Battalion recommended that firing batteries be permanently based at their field firing positions, both for a more efficient response to air attacks and to "impress upon the troops the importance of their mission." To speed up the establishment of these sites, some units surveyed possible sites, negotiated with property owners for access to the land, and then supervised construction of the sites and linking them by radio and commercial telephone lines to AAA operations centers. An additional burden on units was winterizing the sites—a task that often required a good deal of troop labor if it was to be accomplished in time. The experience of establishing operating sites, the 197th Group remarked, "could be compiled in an essay which would embody many elements of pathos and humor."[17]

Once they left Fort Stewart, units had few opportunities to fire their AAA weapons. Although the AFF standard for an AAA gun battalion was four live-fire exercises a year, most managed only one. This was mainly the result of most posts not having ranges suitable for AAA weapons. Many units thus were forced to make long trips to the nearest AAA ranges, something they could not do often without compromising AAA defenses. Dry firing on remote sites was useful, especially in maintaining gun crew proficiency, but it lacked the challenge and excitement of live firing. Radar crews frequently practiced by tracking civilian aircraft, but this was only a partial solution. Civilian aircraft rarely flew along the courses or at the speeds and altitudes expected of enemy bombers. Some units kept sharp by helping nonmobilized guard units' summer training. Once plugged into area air defense networks, operations staffs could get significant practice at their tasks, particularly from ARAACOM, group, and brigade command post exercises.[18]

The greatest drag on maintaining combat readiness, however, was that the AAA Command fell victim to the army's manpower dilemma. While units lost personnel, mainly enlisted men, from discharges for hardship and expiration of enlistment, from release of involuntarily recalled reservists, and from transfers, it was levies for overseas service that gutted AAA units in the ZI. The 736th AAA Gun Battalion lost 10 officers, 2 warrant officers, and 114 enlisted men to FECOM, and 2 officers to EUCOM. The 745th lost 14 officers, 2 warrant officers, and 361 enlisted men in 1951, but gained 14 officers, 4 warrant officers, and 448 enlisted men. The 715th lost four of its five battery commanders and all its battalion staff officers to overseas levies. The commanding general of the Eastern Army Antiaircraft Command was so impressed by the 705th AAA Gun Battalion that in August, 1951, he had its commander transferred to his staff to lead a special training inspection team.[19]

These levies hit guard units especially hard because the most experienced and qualified, and thus first to be levied, tended to be guardsmen. Almost as soon as they joined ARAACOM, units began to lose their guard character. By the end of 1951, only 39 percent of the enlisted guardsmen inducted with it remained in the 736th AAA Gun Battalion. Chief Warrant Officer Walter Hayes of the 703d wrote home that those selected for levies "are not too enthusiastic about going; however, they're adopting what seems to be the only attitude to take ('What the Hell')" and that by mid-July 1951 his battalion was "being torn asunder." Adding salt to the wounds, many qualified officers and enlisted men levied for overseas service did not serve in AAA units. The 713th AAA Gun Battalion found that of 106 enlisted men it sent overseas, only 16 went to AAA gun battalions and only 9 went to AAA automatic weapons units. Many of those soldiers ended up in field artillery units as a result of the merger of the field and coast artillery branches.[20]

Units faced several hurdles when replacing levied personnel. The army, desperately juggling its manpower, had placed AAA units in the ZI on reduced TO&Es, leaving units few qualified or experienced personnel. However, because of the army's racial segregation policy, the 715th AAA Gun Battalion was never short of enlisted men, although their experience level was often on a par with men in white battalions. The 715th, like its white counterparts, suffered from a shortage of officers. During the year, its officer strength dipped as low as 13 percent present for duty. As was the case in the MP battalions, most replacements sent to AAA units were either new soldiers or overseas returnees. Many enlisted replacements were fresh from training centers, but they lacked experience. To make up for this missing expertise, brigades and groups organized unit schools offering training in fire control, gunnery, radar, meteorology, and the duties of gun section chiefs. New junior officers were the usual mix of newly commissioned lieutenants and recalled reservists. The first had training, but no experience, and were often in units only for the six months duty in the ZI required before they could be shipped overseas. The "majority" of officer replacements received by the 736th AAA Gun Battalion in 1951 were Category IV-17 reservists who had been recalled to serve for seventeen months. In the last quarter of 1951, the 703d received fourteen new officers. Seven were reservists, four had just come back from Korea, and three were returnees from elsewhere overseas. The returnees included a number of regulars as well as reservists and guardsmen on extended active duty, but many were short-timers who lacked the motivation to perform their duties in any but the most perfunctory manner.[21]

Personnel turbulence was further aggravated by several other factors. Not all of the returnees and reservists were AAA specialists. For example, of the fourteen officers assigned to the 703d in late 1951, only one was AAA qualified. Many of the enlisted men returning from Korea were promoted and given MOS qualifications by their unit in Korea that made it difficult to fit them into an AAA unit in the ZI. The reduced TO&Es forced many personnel, particularly officers, to carry additional duties, often making it difficult to man remote sites, conduct training, and perform garrison housekeeping duties. The lack of an obvious threat, the slow pace of equipment modernization, and the routines of garrison life, the 736th AAA Gun Battalion noted, made "it difficult for the average soldier to see the full importance of AAA in this defense situation." The lack of any obvious goal in post-cycle training, compared to the ATP, also made it difficult to motivate soldiers. Some units mounted aggressive troop information and education programs, but such efforts never fully counteracted the obvious evidence that the ZI's AAA units were serving in a backwater of the war.[22]

Equipment shortages at mobilization had not been fully rectified by the time many units left Stewart, in part because Third Army held back from filling requisitions due to confusion over how to apply the reduced tables of equipment, and in part because of armywide shortages of many items. The age and worn condition of equipment and a shortage of parts, together with the inexperience of many maintenance personnel, initially helped drag down readiness rates in units. The 716th AAA Gun Battalion's 1st Lt. Donald Perkins recalled that even when his battery had its requisition for three 90-mm guns filled, he "was always upset by the condition of my guns. Those 90-mm guns were beyond service life, which affected their accuracy adversely." Equipment readiness rates in most units gradually improved, though, as parts became available, worn equipment was replaced, and soldiers who had not been levied gained maintenance experience.[23]

Modernization of equipment, particularly 90-mm guns, radars, directors, and generators, proceeded slowly. The arrival of new items could cause difficulties, since many maintenance personnel were unfamiliar with them. The 736th AAA Gun Battalion faced another problem when it received the T-33 fire control system and discovered that its M1A2 90-mm guns could not be used with new system. Ordered by its brigade commander to use the T-33 while at a service practice, the 703d AAA Gun Battalion still could not link it with the guns and found the actual range of the T-33's acquisition radar to be only thirty-five thousand yards—far short of the claimed ninety-thousand-yard range. When it switched back to the SCR-584 radar and M9 director, the 703d fired the best score by a 90-mm gun battalion in the 16th AAA Group.[24]

Units mobilized in 1950 focused on preparing for their return to state control in 1952. The army decided not to retain AAA units in federal service beyond the guardsmen's release dates. Instead, draftees, reservists and Regular Army personnel would gradually replace the departing guardsmen in a unit. When a unit reverted to state control, only its colors would be returned to the state. All equipment would remain with the unit taking over the deactivated unit's mission. Personnel turbulence varied among units, but remained a problem throughout 1952. Units continued to receive the same quality of replacements as they had in 1951, although the army began racial integration of AAA units in the ZI through the replacement system. The 715th AAA Gun Battalion, part of New York City's air defense organization, found the city was very attractive to its Korea returnees and other soldiers with little active duty time left, and many of these soldiers "overstayed passes and furloughs in an attempt to reconnoiter civilian prospects for employment."[25]

Impediments to effective training continued plague units throughout the year. Even though units such as the 713th AAA Gun Battalion conducted programs for "entrenching in the minds of the personnel the importance of this assignment and the seriousness of this mission," many soldiers still did not feel sufficient imminent sense of threat from the Soviet air force to motivate them. Personnel turbulence and the competing demands on the personnel allowed by the reduced TO&Es continued. The 715th reported it had problems manning its operations center because the "best available men" in the battalion were "in great demand in the individual batteries." When a good crew had been put together, personnel turbulence would then break it up. As a result, the battalion developed a system where target plots from the brigade operations center went directly to firing batteries on remote sites as well as to the battalion operations center.[26]

Higher echelon air defense exercises and practice alerts kept units busy with collective training, although live-fire exercises remained rare. Alerts for the underequipped units could be difficult. When the AFF's artillery inspector visited the air defenses around New York City in January, 1952, he ordered all the battalions to move out to their firing positions. The 703d's Chief Warrant Officer Hayes wrote home that "everyone gathered up their broken down equipment, assembled what rolling stock was available and made a bee-line for their positions. Regardless of my description, it went off beautifully. Can't help wondering tho' what those poor fellas are doing to keep warm tonite—no tents, stoves and only half equipped with sleeping bags."

However, the major concern was the degree of individual skill among unit members. As a result, battalions and groups continued to run schools for both officers and enlisted men. Units also sent new personnel to army schools for the training needed to replace departing guardsmen and 1950 draftees. Efforts to get Korea returnees with enough time remaining on their enlistments to attend service schools to learn AAA MOSs met with, the 713th AAA Gun Battalion found, an "unsatisfactory" response. Equipment readiness and modernization also still bedeviled some units in 1952. The 713th's SCR-584 radars, M9 directors and M1A2 90-mm guns "continued to be sources of trouble." The battalion did have valid requisitions on M33 radars and M2 90-mm guns, but none of those items arrived before it was phased out. The 736th, on the other hand, received its T-33 fire control system in 1951 and M2 90-mm guns in March 1952.[27]

Shortly before their remaining guardsmen returned home, guard AAA units were relieved from assignment to ARAACOM and turned over their equipment and sites to newly activated Regular Army units. The guardsmen then left for a post in or near their home state for final processing. The number of guardsmen who remained at demobilization varied, from a low of 4.9 percent in the 736th AAA Gun Battalion to 51.6 percent in the 745th. In most units, a much higher percentage of enlisted men than of officers remained throughout its federal service. Guard AAA units mobilized in 1951 were released from active duty in early 1953, having gone through experiences much the same as those called in 1950.[28]

After returning to state control, guard AAA units began the process of rebuilding. Acquiring the needed personnel, however, was a more important factor in the rebuilding effort despite the fact that units had been forced to turn all of their equipment over to the Regular Army. As in other guard units, rebuilding would take several years and varied from unit to unit, depending in large measure on the legacy of active duty in each unit. The

713th AAA Gun Battalion believed that it had a strong "nucleus of key personnel in each battery" upon which to rebuild. The 715th, on the other hand, did not have this core of experienced personnel upon which to rebuild, although it was in far better shape than the 685th AAA Gun Battalion, which returned home with only twenty-six enlisted men and no officers.[29]

Since Soviet TU-4 bombers never came streaking over the Arctic to attempt the incineration of urban industrial America, evaluation of guard AAA units mobilized and assigned to defend the ZI cannot be based on the evidence of combat. It is clear that army planners regarded this threat as a secondary concern compared to the hot war in Korea and NATO's military buildup, given that early warning of attacks and air force interceptors, not army AAA units, were the key weapons in continental air defense. The personnel turbulence and slow equipment modernization units in the ARAACOM experienced clearly demonstrate the army's priorities. Because of personnel turbulence and equipment shortcomings, guard AAA units faced a major struggle to maintain their combat readiness once they left their postmobilization training sites. Fortunately, during the Korean War the Soviets never had the capability to test that combat readiness by mounting the kind of massive strategic bombing offensive the Allies had inflicted on the Axis during World War II.[30]

Disappointments and Distresses: The 37th Infantry Division

The 37th Infantry Division of the Ohio National Guard had a short and unhappy Korean War. A division with a proud record of service in the two world wars, it was not ordered into federal service until January, 1952. After completing postmobilization training, the 37th remained stateside and by the end of the war had ceased to exist as a guard division. The army stripped almost all the guardsmen from the 37th, using them as individual replacements for units overseas despite the pleas of the division commander and Ohio's governor to keep the troops together. This unhappy experience was not unique to the 37th during the Korean War: three other divisions that mobilized but remained in the ZI suffered the same fate. For these guard divisions, the Korean War truly was a time of "disappointments and distresses."[31]

The 37th Infantry Division during its first thirty-four years earned a reputation as one of the better guard divisions and one that carefully protected its guard and home state character. In 1917, Ohio's adjutant general ignored War Department orders to designate units to serve in a division being formed mainly with units from southern states, and Ohio's governor successfully appealed to the president to allow Ohio to form its own division. Ohio draftees brought the 37th up to full strength, helping to preserve the division's Buckeye identity. Shipped to France in June, 1918, the 37th Division, led by a Regular Army officer, spent seventy-seven days on the line at a cost of 5,387 casualties. In 1940, when the 37th entered federal service a second time, its first large shipment of draftee fillers was from Ohio. The 37th's commander in 1940, Maj. Gen. Robert S. Beightler, was the only National Guard division commander to lead his division from mobilization to demobilization during World War II. Under Beightler, the division maintained a high level of identity as both a guard and an Ohio formation, fighting in the northern Solomons and the Philippines, suffering 5,960 casualties, and earning a reputation as one of the best army divisions in the Pacific.[32]

After the 37th returned to state control, Gov. Frank Lausche gave Brig. Gen. Leo Kreber the job of rebuilding the division. Born in Ohio in 1896, Kreber attended West Point with the class of 1919. Graduating early in 1918, Kreber did not get to Europe before the armistice was signed, although he did spend fifteen months with the Army of Occupation in Germany. He resigned his commission in 1922 and returned to Columbus, where he joined the family business. That same year he was commissioned in the guard as a field artillery officer, and by 1936 commanded the 136th Field Artillery Regiment. He took command of the division artillery in 1940, a position he held until 1946. In January, 1949, Kreber was appointed Ohio adjutant general, giving him the two top positions in the Ohio National Guard, which he would hold until mobilization in 1952. Devoted to both the 37th and the National Guard, Kreber served frequently after 1945 as a vice president of the National Guard Association.[33]

Kreber made his longtime guard associate, Brig. Gen. Kenneth Cooper, the 37th's new artillery commander. Born in 1896, Cooper enlisted in the 37th in May, 1917, and served as an artillery section chief in France. He reenlisted in the guard after the war and held positions from first sergeant to lieutenant colonel. In 1940, he succeeded Kreber as commander of the 136th Field Artillery and spent most of the war as executive officer of the division artillery. When Kreber became Ohio adjutant general, he made Cooper his assistant. Their close relationship led to the marginalization of the assistant division commander, Brig. Gen. Cecil Whitcomb. Born in 1899, Whitcomb enlisted in the 145th Infantry in 1917, served in France with the 37th, rejoined the 145th in 1921, and was commissioned in the guard in 1922. At mobilization in 1940, he commanded a battalion in the 145th, and in 1943 took command of the regiment and led it in combat until May, 1945, after which he served as an assistant division chief of staff and a staff officer in Army Ground Forces. Returning to Ohio, he became the 37th's assistant division commander in 1946.[34]

The division chief of staff in 1951 was Col. Harold Hays. Born in 1897 and commissioned in 1923 as an infantry officer in the 37th, during World War II he was a battalion commander and division personnel officer (G1). Returning to the 37th in 1947 as the G1, Hays became chief of staff in 1949. The four division assistant chiefs of staff, whose average age was thirty-nine, had all served as enlisted men in the interwar 37th. Three had been guard junior officers at mobilization in 1940, and the fourth was commissioned in 1941. Only the intelligence officer (G2) had served with the 37th throughout World War II; the others were transferred out of the division before it entered combat on New Georgia in 1943.[35]

The division's infantry regiment commanders were Cols. S. T. Del Corso (145th), G. C. Schiele (147th), and D. E. Schultz (148th). Del Corso, thirty-eight, and Schultz, forty-five, were longtime Buckeyes who had served as enlisted men during the interwar period in their regiments, were commissioned in their regiments, finished World War II commanding their regiments, and then reorganized their regiments in the postwar guard. Schiele, forty-five, was a reserve officer in 1941 and spent World War II as an instructor at the Infantry School and as a staff officer in China. In 1946, he received a colonel's commission in the guard and command of the 147th. When General Whitcomb retired shortly after the division received its alert notice, Kreber selected Schultz to succeed him. Schultz's executive officer, Lt. Col. Herbert Radcliffe, took command of the regiment and received his colonel's eagle. Radcliffe, forty-three, spent five years as an enlisted man before being commissioned in the 148th Infantry. A company commander in 1940, Radcliffe served with the 148th throughout the war, including tours as regimental operations officer and as a battalion commander. He became Schultz's executive officer when the regiment was reorganized in the postwar guard.[36]

The nine infantry battalion commanders had an average age of thirty-eight. All had been in the 37th at mobilization in 1940, eight as officers. The four field artillery battalion commanders averaged thirty-nine years old. None had been long-serving Buckeyes before World War II; one was a reserve officer who joined the 37th just before mobilization, one was drafted and commissioned during the war, and two had been reserve officers at mobilization in 1941. The four separate battalion commanders, with an average age of thirty-eight, had an uneven level of experience. Major D. E. Putnam (112th Medical Battalion) had no military experience before being commissioned in the guard in 1947. Lieutenant Colonel L. B. Tipton (137th AAA Battalion) was drafted in 1941 and commissioned a coast artillery officer in 1943. A captain at war's end, he joined the guard in 1947. Both Lt. Col. H. E. Gordon (137th Tank Battalion) and Maj. A. E. Szorady (112th Engineer Battalion) were guard enlisted men in 1940 and were commissioned in 1942. They ended the war as captains and rejoined the guard in 1947.[37]

The high point of the Korean War for the 37th was May, 1952. General Collins, the army chief of staff, visited the division for two days and complimented it on its progress in the MTP. Governor Lausche then paid a visit. After a luncheon hosted by the officers' wives, Kreber took the governor on a tour of the division. In the 148th Infantry, Lausche asked one soldier how he liked Ohio. When the man said he was from North Carolina, the governor blushed and replied, "Oh, I forgot I'm not in Ohio." The next day, the division passed in review for the governor, and afterwards Lausche addressed the troops: "We wish that you would not have to be in uniform serving your country, but we must be reasonable about it. No dictator in the world was ever content with his conquests. There is grief, and pain and inconvenience in serving your country. But this sacrifice is repaid many times in future years in the knowledge that you have served your country."[38]

The "grief, and pain and inconvenience" for the 37th soon multiplied significantly, for in May the division received its first overseas levy. These levies affected training by disrupting unit cohesion and lowering morale, especially among guardsmen who suddenly had good reason to fear "Go With Those You Know" was just a hollow slogan. The 37th soldiered on with the MTP, completing battalion ATTs by 26 July and regimental combat team ATTs by 31 August. Slightly ahead of schedule, it finished postmobilization training with a three-day division field exercise in early September, then moved into postcycle training. In mid-October, it reached the highest operational readiness rate it would attain while still mainly an Ohio unit: "65% C," which indicated that the 37th had reached 65 percent of its potential combat effectiveness as an organization, but that "its equipment status *does not* permit operational employment of unit without correction of major equipment deficiencies." [39]

Just as the division reached this readiness rating, the army changed its mission. Struggling with its manpower dilemmas, the army removed the 37th from the General Reserve's tactical unit rolls and designated it a training division for individual replacements. At the same time, the army began siphoning off the division's trained manpower. Although an Army Field Forces study dated 9 April 1952 had warned these levies would cripple mobilized guard and reserve units, the army G3 stated that "a complete drop in the operational readiness of the General Reserve was understood and approved by the Chief of Staff." The 82d Airborne Division would be the only division in the ZI maintained at a high operational readiness rate because of "the difficulties due to personnel limitations in terms of total requirements."[40]

With no plans to send the 37th overseas, the army could use the division to support both the training system in the ZI and rotation programs overseas. And used is how many men in the 37th felt by early October, 1952. The new mission, increasing levies, the isolation of Camp Polk, and a training schedule that remained demanding combined with all the normal aggravations of army life to create feelings of frustration and futility in the ranks. These tensions came into public view with a series of articles in Ohio newspapers that began on 2 October. The headline of the *Akron Beacon-Journal*'s lead story read "Kreber 'On Carpet'?" Datelined Washington, the story listed a number of complaints by members of the 37th that had triggered an investigation by the army's inspector general. Troops were "bitter" about the breaking up of the division and "resentful that they must spend their time in sparsely settled, dreary western Louisiana." The bulk of the article concerned allegations of pressure to buy a copy of the division history and to join the National Guard Association.

The next day, the *Beacon-Journal*'s lead headline read: "Kreber Guaranteed to Sell 37th Book." This story alleged that Kreber had guaranteed the F. J. Heer Company of Columbus $35,000 for seven thousand copies of the book. According to a "reliable source," pressure to buy the book began when sales fell short of that goal and the publisher had to raise the print run to ten thousand in order to make a profit. The story emphasized there was "no indication that the 37th Division or any of its officers would profit in any way by the book sale." However, it also emphasized that Walter Heer, Sr., the firm's president, was chairman of the Franklin County Democratic Party and, as every reader knew, Democratic governor Lausche was running for reelection in 1952. The story quoted Kreber as saying that companies in Texas, Louisiana, and Ohio had bid on the project and that he felt that an Ohio firm should have the job. With a "negotiated low bid," Heer got the job because, according to Kreber, the "Heer firm gave more for the money than any of the other companies that bid on the project." The story concluded by pointing out a major problem with selling the book was that only about seven thousand men in the division were guardsmen.

The *Beacon-Journal* sent a reporter to Camp Polk, where he obviously gained a new perspective on things. A 6 October story on page two was headlined "Pentagon Blamed for Low Morale of 37th" and "Top Brass Kills Spirit of Division." According to the reporter, Kreber was "reluctant to talk about the breakup policy," and that it was "known that Kreber was disappointed, but now feels there is nothing that can be done about it." The story suggested that perhaps the Regular Army did not "want a National Guard division to capture too much attention or glory." It concluded that while hard evidence to back this theory was absent, "it is widely known that Regular Army men look down their noses at National Guard outfits and frequently find ways of putting them in a bad light." One more article appeared the next day, this one on friction within the 37th between guardsmen, draftees, and returnees as a source of low morale, blaming the problem on the army's policy of "dumping three distinct groups" into the division. Then the story faded away.

In Ohio, only the *Beacon-Journal* aggressively followed the story, although the *Cleveland Plain Dealer* did carry an article on 3 October headlined "Army Probe of Low Morale in 37th at Polk Discounted." It quoted a division spokesman as saying that the inspector general's investigation "comes as a complete surprise to us." The *Plain Dealer* contacted the Fourth Army's chief of staff, who denied rumors of disciplinary action against Kreber, adding that the Fourth Army inspector general had investigated the charges in August and nothing came of it.[41]

The 37th's problems reappeared in public with a 16 October *Youngstown Vindicator* story headlined "Youngstowners Charge 'Fix' in 37th Shipments." A soldier had called the paper the night before, claiming there was an investigation at Polk—begun after complaints from men of

Youngstown's Company D, 145th Infantry—of whether some on levy for Korea had bribed soldiers in the 37th's personnel section to change their orders to duty in Europe. In a follow-up article the next day, Kreber was quoted as saying that although the final report was not in, he was satisfied that the charges were groundless and that no further action was being taken. According to the article, Kreber believed the charge was the result of normal soldier complaints caused by being sent where they did not want to go. Fourth Army's inspector general concluded its investigation of the 37th in late 1952. The investigation found no evidence of bribes influencing personnel assignments, of misconduct in the award of the book contract, of pressure on soldiers to buy the book, or "undue pressure" on officers to join the National Guard Association. However, the inspector general did fault the division's senior leaders for overemphasizing NGA membership and purchasing the book, particularly the policy of granting duty-day passes for units in which all personnel bought the book.[42]

These stories and rumors led to the 37th finally making the national media for the first time since a brief notice in the *New York Times* on its alert notification the previous September. *Newsweek*'s 20 October "Periscope" section included a blurb headlined "Low Morale": "The National Guard is having morale trouble again. One major general is voluntarily returning to inactive status while a full-scale investigation is under way at Camp Polk, where the 37th Ohio Guard division is training. Favoritism and low-caliber officers seem to be at the bottom of the trouble."

Kreber did not respond publicly to these allegations. Instead, the 37th's G2, Lt. Col. Archibald Rodgers, wrote to *Newsweek*. Rodgers served in the 37th throughout World War II, including a tour as Kreber's intelligence officer. In the letter, published in the magazine's 24 November issue, Rodgers admitted: "morale is not good in the 37th at the present time. At least it is not good by the standards of the 37th during World War II." However, he noted that morale throughout the military was "far below the standards of World War II." Rodgers blamed this on the nature of the "'police action'," in Korea, which did not "stimulate men to the achievements of a major war" or produce much interest among civilians. Last, Rodgers blamed a military "overburdened with red tape." The excerpt of the letter published concluded with "Yes, sir, morale is not as good in the 37th as it was when we were kicking around Japanese who outnumbered us in the Pacific, but I am certain that morale in the 37th is today far above the average for the Army." In his 1952 command report, Kreber commented on the effects of the change of mission and the levies with his usual understated style: "The change of mission of the 37th Division caused an obvious drop in morale and efficiency."[43]

As the dust settled from all this press notice, the new mission and the levies quickly swamped the 37th. By 31 December its trainee load was 2,019. Between 31 July and 31 December, the division's permanently assigned enlisted strength fell from 14,047 to 7,715. Officer strength in this period actually increased from 939 to 1,099, but that was deceptive. Many experienced officers came down on levy and were replaced by newly commissioned second lieutenants sent to the 37th for a short tour of duty as instructors before going overseas. The division provided 5,965 replacements for all overseas theaters in 1952, with 59 percent going to FECOM. By the end of the year, the change of mission and the massive levies had wrecked the 37th and its sister National Guard divisions. In January, 1953, the army G3 rated the four guard divisions in federal service remaining in the ZI as "Operationally Ineffective."[44]

In late 1952, Kreber and his staff thought they could fulfill the replacement-training mission by converting only the 148th RCT into a training formation. This would allow the rest of the division, even at reduced strength, to continue on with unit training and maintain the cadre essential for the division's return to a combat-ready force. But the trainee load assigned to the 37th "expanded rapidly" and in January, 1953, all three infantry regiments, all of the division artillery battalions, and the engineer battalion had to conduct replacement training. The remainder of the division was placed in general support of training operations. The number of trainees rose rapidly, from 4,678 to its April peak of 10,261.[45]

During those four months, the division continued to lose trained personnel to overseas levies—a total of 2,719, of which 64 percent went to the Far East. In return, it received few permanent replacements, and most of those were short-timers from Korea, fresh graduates of advanced individual training (soon subject to levies themselves), misfits unloaded on the 37th by other units, and "a deluge" of brand-new second lieutenants, many of whom still needed to attend their branch officer basic course.[46]

The 37th struggled on, its Ohio origin now reflected mainly by the division's senior staff and three general officers. The division established its own schools to help the depleted and shaky cadre learn the skills needed for training recruits, perform the minimum housekeeping tasks required to keep the division running, and hold on to a shred of the capability to reconstitute the division as a combat unit. At times the 37th was so short of instructors that it had to borrow men from other units on post. The good instructors the division did possess had to work long hours and on weekends, unlike other units at Polk, which operated almost in peacetime routines. This resulted in a "tendency for poor morale to develop." Equipment shortages forced the division to consolidate vehicles and major weapons systems at division level. This meant that most equipment did not have a dedicated operator, resulting in a steady stream of users who could care less about properly maintaining the equipment and creating more work for the few skilled mechanics. There was also a shortage of expendable supplies, including ammunition. The latter forced the division to restrict rifle firing to just trainees.[47]

With the July, 1953, armistice in Korea, the demand for replacements slackened and the division began to look toward rebuilding itself as a combat-ready force. The rebuilding effort started in November, as the last of the 37th's Ohio guardsmen began to reach their twenty-fourth month of federal service. On 1 January 1954 Kreber turned the division over to Maj. Gen. Phillip D. Ginder, a Regular Army officer returning from Korea, where he had commanded the 45th Infantry Division. Kreber went home to Columbus without fanfare, and Lausche again appointed him Ohio's adjutant general.[48]

In 1952, the Ohio National Guard organized a shadow 37th Infantry Division, creating holding detachments that paralleled the company/battery organization of the 37th. These were designed to provide a home for men, mainly veterans recently released from active duty and, after late 1953, men of the 37th released from federal service, who would be used to rebuild the division when it returned to Ohio. The army endorsed this system in early 1954 by bringing these holding detachments into the NGUS system developed for the four guard divisions mobilized in 1950. Shortly after his return from federal service, Ohio established the 37th Infantry Division (NGUS) with Kreber as the commander. On 15 June 1954 in a ceremony at Fort Riley, Kansas, the army returned the 37th Infantry Division's colors to Ohio. The next day the division in Ohio dropped its NGUS suffix. Neither Kreber nor Lausche attended the ceremony. The Ohio National Guard's 37th Infantry Division was back home. Later that summer, with General Beightler—by then retired from the Regular Army—in attendance, Governor Lausche presented the colors to Kreber and the division during its annual training.[49]

There is little available evidence of what Kreber thought of his two years as a division commander in federal service. He did recommend after the first year that "unit integrity at all levels be maintained as far as possible from activation to combat employment." Given Kreber's efforts to prevent the stripping of his division, it is safe to say that the destruction of the 37th's unit integrity was a bitter disappointment, made even more so by the division's excellent World War II combat record under a guard commander. Kreber remained the 37th's commander until 1956, and continued to serve as adjutant general of Ohio until his retirement in 1959. Korea marked the 37th Infantry Division's final period of wartime service. The army disbanded it in 1968 during a reorganization of the National Guard and replaced it with a separate infantry brigade.[50]

Most Army National Guard units mobilized for the Korean War found their federal service to be deeply unsatisfying. Kept in the ZI either to guard against the Soviet air force or to reconstitute the General Reserve, these units soon fell victim to what John Kendall has so aptly described as the "inflexible response" of army manpower planning. Having planned only for World War III, the army instead had to wage a hot war in Korea while building up its forces for what it saw as the greater long-term threat, a cold war in Europe—and doing both simultaneously with only a relatively small portion of the nation's resources mobilized for these tasks.

Under these conditions, it was only a matter of time before hard-pressed army planners would turn for relief to those guard units not marked for immediate use in Korea. The decision to strip guard units of trained manpower and the sometimes brutal use of the inactive reserves offered the army its only hope for dealing with its dilemma. However, this decision was a calculated risk, for it destroyed the combat readiness of almost the entire General Reserve and severely compromised Army Antiaircraft Command. Had the Soviets come crashing across the West German border or flying over the Arctic, or had American leaders been required to deploy army forces elsewhere in harm's way, the army's capacity to quickly and effectively respond would have been questionable.

The army survived this gamble, but its decisions on how to use mobilized guard units in the ZI spread bitterness and distrust among guardsmen, their families, and their supporters. These emotions would become one of the most powerful and visible reactions to life "under Army orders" for the army guard during the Korean War.

CHAPTER 8

Untold Hardships and Suffering

For the most part, guard units in federal service received little attention from the national press during the Korean War. These units usually appeared in the national press only when something appeared to have gone wrong with them, or when someone wished to score points against the National Guard. *TIME* magazine was especially hostile in 1951. An August article concluded: "until the Defense Department finds the courage to stand up to the politically powerful National Guard Association, U.S. defense is going to waste billions of dollars and much precious manpower on an antiquated and disruptive form of military organization." The *New York Times* briefly noted the departure and return of New York guard units, major milestones such as the deployment of guard divisions to Germany and Korea, and protests by the NGA. Its military affairs correspondent, Hanson Baldwin, occasionally discussed guard issues, but usually in the context of larger issues such as American strategy, force structure, and training exercises.[1] State and hometown newspapers usually gave units mobilized in 1950 extensive coverage until they departed for their training station, whereas units mobilized in 1951 and 1952 usually received far less coverage—with the exception of the four infantry divisions. All nondivisional units suffered a sharp decline in press attention after they left their home stations. Most newspapers decided not to send reporters to check up on these units, and relied on army press releases and letters home from guardsmen for what coverage they did provide. Divisions received greater coverage from the major newspapers in their home states, which often dispatched reporters to training camps, and a few accompanied the four divisions deployed overseas.[2]

While the fate of mobilized units rarely concerned the greater public, there were two groups that cared a great deal about what happened to National Guard units "under Army orders." There were those, most notably the National Guard Association, concerned primarily with defending the guard as an institution. Others, such as mobilized guardsmen and their families, focused on the individual guardsman and his unit's experiences while in federal service. There was some overlap between the concerns of these two groups, most noticeably on the disturbing hollowness of the "Go With Those You Know" slogan, but they had different priorities. The NGA worked on the national level to protect the guard's institutional position, whereas units and their supporters worked mainly on what immediately affected guardsmen and their units. Concern about or opposition to the Regular Army's use of the guard did not lead to opposition to the war, although some in each group eventually questioned the Truman administration's strategy, usually lining up with those who believed the United States had to get to the root of its problems in Asia by destroying the communist regime in China.[3]

Both groups watched carefully for attempts by the Regular Army to slight or injure the guard or guardsmen. Both tried to mobilize countervailing political pressure against the Regular Army by appealing to governors, members of Congress, and crucial constituencies within political coalitions. For the most part, these attempts produced little satisfaction. Major policy decisions—such as not ordering the entire guard into federal service, individual instead of unit rotation in Korea, and stripping units in the ZI for replacements—remained in effect. Even with lower-level issues such as the amount of training a unit received before deploying overseas, retention of guardsmen as unit commanders, and dates for release from federal service, the political pressure mobilized by guardsmen and their supporters rarely had a decisive influence.

"The Rape of Our Army and Air National Guard Units Must Stop"

In September, 1950, the chief, Army Field Forces, Gen. Mark W. Clark, sent a message to "the National Guard in the active service of the United States." Clark told the guardsmen that the Regular Army was "grateful that in this time of world crisis you are once more joined with us to help defeat the enemies of freedom." However, in past wars Americans "had a comfortable margin of time to expand our Army—to properly train and equip a civilian Army. Now there is no such margin of time for preparation. Readiness is vital." He noted that the nation "has long relied heavily on its citizen-soldiery in times of crisis," thus allowing the Regular Army to remain small. This policy worked during World War II, and now, Clark wrote, "the readiness of our National Guard may well mean the difference between victory and defeat in the crisis at hand."[4]

History was also on the minds of many senior guardsmen, including NGA president Ellard Walsh and Maj. Gen. Raymond Fleming, General Cramer's replacement as chief of the National Guard Bureau. For them, the story of the guard in wartime revolved around Uptonian regulars abusing the guard during mobilization, belittling its contributions, and attempting to prevent its postwar reconstruction. Walsh, in particular, was convinced that the inadequate General Reserve and the use of inactive reservists pointedly demonstrated the folly of failing to enact legislation requiring true universal military service after World War II. This would, Walsh believed, have allowed guard and reserve units either to be kept at full or nearly full strength, or provided a vast pool of trained men who would need only quick refresher training before units they were sent to as fillers would be ready to deploy.[5]

During the Korean War, the NGA continued to monitor new legislation the army desired for anything that would adversely affect the guard. Meanwhile, senior guard officers kept close watch on regulars' handling of mobilized units. Active-duty guardsmen bypassed Regular Army channels to keep senior guard officers and key politicians informed of what was happening to units. A number of adjutants general, governors, and members of Congress personally checked up on their mobilized units at training camps in the Zone of the Interior. Politicians of national prominence, such as New York's Thomas Dewey and California's Earl Warren, looked in on their state's units during trips overseas. The NGA was also kept up to date on what was happening to units in federal service via formal and informal channels. State officials, and especially the NGA, publicized the successes of mobilized units, particularly those sent to Korea. The NGA noted in the "Posting the Guard" section of the *National Guardsman* the achievements of units and individuals in federal service. The magazine began a new feature in 1951 titled "In Combat . . . In Korea," which was devoted to the activities of guard units deployed there. Not surprisingly, they did not discuss publicly units with significant problems.[6]

Senior guard officers generally approved of how the army used mobilized guard units between September and November, 1950, and praised the units' performance.[7] At the NGA's annual conference in October, General Fleming reported that while "perhaps earlier than we expected, the National Guard has been put to the test for which it exists—preparedness as an M-Day force. So far, I believe we have met the test well."

Fleming, however, was "concerned with the future when National Guard units are released from federal service." He pledged his and the NGB's commitment to the integrity of guard units, and said that the army chief of staff "has indicated many times that the integrity of National Guard units will be maintained." Fleming further stated that the NGB's position was that "all inducted National Guard units be relieved as complete organizations, returned to State status as complete organizations, and not as individuals to reform themselves into a unit."[8]

For a time it appeared that Fleming and other senior guardsmen would get their way on unit integrity. In December, AFF headquarters instructed commanders of armies in the ZI to avoid, as much as possible, raiding mobilized guard and reserve units for personnel needed to fill units on orders for Korea. This practice, AFF warned, would "jeopardize their training base," and had to be avoided, as "these units are the most important part of our present potential for rebuilding the General Reserve." But with casualties mounting in Korea, the Truman administration's decisions for only partial mobilization and a NATO military expansion, the depletion of the inactive reserve during the summer, and the army's difficulties in expanding its training base, senior guardsmen worried that guard unit integrity would sacrificed as a quick fix for the service's manpower dilemma.[9]

The NGA proposed in December that the remainder of the army guard still in state service be mobilized in several increments, brought to full strength, and used to bring the war to an end. Attempting to tap into increasing unease over the growing number of young draftee casualties in Korea, the NGA claimed that this would end the need to draft eighteen year olds. Given that the army could barely support the guard units it already had in federal service, it was no surprise that the army did not accept the NGA's estimate of the situation.[10]

The rotation policy adopted in 1951 generated the biggest fight between the NGA and the army during the war. The army's decision for individual instead of unit rotation in Korea greatly concerned Walsh and other senior guardsmen. Walsh was convinced the policy was the "crux of our real troubles." The NGA did not oppose rotation per se, but it argued the war's burden should be more widely shared by ordering into federal service "all of the remaining Army National Guard or at least a substantial portion thereof." This policy would allow what Walsh believed was the best solution: "a return to the historic concept of relieving battle-weary organizations and units with comparable organizations and units." The rotation issue, Walsh wrote in late 1951, "has occupied the attention of the Association to a greater degree than any other." The NGA attended "innumerable and seemingly, endless conferences" with the Department of the Army, the NGB, and members of Congress, but "no reasonable solution has been found for the problem and even though a solution is found, such will not undo the damage which has been done." Walsh said it would "not suffice for those in authority to contend there is not a solution, for there is, and it must be found. The rape of our Army and Air National Guard units must stop." He feared that "the maintenance of a strong reserve hereafter may prove an impossible task" as the levies for overseas service on guard units made a mockery of "Go With Those You Know."

The army rejected Walsh's plea for unit rotation. Officially, it cited logistical limitations. Under partial mobilization, the army did not have the funds, material, or supplies to mobilize, train, and deploy a force of guard units in the numbers called for by the NGA. While not officially mentioned, two traditional views of the guard held by many regulars probably affected the decision-making process: Guardsmen were not up to the responsibilities of training large formations and leading them in combat, and guard units brought extensive political baggage with them that regulars found distasteful and difficult to handle.[11] Raymond S. McLain, the most successful guardsman of his generation and a serving Regular Army lieutenant general, supported the army's decision on rotation with another argument. McLain, no fan of the NGA after it had ostracized him because of his role on the Gray Board, disagreed strongly with the association's position. He argued that rotation by units during a partial mobilization would leave a unit "in worse shape the day it is mustered out than the day it was mustered in" because many of the competent soldiers would stay on extended active duty or be integrated into the regulars, while others would leave the guard after returning home to avoid another disruption of their families and careers.[12]

By the time Walsh sounded his warning, most mobilized guard units remaining in the ZI had already suffered heavy losses from personnel levies, and General Kreber's 37th Infantry Division would soon be gutted. For Kreber, a longtime NGA activist and a key figure in Robert Beightler's effort during the last war to keep the 37th a "guard" division, the army's rotation policy was a bitter turn of events, and he sought the help of his governor, who readily obliged. Replying to Governor Lausche's letter objecting to levies on the 37th, Secretary of the Army Pace in June, 1952, explained the reasons for the army's policy and promised that NGB staff officers would visit Kreber and Maj. Gen. Albert Henderson, Kreber's successor as Ohio adjutant general.[13]

On 19 July, Henderson sent Lausche a memo outlining the results of his meeting with the NGB officers. The visitors showed Henderson the levies projected for guard units in federal service during the remainder of 1952. According to Henderson, the figures were "so high that every available army organization will be depleted to such an extent that they will not be available for combat service nor will it be possible to consider the National Guard units as military representatives of the respective states."[14]

Kreber returned to Columbus on 4 July and discussed the situation with Lausche after being briefed on levies planned for the near future. On 22 July he wrote Lausche and suggested the governor again write Secretary Pace, using the enclosed letter prepared by Kreber. He stated that if present trends continued "we cannot hope to have as good an organization as we had last January on coming into active service." He added that Lausche would have the support of every member of Congress if they saw that he was "following up on this—and I quote certain individuals, 'rape of the National Guard.'" In words that would send the blood pressure of an Uptonian regular soaring, Kreber closed his letter with "I hope you and Mrs. Lausche are both well and wishing you every success in the coming elections."[15]

Lausche sent Kreber's draft unchanged to Pace. The answer came in a 22 August letter from Fred Korth, the assistant secretary for manpower and reserve affairs. Korth, after explaining that he was answering Lausche's letter because Pace was "temporarily absent from Washington," reviewed the army's reasons for stripping the General Reserve in the ZI. He stressed that there was no legal requirement to maintain guard unit integrity, although he conceded that it was desirable. Korth mentioned the 37th's fine record and closed by saying: "I share your regret that we are unable to maintain the complete integrity of the National Guard units. I earnestly hope that I have demonstrated that the Army's action in this matter, taken in all good faith, was one of necessity rather than one of choice."[16]

Many guardsmen doubted the army's "good faith" in this matter. Yet neither Ellard Walsh's lobbying at the Pentagon and the Capitol nor Leo Kreber's enlisting the aid of state political figures could stop levies on guard units left in the ZI. Congress, the NGA's major advocate at the national level, was not willing to go beyond rhetorical measures on this issue. It accepted the army's need as too pressing and the NGA's alternative as politically unacceptable in an increasingly unpopular war. State officials had no leverage with which they could move the army to reverse its policy. The failure to prevent or stop the levying of mobilized guard units was, for senior guardsmen, a painful example of how the guard's autonomy had been compromised since 1940, particularly since the start of the Cold War, "by a massive expansion of federal authority in military affairs."[17]

"A Few People Have Had To Bear Untold Hardships"

For guardsmen, their families, and their communities, federal service generated concern focused on individuals and their units. Would guard units be properly prepared for combat? Would guardsmen bear an unequally heavy burden of service compared to other sources of manpower? Would "Go With Those You Know" be honored? Also, the many World War II veterans in the guard shared with their reservist peers a feeling of double jeopardy because twice in their lives, and within such a short period of time, they had been called upon to serve their nation on active duty.

From the time the first guard unit received its alert notice to the time when the last guardsman left federal service, mobilized soldiers and their supporters kept state political figures aware of their concerns. As noted in chapter two, after the unit's alert notice arrived, governors received requests for deferrals or excusals from federal service.[18] Once on active duty, some guardsmen and their families again looked to state political figures for help, this time in obtaining an early release. As in requests for excusal from mobilization, the major reason cited for release from active duty was financial hardship for families created by the absence of their primary breadwinner, often compounded by the illness or disability of other family members. As soon as a unit was called up, however, governors no longer had the authority to grant such requests. Thus, some variation on the theme of "It's a Regular Army matter now" occurs frequently in this correspondence. Governors were generally limited to referring cases to the state adjutant general, who in turn would help constituents navigate the army's bureaucratic reefs. It is worth noting that such pleas for help were not limited to guardsmen. Draftees and recalled reservists also sought state political assistance.[19]

Some family members viewed the question of hardship discharges as a class issue. Mrs. Ann Martin wrote to Pennsylvania governor John S. Fine and complained that it "seems there is no use for a poor person to raise a son so that he can help and then have him taken away from you." Of course, some constituents are more equal than others. In December, 1951, Nanticoke, Pennsylvania, scrap dealer John Allan appealed to Governor Fine for his son's release from federal service. The father claimed his son, an officer who had been levied for overseas service, was needed at home to run the business because he was too ill to manage it on his own. Governor Fine instructed the adjutant general to intervene because "I do know this situation and it is most worthy." The adjutant general reported back six days later that he had obtained a delay in the lieutenant's port call and that he had advised the father on how to appeal for a hardship discharge. In March, 1952, the father wrote to advise Governor Fine that his son had been discharged and that "your assistance has been most deeply appreciated." While the gratitude was no doubt pleasing to the governor, it is doubtful his assistance was any more influential than the army regulations governing hardship discharges.[20]

One case that might have had a larger influence on army policy arose when AFF's 1951 revised mobilization plan provided a four-month period between alert and induction in order to send guardsmen to service schools. Alden Stilson Jr, was a 37th Infantry Division field artillery lieutenant and World War II combat veteran sent to Fort Sill in October, 1951—three months before the division entered federal service. He came down on levy for Korea in 1952 still without any definitive answer on whether or not his school time counted as part of his required twenty-four months of federal service. Stilson believed it should count, but the 37th held that it did not. Angered, Stilson turned to his father and fellow officers for assistance in appealing the division's decision. What especially irritated Stilson and the other officers was that, contrary to the division's claims, they had not volunteered for early active duty but had been ordered by their commanders to attend the service schools. Stilson's father instructed his son to collect statements from others officers in the 37th with a similar complaint. The officers all said that their units had school quotas assigned to them by division headquarters, but what upset them most was that their orders stated they had volunteered for the training.

Alden Stilson, Sr., owned a major engineering consulting firm in Columbus and was a reserve colonel in command of an engineer brigade. He used the officers' statements solicited by his son in a letter-writing campaign during the fall of 1952. Stilson wanted the army to change his son's active duty start date to October, 1951, instead of January, 1952. He wrote to and talked with Governor Lausche several times and also contacted Sen. John Bricker in Washington. In December, the army decided that the basic active service date for those sent to schools in 1951 should be the day they reported for training. Exactly how much influence the senior Stilson's efforts had on this decision is impossible to say, although he did get a personal letter from the army's adjutant general announcing the decision. For his part, Stilson gave Lausche a good deal of the credit. He told the governor that he would make sure the "boys" did not forget "that their Governor has an interest in their welfare and in giving them their just due." Lausche answered that if "I at all contributed to the solution . . . I am more than repaid by the graciousness of your letter."[21]

Another source of grievances, and thus of appeals to politicians for help, was the belief among some guardsmen and their families, particularly World War II veterans, that the guard should be mobilized only for defense of the continental United States or for World War III with the Soviets. Mobilization for a war in Korea was very frustrating for these guardsmen, especially those stripped from their unit for service in Korea, or whose unit went to Europe instead of Korea.

Frustration grew into anger for some in 1951 when guardsmen and their families learned the Defense Department planned an early release for involuntarily recalled inactive reservists, and the Selective Service system planned to hold draft deferment examinations for undergraduate college students. Sergeant Ellsworth Linker, a World War II veteran of the 28th Infantry Division serving in Korea with Pennsylvania's 176th AFA Battalion, wrote Governor Fine about the early release of reservists, and noted that guardsmen who were veterans of the last war "deserve a break also." Sergeant George Harris, serving in Korea with North Carolina's 378th Combat Engineer Battalion, complained to his governor about the same issue, arguing that "six months in this stinking hole is enough for anybody."[22]

Writing Governor Fine in April, 1951, shortly after his unit received its alert notice, a World War II veteran attending graduate school complained that it was "grossly unfair" for him to be called up when "non-veteran freshman can be deferred." In Pittsburgh, orders to Germany for the 28th Infantry Division were the last straw for some, sparking a heated exchange in the *Post-Gazette*'s letters section during August and September, 1951. "Two Veterans' Wives" on 31 August asked why their husbands had to go to Germany when "there are single men, in and out of uniform, who have never served overseas?" Another veteran's wife on 5 September wrote that she "wholeheartedly" agreed with her two peers and that she was "furious" at college draft deferments. The wives writing to the *Post-Gazette* also attracted some spirited rebuttals, including one on 13 September from a mother with a son serving in Korea who wrote that the government should send to Korea "married men from 21 to 30 who are hiding behind baby buggies."[23]

For many guardsmen, their families, and their communities, alert notices in 1950 and early 1951 brought with them fears that units would be sent in harm's way unprepared for combat. These fears were enhanced by news reports from Korea of poorly prepared Regular Army units being forced back down the peninsula with heavy losses. This was a constant, if low-key concern in Oklahoma about their Thunderbirds. Wyoming's adjutant general used the possible political repercussions of poorly prepared guard units committed to combat as a tool in his efforts to help the 300th AFA Battalion. Relatives of 40th Infantry Division soldiers lodged similar complaints when it was ordered to Korea. The army's levies on guard units left in the ZI meant that this concern extended to units not ordered to Korea. Shortly after the 31st Infantry Division entered federal service in January, 1951, Mississippi's Sen. John Stennis requested "that these men be thoroughly and fully trained before being shipped out for service in Korea." The practice of assigning guardsmen levied from units in the ZI to positions for which they did not have the proper training or experience also generated concern. A Pennsylvania AAA officer's wife wrote her governor to complain that assigning her husband to a field artillery unit in Korea was "ridiculous." Some concerned family members contacted their governors when rumors of lack of preparedness for combat surfaced in the hometowns of units ordered to Korea. One woman claimed that the

987th AFA Battalion's commander had returned to Ohio shortly before deploying and said that his unit was "well trained when he knew it was not true."[24]

The greatest amount of concern expressed over a unit's preparedness for combat service came from Arkansas, home of the 936th and 937th FA Battalions and Secretary of the Army Pace. Shortly after the two units sailed for Korea before completing their ATPs, rumors began circulating in the state that they would be committed to combat upon arrival. Arkansas politicians began sending letters and telegrams to the president, Secretary Pace, Gen. Douglas MacArthur, and General Ridgway demanding, as Rep. Boyd Tackett said in a telegram to Ridgway, that the battalions "will not be committed to combat until they are trained." Since Eighth Army, well aware of the battalions' deficiencies, already had planned a training program for the new units, it is unlikely that the politicians' efforts did more than reinforce regulars' negative perceptions about guard units. When General Ridgway on 7 March 1951 mentioned this political interest to General MacArthur, MacArthur "laughed and made some remark about the politicians."[25]

Arkansas further reinforced these perceptions later in 1951 when Lt. Col. W. L. Bush, the 936th's commander, organized a meeting of guard officers in I Corps to complain about what he considered to be unfair treatment of guard officers. When Lt. Gen. John W. O'Daniel, the I Corps commander, learned of this meeting, he ordered his inspector general to investigate. The investigation cleared the other officers, who were "pretty much disgusted with" Bush. O'Daniel recommended that no action be taken against Bush, as he was now "plenty scared, as he should be," but asked that Bush not be retained past his rotation date as he was "of no further use here."[26]

Action was taken against two mobilized guard generals for their public comments, but in both cases it was for the officers' critiques on American conduct of the war. Brigadier General Walter J. Hanna, the 31st Infantry Division's assistant commander, said in early 1951 that U.S. troops had not been properly prepared for the rigors of combat, that they would be kicked out of Korea before they could pull out, and that the nation was facing the worst plight in its history. In early May, Hanna was relieved and transferred out of the 31st. Third Army claimed that the action was an "internal division matter," but the Dixie Division's commander, Maj. Gen. A. G. Paxton, made no public comment on the matter. Hanna, at his own request, was released from federal service. A year later, Maj. Gen. Daniel H. Hudelson, returning home from command of the 40th Infantry Division in Korea, told reporters that U.S. forces there "simply don't have the manpower to stand up against the Communist hordes, even though our equipment is the best." Before releasing him from active duty, Sixth Army's commanding general gave Hudelson an official reprimand.[27]

The return of guard units to state control was another topic that concerned guardsmen and their supporters. Beginning in mid-1952, the army began releasing units from federal service as it had done at the end of World War II: Returning guardsmen as individuals or in small groups, spread out over a period of days or weeks. They also came back without their unit equipment, which the army retained.[28] Some units' colors, especially those that had deployed overseas, did not return to state control until several years after their guardsmen did because the army decided to keep their unit designations in federal service. This decision angered many guardsmen and the units' communities, who turned to local and state politicians for relief, but to no avail.[29]

The army's treatment of mobilized guard units created bitterness among some guardsmen and reinforced traditional guard prejudices against the Regular Army. According to Idaho's adjutant general, "a lot of people have lost their confidence in planning at the higher levels . . . it appears sometimes to Unit Commanders that the Department of Defense and the Department of the Army just don't give a damn what happens to their organizations." Sergeant Harris predicted that after Korea, the army would "find it much harder the next time to find veterans to volunteer their services to the guard because of the unscrupulous treatment they have received. They have learned their lesson." Although Ellard Walsh's warning that the guard's experience during the Korean War would cripple the postwar guard did not come to pass, it is clear that the guard was not very successful at recruiting Korean War veterans. Moreover, from 1951 to at least several years after the armistice, the destruction of unit integrity in many guard units left a legacy that added an additional obstacle to recruiting.[30]

These developments made all the more crucial the pool of seventeen- to eighteen-and-a-half year olds who could receive a draft deferment for enlisting in the guard. Foreshadowing what would occur fifteen years later, the guard became entangled in the issue of draft deferments as it continued to recruit for units remaining in state service. Both the NGB and some units made references in their recruiting to the fact that men eighteen-and-a-half or younger would be exempt from the draft if they enlisted in the guard. These references aroused concern over how this effort would affect the quality of manpower available for the Regular Army, as that age group came to dominate the enlisted strength of guard units that had not been mobilized. In early 1953, when Assistant Secretary of Defense John A. Hannah proposed that this draft exemption be removed, Ellard Walsh and the NGA mobilized to defeat the proposal. That age group continued to dominate the guard's enlisted force through the mid-1950s.[31]

In the end, there was little guardsmen could do to influence significantly life "under Army orders" for either units or individuals. In a few instances, their efforts may have had some effect, such as the return of purged officers to the 272d FA Battalion or the revision in Lieutenant Stilson's basic active service date. A type of success did occur when the army declined to take on the heart of the former Confederacy when it did not racially integrate the 31st Infantry Division, even after it had lost most of its guardsmen to levies. Integration finally occurred after the 31st's senior guard officers left the division. The army also allowed the Dixie Division's band to continue to wear the modified Confederate uniform its members wore while in state service.[32]

However, when the army believed an issue—such as which units to mobilize, the use of levies for overseas service, or the retention of unit colors in federal service—was crucial to accomplishing its assigned missions, no protests from guardsmen or their supporters could get the army to change its mind. As governors and other political figures came to realize, the alternative courses of action in many cases would be even more unpopular at the national level. Generally, all they could offer guardsmen and their supporters was the cold comfort given by North Carolina's Gov. W. Kerr Scott: "we must remember that there have been many critical times in the history of this great Country of ours in which a few people have had to bear untold hardships and suffering in order to preserve our free way of life."[33]

Conclusion

The Army National Guard's mobilization for the Korean War was, overall, more efficient than the guard mobilizations for the world wars. This was partly a matter of scale: Only 43 percent of the army guard entered federal service in 1950–52, as opposed to 100 percent of the guard in the world wars. Despite the difficulties it encountered, the army guard in 1950–52 faced nothing like the difficulties that bedeviled units in both 1917 and 1940–41. On both those occasions crippling equipment shortages, sweeping changes in unit structure accompanied by major changes in doctrine, and significant numbers of leaders too old for their positions plagued the guard.

Still, like the Regular Army and the nation both institutions served, the Army National Guard in 1950 was ill prepared for the challenges created by the Korean War. The war caught the guard while it was still rebuilding after World War II and, like the Regular Army, had major personnel problems and equipment deficiencies. After the war began, both components suffered from the army's personnel dilemma, its small inventory of equipment and supplies, and the restrictions on resources created by the Truman administration's decision for only a partial national mobilization.

Between 1945 and 1950, both the NGA and the NGB used the symbolism of the minutemen when arguing that the guard had a crucial role in the Cold War. However, they and the AFF understood that guard units would not be able to spring to arms and enter combat on or shortly after M-Day. Army Field Forces plans for training mobilized units—grounded in lessons learned from World War II—were generally sound and the AFF devoted much effort to supervising their execution. During 1950 and 1951, the actual course of events, particularly developments in Korea and the decision for a limited mobilization, undermined the assumptions that had guided mobilization planning. Without effective contingency plans, the army had to improvise on the run, kicking up sand that generated significant friction for mobilized guard units.

Limited mobilization also raised questions of fairness and equality of sacrifice, particularly concerning which units to order into federal service and which units to deploy overseas. Most guardsmen and their families did not feel the sense of betrayal widespread among involuntarily recalled inactive reservists. However, many did wonder why they had to put their civilian lives on hold when the majority of guard units mobilized went either to Europe or remained in the ZI. Levies for overseas service on units in the ZI only intensified these feelings, especially among the many World War II veterans. The destruction of unit integrity by personnel levies was a major blow to a force recruited to a significant degree on the promise that those who signed up would "Go With Those You Know." This decision, which for older guardsmen rubbed salt in similar wounds from the world wars, did much to destroy the army's credibility with many guardsmen and their supporters, and helped perpetuate guard–Regular Army tensions.

Guardsmen and their supporters were not shy about voicing their displeasure over real or imagined injuries and insults to mobilized units and individuals. Congress, the Department of the Army, and senior commanders all heard from those who were upset over the treatment of guardsmen in federal service. These efforts to change Regular Army decisions concerning mobilized guard units rarely had much effect. The army, Congress, and the president deemed alternatives proposed by guardsmen on major issues such as unit rotation to be too costly both politically and fiscally. In other cases, such as training, the army believed the complaints to be unwarranted intrusions into areas of its professional expertise. The Korean War did not change the guard's position as the army's first-line combat reserve force, but the army's dominance over the fate of mobilized guard units also did not change.

One area of political sensitivity for the Regular Army and the guard was the role of African Americans in both institutions. Race does not appear to have affected army decisions on which units to order into federal service. However, once they were on active duty, guard units became caught up in the controversies generated by army racial policies and efforts by African Americans to improve their condition in American society. The army preferred to avoid this issue if possible when it came to guard units in federal service. In the ZI, the army rarely tried to change the racial composition of a guard unit until 1952, and then usually only when most of its original guardsmen were gone. Guard units sent overseas generally were integrated as part of the theater commander's integration program. White guardsmen met this policy without overt resistance, although some disliked it and others, particularly unit commanders in Europe, complained that black units used the integration process to unload all their problem soldiers.

African American units had to deal with all of the problems that affected white guard units as well as some that were rooted in army and guard policies concerning African Americans or the prejudices of white officers. Still, the great majority of black guard units performed along the same curve as white guard units. When a black guard unit failed, as did the 272d FA Battalion, the effects of the army's racial policies—and the general racial climate of early 1950s America—played a part. Nevertheless, as the case of the 272d FA Battalion showed, the most important reasons for unit failure were the universal military sins of poor leadership and inadequate training.

The 272d FA Battalion's performance demonstrated that in the guard, as in the Regular Army, the quality of a unit's leadership was the most important variable in determining its success or failure. Many senior guard officers were well aware of this and emphasized the importance of recruiting skilled and experienced officers and NCOs after 1945. However, the demand for these leaders outstripped the available supply. Correspondence courses just did not provide the same depth of training as did attendance at army schools, and very limited training time made it difficult for leaders to practice their craft. Once in federal service, guard units benefited from infusions of trained and experienced reserve leaders, and a small number of regulars. With access to army schools and time to practice their craft, guard leaders generally performed as well as those in Regular Army units during this period: a small number were revealed as incompetent, some muddled through, the great majority did a good job, and a few excelled.

One variable in examining guard unit performance is how much of its guard character a unit retained when it deployed. As in the world wars, guardsmen usually became a minority in units once fillers arrived at the training site. But if the core of a unit—leaders and key staff officers—

remained mainly guardsmen, then the unit can be considered guard in character. For World War II, one can compare the combat performance of units that retained and units that lost their guard character. This comparison cannot be made for the Korean War, as only a minority of units went to Korea, and most of these units retained the greater part of their guard character because they were protected from significant personnel levies before deploying. Units sent to Germany varied in the degree to which they were guard in character at deployment, but most retained a far greater degree of guard character in federal service than did units that remained in the ZI.

One lesson learned from the Army National Guard's experience during the Korean War is that the degree to which a unit retained its guard character is important only insofar as that factor affects more universal military truths. Looking at the range of unit performance best summarizes this conclusion. The most notable failure in this study, the 272d FA Battalion, was the result of an unfortunate intersection of almost every negative influence on unit performance possible during this period: inadequate prewar preparation, a poor choice of mobilization training site, little effective supervision by higher headquarters, extreme personnel turbulence, a large number of poor quality fillers, the racial climate of the period, and, most importantly, leadership unequal to the demands placed upon it. In the 272d, that leadership was initially guard, then mainly guard overlaid with regulars and reservists in senior positions. At the other extreme, the success of nondivisional field artillery battalions sent to Korea in early 1951 occurred under guard leadership, leavened with reservists at the battery level, despite significant obstacles. For most of these units, success was the result of continuity with the 1940 troop list and the resulting good prewar preparation, good fillers, completion of a well-designed training program before commitment to combat, and leadership equal to the demands placed upon it. The 45th Infantry Division's senior leaders in Korea were mainly guard officers, whereas a heterogeneous mix typical of the army in 1952 dominated the junior leadership ranks. The result was performance similar to that of other army divisions in Korea—and a guard commanding general who was just as frustrated by his unit's performance as many of his Regular Army peers were by theirs. When one considers the course of the war's first six months, it is clear that Korea again demonstrated the need for both regulars and guardsmen to insist on creating and sustaining high quality leaders in their units.

During the Korean War there were no massive antiwar protests or attempts to block the mobilization of guard units, as there were during the Vietnam War. Much of the reason for this difference is in the nature of the two wars and in the character of American society during those periods. Still, the large numbers of guardsmen and reservists who boarded trains and left their loved ones behind to honorably perform their duties between 1950 and 1952 provided the Truman administration an important sign of consent from the people for the decision to go to war over a place most Americans knew nothing about. Lyndon Johnson's refusal to risk obtaining similar consent for America's next war was one of his many mistakes.

APPENDIX A

Assignment of Mobilized Army National Guard Units

As of September, 1951

In September, 1951, mobilized guard units were either assigned to or on orders to the following areas:

Units	*No. Mobilized*	*Far East*	*Europe*	*Zone of the Interior*
Divisions	6	2	2	2
FA Battalions	26	10	4	12
FA Observation Battalions	4	0	0	4
MP Battalions	5	0	1	4
Engineer Battalions	16	6	2	8
Tank Battalions	4	0	2	2
Quartermaster Companies	2	0	0	2
Medical Companies	15	1	6	8
Truck Companies	21	6	0	15
Ordnance Companies	20*	3	4	12
Engineer Bridge Companies	8	3	1	4
AAA Operations Detachments	13	0	0	13
SRMUs	25	0	0	25
Bands	15	0	0	15
Medical Battalion HQs	3	0	2	1

Units	*No. Mobilized*	*Far East*	*Europe*	*Zone of the Interior*
Truck Battalion HQs	7	1	2	4
Ordnance Battalion HQs	5	2	2	1
AAA Brigade HQs	3	0	0	3
Engineer Group HQs	3	1	1	1
Ordnance Group HQs	1	0	0	1
Medical Group HQs	1	0	0	1
Quartermaster Group HQs	2	1	0	1
FA Group HQs	5	0	0	5
AAA Group HQs	11	0	0	11
AAA Gun Battalions	43	3	0	40

Note: In addition to these three main areas, part of an RCT was sent to Iceland, an RCT was stationed in Puerto Rico, and an RCT and ordnance company were sent to Alaska. In early 1952, two additional infantry divisions were activated and remained in the Zone of the Interior.

Source: Adjutant general, "Directory and Station List of the United States Army, 4 Sept. 1951," U.S. Army Center of Military History, Washington, D.C.

APPENDIX B

Officer Profiles

TABLE B-1: REGIMENTAL AND GROUP COMMANDERS

Total: 25 (18 infantry, 4 AAA, 2 quartermaster, 1 field artillery)
Pre–World War II NG officers: 22 (88%)
Pre–World War II NG enlisted men: 0
Pre–World War II ORC: 3 (12%)
World War II commission in same branch as post-1945 NG: 0
World War II commission in different branch: 0
World War II enlisted men commissioned in post-1945 NG: 0
No World War II service: 0
Branch school graduates: 15 (60%)
College graduates: 9 (36%)
Born in state: 19 (76%)
Born out of state: 6 (24%)
Average age: 46.6

TABLE B-2: BATTALION COMMANDERS

Total: 101 (48 infantry; 21 FA; 9 engineer; 8 AAA gun; 5 tank; 4 AAA automatic weapons; 3 MP; 1 signal, 1 ordnance; 1 transportation)
Pre–World War II NG officers: 60 (59.4%)
Pre–World War II NG enlisted men: 10 (9.9%)

Pre–World War II ORC: 22 (21.7%)
World War II commission in same branch as post-1945 NG: 15 (14.9%)
World War II commission in different branch: 4 (4%)
World War II enlisted men commissioned in post-1945 NG: 0
No World War II service: 0
Branch school graduates: 42 (41.6%)
College graduates: 48 (47.5%)
Born in state: 72 (71.3%)
Born out of state: 29 (28.7%)
Average age: 38.8

TABLE B-3: COMPANY GRADE OFFICERS AND MAJORS

Total: 1,709[a]
Pre–World War II NG officers: 80 (4.7%)
Pre–World War II NG enlisted men: 394 (23%)
Pre–World War II ORC: 47 (2.7%)
World War II commission in same branch as post-1945 NG: 317 (18.5%)
World War II commission in different branch: 483 (28.3%)
World War II enlisted men commissioned in post-1945 NG: 699 (40.9%)
No World War II service: 83 (4.9%)
Branch school graduates: 145 (8.5%)
College graduates: 406 (23.8%)
Born in state: 1,312 (76.8%)
Born out of state: 397 (23.2%)
Average age:
- Majors: 36.2
- Captains: 32.6
- 1st Lieutenants: 29.4
- 2d Lieutenants: 27.5

Commissioned after mobilization alert: 254 (14.9%)

[a]Sample drawn from 11 infantry regiments, 20 FA battalions, 7 AAA battalions, 9 engineer battalions, 3 tank battalions, 3 MP battalions, 2 truck companies, 2 AAA group headquarters, 2 AAA operations detachments, and 1 ambulance company.

Note: Totals of branch school graduates in all three tables include those who attended a peacetime special National Guard course and those who attended a wartime course between 1941 and 1945.

Source: Officer rosters found in unit records, unit command reports, and unit yearbooks, checked against the *National Guard Register 1951.*

APPENDIX C

Comparison of General Officers in the Army National Guard and Regular Army, 1950

This appendix compares, with one exception, the backgrounds of Regular Army and Army National Guard general officers filling the following positions at or shortly after the start of the Korean War:

- Division commander
- Assistant division commander
- Division artillery commander
- Armored division combat command commander
- Corps artillery commander
- AAA Brigade commander

The exception is corps artillery commanders. In 1950, the Regular Army filled these positions with colonels, whereas the National Guard filled them with brigadier generals. Later in the war, Regular Army corps artillery commanders were brigadier generals.

TABLE C-1: DIVISION COMMANDERS

	RA	NG
Number	10	27
Average age	53.4	54.6
(Oldest/Youngest)	(56/50)	(61/47)

	RA	NG
World War I veterans	5	22
(Served with NG unit)	(0)	(14)
College graduates	6	18
(USMA)	(4)	(2)
Attended branch school	10	12
Attended C&GS course	10	0
Attended NG/WWII C&GS course	n/a	15
Most senior World War II position		
Division commander	4	1
Assistant division commander	1	1
Division artillery commander	0	5
Corps artillery commander	1	0
Infantry regiment commander	0	1
Armored division combat command commander	0	1
Field artillery group commander	0	2
Engineer regiment/group commander	0	2
Cavalry regiment commander	0	1
AAA regiment commander	0	1
Regimental executive officer/ battalion commander	0	2
Higher-echelon unit staff officer	3	3
Nonunit staff officer	1	7
Average years of service	32	29.8
Average years of guard service	n/a	21.8

TABLE C-2: ASSISTANT DIVISION COMMANDERS

	RA	NG
Number	9	25
Average age	51.3	52.4
(Oldest/Youngest)	(58/47)	(60/42)
World War I veterans	3	15
(Served with NG unit)	(0)	(7)
College graduates	8	11
(USMA)	(6)	(0)
Attended branch school	9	20
Attended C&GS course	9	n/a

Attended NG/WWII C&GS course	n/a	12
Most senior World War II position:		
Assistant division commander	1	1
Infantry regiment commander	2	7
Field artillery group commander	0	1
Cavalry group commander	1	0
AAA group commander	0	2
Regimental executive officer/ battalion commander	0	4
Higher-echelon unit staff officer	2	5
Nonunit staff officer	3	5
Average years of service	29.4	29.6
Average years of guard service	n/a	23.1

TABLE C-3: DIVISION ARTILLERY COMMANDERS

	RA	NG
Number	9	25
Average age	52.1	52
(Oldest/Youngest)	(55/47)	(60/44)
World War I veterans	3	17
(Served with NG unit)	(0)	(9)
College graduates	9	19
(USMA)	(7)	(1)
Attended branch school	9	13
Attended C&GS course	7	0
Attended NG/WWII C&GS course	n/a	8
Most senior World War II position:		
Division artillery commander	1	1
Corps artillery commander	3	0
Infantry regiment commander	1	0
Field artillery group commander	0	1
Quartermaster regiment commander	0	1
Battalion commander	0	7
Higher-echelon unit staff officer	3	8
Nonunit staff officer	1	7
Average years of service	30.2	28.8
Average years of guard service	n/a	19.3

TABLE C-4: AAA BRIGADE COMMANDERS

	RA	NG
Number	4	13
Average age	52.8	53.5
(Oldest/Youngest)	(59/48)	(60/46)
World War I veterans	2	10
(Served with NG unit)	(0)	(5)
College graduate	2	4
(USMA)	(2)	(2)
Attended branch school	3	9
Attended C&GS course	3	0
Attended NG/WWII C&GS course	n/a	1
Most senior World War II position:		
AAA Brigade commander	3	1
AAA regiment/group commander	0	5
AAA battalion commander	0	4
Quartermaster battalion commander	0	1
Higher-echelon unit staff officer	0	1
Nonunit staff officer	1	1
Average years of service	30.5	29.6
Average years of guard service	n/a	21.2

TABLE C-5: CORPS ARTILLERY COMMANDERS

	RA	NG
Number	5	4
Average age	50.8	51.8
(Oldest/Youngest)	(56/46)	(54/48)
World War I veterans	1	3
(Served with NG unit)	(0)	(2)
College graduates	5	3
(USMA)	(4)	(0)
Attended branch school	5	2
Attended C&GS course	3	0
Attended NG/WWII C&GS course	2	1
Most senior World War II position:		
Division artillery commander	1	0
Field artillery group commander	3	0

Field artillery battalion commander	0	3
Engineer battalion commander	0	1
Higher-echelon unit staff officer	1	0
Average years of service	29.2	27.8
Average years of guard service	n/a	22.5

TABLE C-6: COMBAT COMMAND COMMANDERS

	RA	**NG**
Number	2	4
Average age	51.5	48.5
(Oldest/Youngest)	(54/49)	(55/43)
World War I veterans	1	2
(Served with NG unit)	(0)	(2)
College graduates	1	0
(USMA)	(1)	(0)
Attended branch school	2	3
Attended C&GS course	2	0
Attended NG/WWII C&GS course	0	2
Most senior World War II position:		
AAA brigade commander	1	0
Cavalry squadron commander	0	1
Higher-echelon unit staff officer	0	2
Nonunit staff officer	1	1
Average years of service	31	26
Average years of guard service	n/a	20.5

Sources: Army Register 1951; National Guard Register 1951; Army, Navy, Air Force Journal, 1946–51; *Coast Artillery Journal,* 1946–50; *Register of Graduates of the United States Military Academy;* Information Office, *General Officers of the National Guard of the United States;* and Clay Blair, *The Forgotten War: America in Korea, 1950–1953.*

NOTES

Preface

1. John K. Mahon, *History of the Militia and the National Guard*, p. 209; National Guard Bureau, "Induction and Release of Army National Guard Units, 1950–1956," copy in U.S. Army Center of Military History, Washington, D.C.
2. The Air National Guard's experiences during the war are well covered by Charles J. Gross in *Prelude to the Total Force: The Air National Guard, 1943–1969*.
3. Warren J. Williams, ed., *A Revolutionary War: Korea and the Transformation of the Postwar World*, pp. 1–12. Of course, the Korean War must compete with these other wars against the still very large shadow cast by the American Civil War.
4. See Appendix A for the distribution of mobilized army guard units.
5. James F. Schnabel, *Policy and Direction: The First Year*, pp. 120, 122–25, 344–45, 385; Walter G. Hermes, *Truce Tent and Fighting Front*, pp. 202–204; and Billy C. Mossman, *Ebb and Flow: November 1950–July 1951*. National Guard units appear in two other books published by the army concerning the Korean War, but they are not identified as guard. See Russell A. Gugeler, *Combat Actions in Korea*, pp. 155, 222–35; and John G. Westover, *Combat Support in Korea*, pp. 93–94, 218. The only exception to the Army's treatment of the guard during the war is Thomas S. Grodecki, "From Powder River to Soyang: The 300th Armored Field Artillery in Korea, A Case Study of the Integration of the Reserve Components into the Active Force," copy in the U.S. Army Military History Institute, Carlisle Barracks, Pa. (hereafter USAMHI).
6. "Mobilization in the Korean Conflict" (study prepared for the Office of the Assistant Secretary of Defense for Manpower, Reserve Affairs, and Logistics by the Historical Evaluation and Research Organization of Dunn Loring, Va., 1982); I. Heymont and E. W. McGregor, "Review and Analysis of Recent Mobilizations of U.S. Army Reserve Components" (study prepared for the U.S. Army Strategic Studies Institute by the Research and Analysis Corp. of McLean, Va., 1972); "Historical Resume, Division Force Structure, Active and Reserve, 1935–1965" (Washington: Office of the Chief of Military History,

1963); Elva Stilwaugh, "Personnel Policies in the Korean Conflict" (Washington: Office of the Chief of Military History, n.d.); Samuel J. Newland, *The Militia's Role in National Defense: A Historical Perspective.*

7. William Berebitsky, *A Very Long Weekend: The Army National Guard in Korea, 1950–1953.* An area that Berebitsky does not discuss, except in passing, because of the sources he uses, is the reactions to mobilization and federal service in units' communities and states, and the interplay between state and federal officials over the use and treatment of mobilized guardsmen by the Regular Army.
8. Mahon, *History of the Militia,* pp. 208–10; Jim Dan Hill, *The Minute Man in Peace and War: A History of the National Guard,* pp. 503–14. Because Hill's book does not examine in detail the mobilization experience of guard units during the war, his argument about proper U.S. strategy does not consider the actual status of guard units in June, 1950, the army's and industry's ability to support a total guard mobilization during the summer of 1950, or the nation's capacity to transport significant guard forces to Korea before the Inchon landing and Chinese intervention. Hill argues that the Chinese forces in Korea could have been dealt with by stationing several American divisions on Formosa, which would have posed such a threat to Chinese seaports that Mao Tse-tung would have withdrawn his forces from Korea. Martha Derthick's discussion of the Korean War in *The National Guard in Politics* (pp. 111–13) is brief and concerned with the effects of the war on the National Guard Association's political strength.
9. See, for example, Virginia Brainard Kunz, *Muskets to Missiles: A Military History of Minnesota;* Richard Cropp, *The Coyotes: A History of the South Dakota National Guard;* Robert Hawk, *Florida's Army: Militia/State Troops/National Guard, 1565–1985;* Brian D. Fowles, *A Guard in Peace and War: The History of the Kansas National Guard, 1854–1987;* and Peter H. Haraty, ed., *Put the Vermonters Ahead: A History of the Vermont National Guard, 1764–1978.*
10. Kenny Franks, *Citizen Soldiers: Oklahoma's National Guard,* pp. 142–55; Richard Seiverling, "Post World War II–Korean War," in *The First Century: A History of the 28th Infantry Division,* ed. Uzal W. Ent, pp. 178–96; Jerry Cooper with Glenn Smith, *Citizens as Soldiers: A History of the North Dakota National Guard,* pp. 386–98; Richard C. Roberts, "History of the Utah National Guard: 1894–1954" (Ph.D. diss., University of Utah, 1973), pp. 457–513.
11. "Regular" is a relative term here. Most Regular Army units in Korea after the early days of the war were filled with a mix of personnel sources. Most enlisted men were draftees and many of the NCOs and junior officers were reservists. Only the field grade and general officer ranks remained dominated by regulars. However, these had always been the positions in the guard about which regulars had the greatest doubts during earlier wars.
12. Jerry Cooper, *The Militia and the National Guard Since Colonial Times: A Research Guide,* pp. 117–30; Derthick, *National Guard in Politics,* pp. 101–14. The quote is from "45th Will Keep Training, Grant Short Furlough," *Daily Oklahoman,* 25 Feb. 1951, p. 18.

Chapter 1. Rearming the Minutemen, 1945–50

1. Robert S. Beightler to Maj. Gen. John F. Williams, 21 Apr. 1945, Robert S. Beightler Papers, box 1, folder 2, Ohio Historical Society (hereafter Beightler Papers). On the guard during World War II, see Mahon, *History of the Militia,* chap. 13.
2. Beightler to Maj. Gen. Ellard A. Walsh, 11 Oct. 1945, box 1 folder 4, Beightler Papers. On guard–Regular Army relations, see Maj. Gen. Bruce Jacobs, "Tensions Between the Army National Guard and the Regular Army," *Military Review* 73, no. 10 (Oct., 1993): pp. 5–17. A bitter early postwar assessment of guard–Regular Army relations during the war is Maj. Gen. James E. Edmonds, "It's Up to Congress," pt. 2, *National Guardsman* 3, no. 1 (Jan., 1949): pp. 8–10, 29.
3. The writings of Emory Upton, a brilliant young officer during the Civil War and postwar theorist, had, since the 1880s, heavily influenced much of the Regular Army's thinking on reserve forces policy. Disgusted by the waste and stupidity he saw during the Civil War, Upton blamed this on the amateurishness of militia officers, a too-small prewar professional army, and the interference of politicians in military matters. Upton greatly admired the German system of a large professional army backed by a large centrally controlled reserve force maintained by universal male conscription. See Russell F. Weigley, *Towards an American Army: Military Thought from Washington to Marshall,* pp. 100–128.
4. Derthick, *National Guard in Politics,* pp. 75–76, 91–92.
5. This and the preceding three paragraphs are based on Col. Bruce Jacobs, "Out of the Ashes of Victory," *National Guardsman* 25, no. 8 (Aug.–Sept., 1971): pp. 5–8; Derthick, *National Guard in Politics,* pp. 76–77, 93–96; Lt. Gen. L. J. McNair, memorandum for General Marshall, Subject: "High Commanders," 7 Oct. 1941, box 76 folder 31, George C. Marshall Papers, George C. Marshall Library, Virginia Military Institute, Lexington, Va. (hereafter Marshall Library).
6. This section is based on Derthick, *National Guard in Politics,* pp. 58–69 and Mahon, *History of the Militia,* pp. 195–97. The quote is from a memorandum for the chief of staff from the General Staff committee on National Guard policy, 14 Sept. 1944, as quoted in Derthick, *National Guard in Politics,* p. 67. Universal Military Training differed from the wartime draft in two ways. All able-bodied men would serve, remaining on active duty only long enough to become trained. They would then join the guard or Organized Reserve Corps for a mandatory length of time. Some senior guardsmen had doubts about basing the postwar guard on UMT, which they believed an American people weary of military burdens would not allow Congress to pass. See Robert S. Beightler to Maj. Gen. John F. Williams, 20 Aug. 1945, box 1, folder 3, Beightler Papers.
7. This section is based on John M. Kendall, "An Inflexible Response: United

States Army Manpower Mobilization Policies, 1945–1957" (Ph.D. diss., Duke University, 1982), pp. 52–77.

8. This and the preceding paragraph are based on E. A. Walsh to Lt. Gen. Raymond S. McLain, 18 Aug. 1948, and Walsh to Maj. Gen. Ralph Loveland, 15 Dec. 1948, box 29; and Walsh to Col. George A. Fisher, 11 Oct. 1948, box 16, National Guard Association of the United States files, Ellard A. Walsh Papers, National Guard Association of the United States, Washington, D.C. (hereafter Walsh Papers); Mahon, *History or the Militia*, pp. 198–205; Derthick, *National Guard in Politics*, pp. 72–74; Kendall, "An Inflexible Response," pp. 116–31. My thanks to Prof. John Kennedy Ohl for providing me copies of the Walsh letters.
9. "General Cramer Dead in Germany," *New York Times*, 21 Feb. 1954, p. 69; "National Guard Gets New Boss," *LOOK*, 18 Nov 1947, p. 104; extract from officer efficiency report on Cramer by Lt. Gen. Matthew B. Ridgway, Aug., 1950, box 16, file "Historical Record August–October 1950," Matthew B. Ridgway Papers, USAMHI (hereafter Ridgway Papers); Derthick, *National Guard in Politics*, pp. 102–105. Cramer's feud with the air force triggered a major investigation by the army and air force inspectors general. See Report of U.S. Army and U.S. Air Force Inspectors General, 24 Jan. 1950, "Status Chief, National Guard Bureau," Army Chief of Staff Decimal File 1950, box 593, Record Group (RG) 319, National Archives, College Park, Md. (hereafter NA). The air force inspector general, in a separate recommendation, called for Cramer's removal.
10. Kenneth F. Cramer, "M-Day and the New National Guard," *Army Information Digest* 2, no. 9 (Sept., 1947): pp. 2–7; "The National Guard in the Post-War Military Establishment," *Military Review* 28, no. 3 (June, 1948): pp. 3–9; and "The National Guard—Our Modern Minutemen," *Coast Artillery Journal* 91, no. 4 (July–Aug., 1948): pp. 27–29.
11. Cramer, "The National Guard—Our Modern Minutemen," p. 29.
12. This process can be followed at the national level with the state decimal files of the National Guard Bureau, RG 168, NA. The state perspective on this process is harder to reconstruct, given the wide difference in available archival material among the states I have sampled. Pennsylvania's experience is well documented in the archives of the Pennsylvania Historical and Museum Commission, Harrisburg, Pa. (hereafter PHMC). See MG 156, the Edward Martin Papers (hereafter Martin Papers); MG 190, the James H. Duff Papers (hereafter Duff Papers); and RG 19, Department of Military Affairs. The manuscript and oral history collections at USAMHI are also useful. Two good secondary works are Cooper and Smith, *Citizens as Soldiers*, pp. 375–86; and Roberts, "History of the Utah National Guard," pp. 426–46.
13. The most dramatic shift occurred with the 45th Infantry Division. In 1940 it had drawn on Oklahoma, Colorado, Arizona, and New Mexico. In 1946, Oklahoma guardsmen successfully lobbied to make the 45th an all-Oklahoma division. This was quite a coup, given the Thunderbirds' outstanding record during

the war, and Oklahomans took a very possessive interest in "their" division (Franks, *Citizen Soldiers*, pp. 140–41).

14. For example, the 2d Battalion, 117th Infantry, became the 168th MP Battalion (Tennessee); the 197th Coast Artillery Regiment became the 197th AAA Group (New Hampshire); a battalion of the 115th Cavalry became the 300th AFA Battalion (Wyoming); a battalion of the 372d Infantry became the 272d FA Battalion (Massachusetts).
15. For example, the 44th Infantry Division (Illinois) included the 129th and 130th Infantry Regiments, and the 196th Regimental Combat Team (South Dakota) drew on the 147th FA Battalion.
16. The Duff Papers and the Department of Military Affairs records in the PHMC provide a good view of this for Pennsylvania. See also the manuscript collections and oral histories at USAMHI; Roberts, "History of the Utah National Guard"; Cooper and Smith, *Citizens as Soldiers;* and Col. Sherwood Dixon, "The Impossible Takes Longer," *Infantry Journal* 62, no. 4 (Apr., 1948): pp. 27–30.
17. This did not stop charges that the Ohio National Guard was still a "Jim Crow Guard." See "Ohio Still Planning To Set Up Jim Crow Guard," *Cleveland Call and Post*, 18 Oct. 1947, p. 1; and "Ohio Guard to End Jim Crow? 'Brass in Dark'," ibid., 8 Dec. 1951, p. 3B.
18. Charles Johnson, *African American Soldiers in the National Guard: Recruitment and Deployment During Peacetime and War*, pp. 165–79. The problems of ordering desegregation of a state's National Guard can be followed in boxes 374 and 377 of the G. Mennen Williams Papers, Bentley Historical Library, Ann Arbor, Mich. (hereafter Williams Papers). General Cramer's Connecticut was another state that integrated its guard by 1950. This caused some concern in Connecticut in 1950 when the 43d Division mobilized and went to Camp Pickett, Va. See "Guardsmen Will Not Be Jim Crowed in Virginia, Connecticut Promises," *Pittsburgh Courier*, 19 Aug. 1950, p. 17.
19. Beightler to Williams, 20 Aug. 1945.
20. Daniel B. Strickler, *The Memoirs of Lieutenant General Daniel Bursk Strickler*, pp. 145–62; A. G. Paxton, *Three Wars and a Flood*, pp. 73–74; Kenneth R. Scurr, *Reflections of Service: 147th Field Artillery Group, 1917–1977*, pp. 63–68; manuscript and oral history collections, USAMHI; Dixon, "Impossible Takes Longer," pp. 27–30; Cooper and Smith, *Citizens as Soldiers*, pp. 375–86; Franks, *Citizen Soldiers*, pp. 140–41.
21. LaVern Weber Oral History, USAMHI. Born in 1923, Weber graduated from Marine Corps Officer Candidate School in 1945, but did not see combat before the war ended. See also Robert L Stockton file, Korean War Veterans Survey, USAMHI (hereafter Korean War Survey).
22. This section is based on Derthick, *National Guard in Politics*, pp. 78–82; editorials in the *National Guardsman*, 1948–50; manuscript and oral history collections, USAMHI; and the analysis of guard general officers' careers in Appendix

C. A good expression of this generation's belief in the importance of the guard as a *state* institution is Col. Elbridge Colby, "What of the National Guard," *Infantry Journal* 60, no. 2 (Feb., 1947): pp. 9–15. The quote is from Gov. John W. Bricker to the Secretary of War, 31 May 1939, box 1, folder "Adjutant General W–Z," John W. Bricker Papers, Ohio Historical Society, Columbus.

23. This discussion is based on manuscript and oral history collections at USAMHI; the analysis in Appendix B of officer backgrounds in selected units; Dixon, "Impossible Takes Longer"; Cooper and Smith, *Citizens as Soldiers;* Derthick, *National Guard in Politics,* pp. 92–93; "The President's Page—Operation Circulation," *National Guardsman,* Feb., 1949; "New Pay Table," *National Guardsman,* Nov., 1949, p. 7; "Report of Staff Training Visit, 5–13 September 1950" in Second Army Command Report, 1950, vol. 5, box 943, RG 407, NA.

24. This discussion is based on the same sources listed in note 23. A particularly dramatic example of premobilization commissioning occurred with Pennsylvania's 28th Reconnaissance Company: Out of seventy enlisted men, twelve received commissions. "12 in City Troop Pass Officer Test," *Philadelphia Inquirer,* 1 Sept. 1950, p. 5.

25. National Guard Bureau, "Progress and Status of the Army National Guard, 31 August 1950," copy in Col. Cyrus A. Dolph III, "The National Guard" (student thesis, U.S. Army War College, 23 Feb. 1951).

26. Information on enlisted guardsmen is sparse compared to that on officers. This section is based on the manuscript, oral history, and Korean War Survey collections at USAMHI; Dixon, "Impossible Takes Longer"; Cooper and Smith, *Citizens as Soldiers;* Roberts, "History of the Utah National Guard"; Col. Charles L. Southward, "Training the National Guard" (student thesis, U.S. Army War College, 15 Mar. 1954), pp. 15–17; "As We See It: Things the Recruit Must Know," *National Guardsman,* Jan., 1949; and the monthly column "Posting the Guard," ibid., 1948–50. The large numbers of underage enlistees, particularly in small town areas, became quite noticeable when units mobilized in 1950. The 28th Infantry Division (Pennsylvania) lost 3.8 percent of its strength to underage enlistees, the 45th Infantry division (Oklahoma) lost 16 percent, and the 278th Regimental Combat Team (Tennessee) lost 10.5 percent (Memorandum, "Report on Divisions and RCT's inducted into Federal Service," 27 Nov. 1950, National Guard Bureau, Army National Guard Decimal File, 1949–50, box 1083, RG 168, NA).

27. "Washington Report," *National Guardsman,* Feb., 1950, p. 6.

28. As the headline to a two-page ad proclaimed in *Collier's,* 22 Mar. 1947.

29. Information Office, National Guard Bureau, "A Review of Progress of the National Guard Through a Continuous Program of Public Information, 1 Sept. 1947–1 January 1950," copy in the USAMHI library; Maj. Gen. Kenneth F. Cramer to F. Clayton Hepler, Gardner Advertising Co., 30 Aug. 1950, Army National Guard Decimal File, box 1059, RG 168 NA; Morton Bailey, *Saturday Evening Post,* to Gov. G. Mennen Williams, 3 Jan. 1949, box 373, Williams Pa-

pers. See also a series of articles by Cramer in the *National Guardsman:* "Organized Labor Backs the National Guard," July, 1949; "Business and Industry Back the Guard," Sept., 1949; and "The Guard's New Radio Show," Oct., 1949.

30. "Address by Major General Kenneth F. Cramer," *Official Proceedings of the National Guard Association of the United States General Conference 1948*, pp. 142–43; "The First to Fight," *Newsweek* 30, no. 12, 22 Sept. 1947, pp. 27–28; and "Operation 88,888," *Collier's*, 8 Nov. 1947, p. 94. The weekly progress of "Operation 88,888" can be followed in issues of the *Army Navy Journal* from 27 Sept. to 6 Dec. 1947. Local activities can be sampled in the following 1947 newspaper articles: "National Guard Opens Drive Today," *New York Times*, 16 Sept., p. 13; "Tributes Are Paid to National Guard," ibid., 17 Sept., p. 25; *Washington Post*, 17 Sept., p. B1; "Guard Gives Youth A Chance," *Boston Herald*, 16 Sept., p. 18; "State Joins in Drive for Guard Recruits," *Atlanta Constitution*, 16 Sept., p. 21; "100 Men Inducted By 138th Infantry," *St. Louis Post Dispatch*, 17 Sept., p. 12A; and "Recruit Drive To Test Stark's Guard Loyalty," *Canton (Ohio) Repository*, 14 Sept., p. 15.
31. Examples of all of these themes can be found in ads placed by the National Guard Bureau in *Collier's* during 1947. See the following issues: 22 and 29 Mar., 12 and 26 Apr., 3 and 24 May, 23 Aug., 20 Sept., 18 Oct., 15 Nov., and 13 Dec. The quotes are drawn from these ads. Blatant examples of the serving with your buddies and neighbors theme can be seen in recruiting ads placed in the *Daily Oklahoman*, p. 20, and the *Providence Journal*, p. 5, on 15 Aug. 1950 when the 45th and 43d Infantry Divisions were mobilized.
32. National Guard Bureau, Draft of "Notes and Comments for Unit Commanders—The Three Year Training Plan," Army Decimal File, box 1102, RG 168, NA; Col. Thomas L. Martin, "New National Guard Training Plan," *Infantry Journal* 62, no. 9 (Sept., 1948): pp. 32–36; Army Field Forces, "Report of Staff Visit to National Guard Units of Texas and Oklahoma," 11 Jan. 1950, box 26 (Inspection Reports), RG 337, NA; manuscript and oral history collections, USAMHI.
33. National Guard Bureau, *Annual Report of the Chief, National Guard Bureau, 1949*, pp. 18–19; Scurr, *Reflections of Service*, p. 67. On life as an instructor with a guard unit, see Lt. Col. R. C. Williams, "In Conclusion . . . ," *National Guardsman* 4, no. 3 (Mar., 1950): pp. 10–11, 20; and "National Guard Instructor," *Infantry Journal* 62, no. 2 (Feb., 1948): pp. 11–13. See also Chief, Army Field Forces, "Notes for Instructors and Adviser-Instructors Army National Guard," Feb., 1950, copy in Southward, "Training the National Guard." When George C. Marshall was assigned this duty in the 1930s, he said it "put him off the main career road to high command in the Army" (quoted in Forrest C. Pogue, *George C. Marshall: Education of a General, 1880–1939*, p. 282).
34. National Guard Bureau, *Annual Report of the Chief, 1949*, pp. 33–36; Francis S. Greenlief Oral History, USAMHI. The lack of modern armories also caused

security problems. In 1951, for example, thieves broke into a garage rented by New Jersey's 114th Armored Infantry Battalion and stole a large number of weapons ("Arsenal in Jersey Looted of Machine Guns, Pistols," *New York Times*, 3 Sept. 1951, p. 13).

35. See Lt. Gen. Raymond S. McLain, "Comments on Certain Aspects of the National Guard," 8 Aug. 1951, copy in USAMHI.
36. Shortages of equipment are mentioned constantly in the command reports of guard units mobilized for the Korean War found in RG 407, NA. The statistics for Pennsylvania units are taken from the units' 1950 Training Inspection Reports (NGB Form 115), box 1, RG 19, PHMC. Many guard units also lacked sufficient numbers of field manuals and technical manuals. Officers of the Ohio National Guard purchased their own copies instead of waiting for the adjutant general's office to finally deliver them (Col. W. R. Smith, "Staff Visit to Camp Atterbury, 18–20 Aug. 1948," box 1 [Combat Arms Advisory Group], RG 337, NA).
37. Strength figures are from National Guard Bureau, *Annual Report of the Chief, 1950*, p. 45. The Air National Guard's strength stood at 44,728.

Chapter 2. Limited Mobilization during a Limited War

1. Schnabel, *Policy and Direction*, pp. 42–60; Russell F. Weigley, *History of the United States Army*, pp. 485–504; Kendall, "An Inflexible Response," chap. two; William W. Epley, *America's First Cold War Army, 1945–1950;* J. Lawton Collins, *War in Peacetime*, pp. 66–85; Clay Blair, *The Forgotten War: America in Korea, 1950–1953*, pp. 3–61; Faris R. Kirkland, "Soldiers and Marines at Chosin Reservoir: Criteria for Assignment to Combat Command," *Armed Forces and Society* 22, no. 2 (winter, 1995–96): pp. 257–74.
2. Schnabel, *Policy and Direction*, pp. 83–99, 117–36; Kendall, "An Inflexible Response," pp. 166–72.
3. Studies by an interservice committee in 1950 had recommended a list of sites critical enough to warrant AAA defense, but only at the Hanford nuclear weapons production facility had a Regular Army AAA gun battalion been deployed by the start of the Korean War. The Army Antiaircraft Command was not established until July, 1950. The army filled the first two increments of guard units called to active duty with AAA units to implement the AAA defense plan and give the Army Antiaircraft Command operational units. See Stephen P. Moeller, "Vigilant and Invincible: United States Army Air Defense Command," *Air Defense Artillery*, (May–June, 1995): pp. 7–13.
4. The army tapped inactive and volunteer reservists instead of reservists in organized units because, fearing that war in Korea might lead to an even larger conflict, it wanted to maintain those units for future mobilization. As almost all reservists in inactive or volunteer status had not expected to be called for anything short of World War III and had not been attending drills or receiving pay, this decision was extremely unpopular and later led Congress to man-

date their early release from active duty in 1951, generating in the process significant personnel turbulence for guard units deployed to Korea that had received large numbers of enlisted reservists as fillers in 1950. The inactive and volunteer reserves also proved inadequate to demands for junior combat arms officers, forcing the army later to tap reserve units that had not yet been mobilized for individual officers. See Schnabel, *Policy and Direction*, pp. 120–22; Kendall, "An Inflexible Response," pp. 180–83, 206–10; "Mobilization in the Korean Conflict," pp. 5–25; and Richard B. Crossland and James T. Currie, *Twice the Citizen: A History of the United States Army Reserve, 1908–1983*, pp. 94–100.

The major exception to this generalization was guard units selected for deployment to Korea in 1950. They received large numbers of enlisted reservists as fillers and some officer reservists. See chapter three.

5. Some guardsmen hoped that the draft extension law would help recruiting for guard units ("45th Hears Draft News, Opens Armory Doors to Enlistments," *Daily Oklahoman*, 8 July 1950, p. 5).
6. This and the preceding paragraph are based on Schnabel, *Policy and Direction*, pp. 122–23; Kendall, "An Inflexible Response," pp. 172–73; and "Mobilization in the Korean Conflict," pp. 25–26. The war in Korea, and the belief that Stalin was really calling the shots for North Korea, generated a great deal of concern among Americans that World War III and Soviet atomic strikes against the United States were not far off. See the following 1950 articles: "Clay Calls 'Full Speed Ahead' On A-Defense; Finds City Ideal Target," *New York Post*, 10 Aug., p. 3; "Here's the Stark Story If A-Bomb Strikes," ibid. 13 Aug., p. 1; "U.S. 'In Poor Shape To Repel A-Bombs'," *St. Paul Dispatch*, 12 Aug., p. 1; "U.S. Air Defense Now Inadequate To Meet Attack," *Augusta Herald*, 22 Aug., p. 6; "Bomb Shelters For Seattle Urged In Defense Appeal,' *Seattle Post-Intelligencer*, 6 Sept., p. 5; and "Defense of State Stressed by Duff," *Philadelphia Inquirer*, 8 Aug., p. 7.
7. The first two increments mobilized in 1950 contained 19 AAA gun battalions, 7 AAA group and brigade headquarters, 24 AAA operations detachments and radar maintenance units, 3 combat engineer battalions, 1 field artillery battalion, 1 separate engineer company, 1 ordnance company, 1 ordnance battalion headquarters, and 1 engineer group headquarters. See "Mobilization in the Korean Conflict," pp. 26–27; Kendall, "An Inflexible Response," p. 173; and National Guard Bureau, "Induction and Release of National Guard Units, 1950–1956," copy in the U.S. Army Center of Military History.
8. The following nondivisional units were mobilized later in 1950: Puerto Rico's 296th Infantry (to replace the Regular Army's 65th Infantry, normally stationed on the island, but deployed to Korea); one tank battalion; one engineer group headquarters; and sixteen bands ("Induction and Release of National Guard Units").
9. These units, arriving during February and March, 1951, together with the transportation units that arrived earlier, would greatly assist in Eighth

Army's defeat of the Chinese 1951 spring offensives. See Berebitsky, *A Very Long Weekend*, pp. 14–25, 268–69; Schnabel, *Policy and Direction*, pp. 134–36; "Mobilization in the Korean Conflict," pp. 30–31; and Scurr, *Reflections of Service*, pp. 71–72.

10. Many veterans of the guard divisions that had served during one or both of the two world wars had developed a bond of affection and pride. The divisions also tended to monopolize national attention concerning the guard after 1917. See Mahon, *History of the Militia*, chap. 13; Jacobs, "Tensions Between the Army National Guard and the Regular Army," pp. 5–17; William Donnelly, "Keeping the Buckeye in the Buckeye Division: Major General Robert S. Beightler and 37th Infantry Division, 1940–1945," *Ohio History*, no. 106 (winter–spring, 1997): pp. 42–58; and the discussions of the 45th Infantry Division in chapter four, the 28th Infantry Division in chapter five, and the 37th Infantry Division in chapter six.
11. The regimental combat teams were needed to cover missions in peripheral areas providing locations for bases such as Iceland and Alaska that did not require an entire division. General Collins did not want to violate the integrity of divisions (and risk the wrath of the NGA) to provide units for this type of mission when the separate RCTs were available. See Schnabel, *Policy and Direction*, pp. 122–25; and "Mobilization in the Korean Conflict," pp. 27–30.
12. Interestingly, only three of the six divisions designated by the NGB in 1948 as priority divisions of the mobile strike force were on the AFF's recommendation list in 1950: the 28th, 31st, and 45th. Missing from the AFF's list were the 26th (Massachusetts) and 43d (Connecticut, Rhode Island, and Vermont) Infantry and the 49th (Texas) Armored Divisions.
13. These selections meant that each numbered army in the continental United States provided either a division or a RCT. See Schnabel, *Policy and Direction*, pp. 124–25; Kendall, "An Inflexible Response," pp. 105, 173–75; and "Mobilization in the Korean Conflict," pp. 28–29. A *LIFE* magazine editorial argued that concern over the political implications of mobilizing guard divisions "was a sure sign of Washington's failure to face the implications of the Korean war." The editorial writer agreed with General Clark that guard divisions "ought to be called up in the order of their fitness" ("Questions For Washington," 7 Aug. 1950, p. 30).
14. Although he was out of Washington, Cramer could not stay out of controversy. Complaints from guardsmen, draftees, and their families over Cramer's policies and command style led to press criticism and calls from politicians in the 43d's home states for an investigation. Lt. Gen. James A. Van Fleet's Second Army headquarters (in whose area the 43d was stationed on active duty) investigated and cleared Cramer of any wrongdoing. However, Army Field Forces remained dubious of both Cramer's abilities as a division commander and of the abilities of the 43d's senior leaders right up to the time the division deployed to Germany in 1951. See diary entry for 2 Oct. 1950, "Historical Record Aug.–Oct. 1950" file, box 16, Ridgway Papers; "Officers and Men at

Camp Pickett Are Restless Under Restrictions," *Providence Journal*, 1 Oct. 1950, p. 16; "Green, Fogarty, Forand Ask 43rd Div. Complaints Probe," ibid., 7 Oct. 1950, p. 1; "Probers Report on Pickett," *Army Times*, 2 Dec. 1950, p. 1.; "The Troubled 43rd," *TIME*, 4 June 1951, pp. 23–24; and Gen. Mark W. Clark, memorandum for Gen. J. Lawton Collins, 1 Oct. 1951, Subject: "Suitability of Maj. Gen. Kenneth F. Cramer for Continuation in Command of the 43d Infantry Division," Army Field Forces Decimal File 1951–52, box 38, RG 337, NA.

15. This and the preceding paragraph are based on "D.C., Virginia Military Units Called Up," *Washington Post*, 24 July 1950, p. 1; Berebitsky, *A Very Long Weekend*, p. 8; "6,000 Guardsmen Arrive At Gap For Drills," *Philadelphia Inquirer*, 9 July 1950, p. 1; "2000 Guardsmen Back From Camp," ibid., 23 July 1950, p. 1; "City Guardsmen Arrive At Camp," ibid., 30 July 1950, p. 1; "Duff Warns Guardsmen 'Serious Business' Ahead," *Pittsburgh Post-Gazette*, 10 July 1950, p. 13; "National Guardsmen Leave With Uncertain Feeling as to Whether Two-Week Training May Be Lengthened by Call to Federal Service," *Providence Journal*, 21 July 1950, p. 7; "R.I. Reservists Remain Uncertain As to Summons for Federal Duty," ibid., 22 July 1950, p. 1; "Bristol Battery Described as Serious, Determined About Training," ibid., 24 July 1950, p. 12; "Vinita Guardsmen Ready for Duty," *Daily Oklahoman*, 7 July 1950, p. 15; "Guardsmen Here Expecting Call For Early Date," *Augusta Herald*, 21 July 1950, p. 1; "'How Soon?' Is Uniform Topic of the Day Among Reservists," *Canton (Ohio) Repository*, 23 July 1950, p. 1; Col. P. J. C. Murphy, "Report of Staff Visit to the 43d Infantry Division, Pine Camp, New York," 3 Aug. 1950, Army Field Forces Decimal File 1949–50, box 178, RG 337, NA.

    Col. Kenneth Scurr, commander of the 196th RCT, claimed in his memoirs that an AFF inspector visiting the RCT at its summer training in June 1950 told him that the 196th would be among the first units ordered to active duty for the Korean crisis (Scurr, *Reflections of Service*, p. 68).

    Passed over in favor of the 43d Infantry Division, a "majority" of guardsmen in the 26th Infantry Division believed it was only a matter of time before they, too, would enter active duty. (They never did.) "Y-D Just Misses Being Called Up; Is Getting Ready," *Boston Globe*, 1 Aug. 1950, p. 1.

16. "MP Battalion From District Is Federalized," *Washington Post*, 4 Sept. 1950, p. 1B; "Battery D Recruits Put Through Paces, Say Life in Army Is Great," *Providence Journal*, 20 Aug. 1950, p. 18; and Col. P. J. C. Murphy, "Report of Staff Visit to the 43d Infantry Division, Pine Camp, New York," 3 Aug. 1950, Army Field Forces Decimal File 1949–50, box 178, RG337, NA.

    Robert Stockton, a 1950 high school graduate, recalled his initial reaction on hearing that his 45th Infantry Division had been alerted was "this changed college plans" (Stockton file, Korean War Survey).

    The mother of a seventeen-year-old guardsman wrote the Pennsylvania governor asking him to intervene to support her application for the discharge of her son, who she claimed was illegally enlisted in the guard at the age of fifteen. Mrs. Martha Moyer Lowe to Gov. James Duff, 16 Aug. 1950, Official Papers 1947–51, subject file, box 13, Duff Papers.

17. "45th Packed With Know-How," *Daily Oklahoman,* 8 Aug. 1950, p. 3.
18. Ibid.; and "Veterans of 45th Are Ready for Job," ibid., 9 Aug. 1950, p. 9.
19. Weber Oral History. General Clark's remarks did not sit well with some. Mrs. J. Sterl Long of Billings wrote to the *Daily Oklahoman* that as the mother of a Thunderbird, she "wasn't proud of that statement." She noted that "these boys are the same boys whose mothers have taught them to live by the Ten Commandments, one of which is 'Thou shalt not kill.'" Her son, a World War II veteran, will "go again—not as a killer of men—but to protect a heritage he is proud of" ("No Killer, but the Protector of a Heritage," 20 Aug. 1950, p. 26).
20. This and the preceding paragraph are based on "Goodbye for Now, Stew Is Gone Again," *Daily Oklahoman,* 3 Sept. 1950, p. 1; "It's the Waiting That's Tough," *Seattle Post-Intelligencer,* 11 Aug. 1950, p. 19; *Providence Journal,* 30 July 1950, p. 15; "Many Problems Face Men In 43rd," ibid., 7 Aug. 1950, p. 8; "Veterans of 45th Are Ready for Job," *Daily Oklahoman,* 9 Aug. 1950, p. 9; James D. Christie, Joe E. Whitesides, and Max C. Wurster files, Korean War Survey; Murphy, "Report of Staff Visit"; and Scurr, *Reflections of Service,* p. 69.
21. See results of questionnaires sent to state adjutants general by Lt. Col. William B. Rose compiled in his 1954 Army War College thesis, "Training the National Guard," copy in the archives, USAMHI. Also see Gov. G. Mennen Williams to Secretary of the Army Frank Pace, 15 Mar. 1951, box 375, Williams Papers; Ellard A. Walsh to Maj. Gen. John H. Manning, 25 Aug. 1950, box 1.1, Walsh Papers; and the following 1950 stories in the *Seattle Post-Intelligencer:* "Company K, National Guard Stands Ready To Do Its Job; Korea Duty Beckons," 3 Aug., p. 7; "Reserves Get Brush-Off In Quest Of Jobs," 1 Sept., p. 1; "Jobs Pledged To Reservists," and 2 Sept., p. 1.
22. Some Regular Army headquarters were concerned over the caliber of senior guard officers entering federal service. For example, on 1 August, Second Army ordered senior army instructors in the army area to "furnish confidential biographical information" on commanders and key staff officers of major guard units, including separate battalions (G3 Section, Command Report, 1950, Second Army, box 943, RG 407, NA).

    New Mexicans lived with the memory of the 200th Coast Artillery Regiment, lost on Bataan. The AAA gun battalions in the postwar New Mexico guard all traced their ancestry to that regiment, and a few of its survivors had joined the postwar guard ("Silver City Goes To War Again," *LIFE,* 7 Aug. 1950, pp. 25–29).
23. "45th Leaders Keep Studying, Watching News," *Daily Oklahoman,* 10 July 1950, p. 12; "Straight From the Feedbox; 45th to Have Regular Camp," ibid., 20 July 1950, p. 1; "Discharges Halted By 45th Division," ibid., 21 July 1950, p. 1; and ibid., 3 Aug. 1950, p. 18.

    No doubt the fate of Oklahoma's Marine Corps Reserve 20th Infantry Battalion fanned these fears. Within a month of its arrival at Camp Pendleton,

California, the battalion was broken up and its members distributed among units of the 1st Marine Division (ibid., 13 Aug. 1950, p. 1).

24. "2nd D.C. Guard Unit Called For Service; All-Negro Command Gets Orders," *Washington Post,* 26 July 1950, p. 1; "372d Battalion Ready For Active Duty," *Cleveland Call and Post,* 12 Aug. 1950, p. 6C; "N.C. Guard Is Ready If Call Comes," *Raleigh News and Observer,* 3 Sept. 1950, p. 1-IV; "Veteran Soldier Praises Local Battalion's Spirit," *Canton (Ohio) Repository,* 23 Aug. 1950, p. 5; "Troops of 5 R.I. Guard Units Win Praise Of Governor, Officers in Camp Review," *Providence Journal,* 7 Aug. 1950, p. 1; and "Battery D Recruits Put Through Paces." Governor Duff is quoted in "Penna.'s Own 28th Inducted With Simple Roll Call," *Philadelphia Inquirer,* 6 Sept. 1950, p. 2. General Cramer said that he and his 43d Infantry Division "are very happy the Forty-Third Division was among the first National Guard divisions selected for active duty" ("43rd Division of New England Among 4 Guard Units Called," *New York Times,* 2 Aug. 1950, p. 1).
25. "Penna.'s Own 28th Inducted"; "Home Guard Planned for State Defense," *Philadelphia Inquirer,* 19 July 1950, p. 1.; "New York Guards Alerted By U.S.," *New York Times,* 24 July 1950, p. 1; "State Guards Take Over Armory Here," *Augusta Herald,* 8 Aug. 1950, p. 9; "A State Guard May Be Needed," *Nashville Banner,* 5 Aug. 1950, p. 4.
26. Sen. John Stennis to Maj. Gen. Kenneth F. Cramer, 16 Aug. 1950, file 325.452, National Guard Bureau Decimal File 1949–50, box 1083, RG 168, NA. The 31st would get its shot at glory when the army brought it into federal service in January, 1951. The chief of staff's selection of the 43d over the higher-rated 26th Infantry Division was received with "divided sentiment" by Massachusetts Guardsmen of the Yankee Division ("Y-D Just Misses Being Called Up").
27. The same *Washington Post* article also charged that the Regular Army had not been properly prepared in training, equipment, and morale for combat operations. It blamed as the root cause "a people who congenitally seek the easy way out until they find themselves in a corner from which escape is only the toughest way of all" ("'M-Day Force' Still Mainly on Paper," 30 July 1950, p. 3B). See also "Farewells . . . Tears . . . Wonder," *Logan Herald-Journal,* 25 Aug. 1950, p. 1; "A Call to Arms," *Providence Journal,* 2 Aug. 1950, p. 11; and "Pennsylvania's 28th Division To Serve U.S. Again," *Philadelphia Inquirer,* 3 Aug. 1950, p. 22.

    A 21 July *Washington Post* editorial expressed the hope, somewhat unrealistically, that in selecting which divisions to mobilize, senior army leaders would "be less concerned with any possible political complaints than with meeting their needs in short order" ("Reservists To Duty," 21 July 1950, p. 18). The paper reiterated its concern in "More Men Called," 29 July 1950, p. 6.
28. "In the Finest Tradition," *Charlotte News,* 24 Aug. 1950, p. 12A; "Moorehead City's Battery Gets Call," *Raleigh News and Observer,* 17 Sept. 1950, p. 6; and "Battery D Recruits Put Through Paces." See also "'Fighting Civilians' At Armory Await Call To Training To Man A-A Guns," *Seattle Post-Intelligencer,* 15

Aug. 1950, p. 5; "Ave Atque Vale," *Providence Journal,* 12 Sept. 1950, p. 9; and "Pennsylvania's 28th Division To Serve."

29. "Partial to the 43rd?" *Providence Journal,* 8 Oct. 1950, p. 1-III; "Remember the 705th," ibid., 22 Oct. 1950, p. 1-III; "2 City Guard Units Get Active Duty," ibid., 24 July 1950, p. 1; and "Guard Unit Federalized," ibid., 14 Aug. 1950, p. 11. On the 47th, see the following 1950 *Providence Journal* articles: "Guard To Try Korea Tactics At Ripley," 12 Aug., p. 4; "Ripley Troops Concentrate on Arms Use," 14 Aug., p. 9; "Mill Citian's Pet Coyote, K-9 Vet, Is Ripley Mascot," 18 Aug., p. 1; "Youngdahl To See Troops at Ripley," 24 Aug., p. 4; and "Troops Reviewed By Youngdahl," 26 Aug., p. 4.

30. "45th to Train at Camp Polk for Duty; Recruits Are Sought," *Daily Oklahoman,* 2 Aug. 1950, p. 1; "The Guard Turns Out," ibid., 3 Aug. 1950, p. 18; ibid., 25 Aug. 1950, p. 4; "Send-Off Gift Sought for 45th," ibid., 29 Aug. 1950, p. 1.

    Pennsylvania was not far behind Oklahoma when it came to the 28th Infantry Division. Although the state had many other guard units in addition to the "Bloody Bucket" division, it is clear that the 28th was first in the Keystone State's affections. See "Pennsylvania's 28th Division To Serve"; "28th Lauded by Pershing," *Philadelphia Inquirer,* 2 Aug. 1950, p. 2; and "28th Division Proves It's Ready For Duty," *Pittsburgh Post-Gazette,* 7 Aug. 1950, p. 1.

31. A copy of the information handed out to commanders and their staffs by the AFF at the conference can be found in Headquarters, Army Field Forces, Secret Decimal Correspondence File 1949–50, box 190, RG 337, NA.

32. "Pawtucket Armory Resumes Full-Time Army Role Today," *Providence Journal,* 14 Aug. 1950, p. 22; "If You've Got To Go, Go With Friends!" ibid., 17 Aug. 1950, p. 9; "45th to Train at Camp Polk for Duty; Recruits Are Sought," *Daily Oklahoman,* 2 Aug. 1950, p. 1; "National Guard Unit Here Seeks Recruits," *Augusta Herald,* 25 July 1950, p. 1; "National Guard Negro Battalion Alerted For Duty," *Boston Globe,* 12 Aug. 1950, p. 1; and Thomas S. Grodecki, "From Powder River to Soyang," pp. 18–19.

33. 130th FA Group Command Report, 1950, box 4685, RG 407, NA. Most units' 1950 command reports mention a recruiting campaign conducted between alert and induction, but few reveal the results of the campaign.

34. *Daily Oklahoman,* 20 Aug. 1950, p. 16; and ibid., 13 Aug. 1950, p. 16.

35. Ibid., 15 Aug. 1950, p. 20; G1 Section, 45th Infantry Division, Command Report, 1950, box 4257, RG 407, NA.

    The 45th also tried to use its wartime esprit as a recruiting tool, getting a special dispensation from the Department of the Army that would allow World War II Thunderbird veterans living anywhere in the country to enlist for a guaranteed assignment in the division after it entered active duty. There is no evidence that many veterans outside of Oklahoma accepted this offer ("Veterans of 45th May Go Back to Old Outfits," *Daily Oklahoman,* 5 Aug. 1950, p. 2).

36. 45th Infantry Division Command Report, 1950; "Missing State Draftees Stop By 45th First," *Daily Oklahoman,* 9 Aug. 1950, p. 1; and William T. Craig, *Lifer! From Infantry to Special Forces,* pp. 16–17.

While at Camp Polk, a sheriff from Oklahoma came for Craig armed with a federal warrant for failure to report for induction on Sept. 15. The sheriff returned to Oklahoma without a prisoner when Craig produced his army identification card (which showed his date of entry on active duty) and pointed out to the sheriff that he would "look like an idiot" for arresting a soldier on active duty who had ignored an induction notice dated fourteen days after he went on active duty (Craig, *Lifer!*, pp. 21–22).

37. The shorthanded 235th FA Observation Battalion promoted six enlisted men to warrant officer after the alert—two to be unit administrators, one to be an assistant radar officer, one to be the assistant supply officer, one to be the assistant survey officer, and one to be the battalion motor officer.
38. The conclusions concerning warrant and company grade officers is based on checking unit officer rosters against the *National Guard Register 1951*. On the Philadelphia City Troop, see "12 in City Troop Pass Officer Test," *Philadelphia Inquirer*, 1 Sept. 1950, p. 5.

    The 1950 annual federal inspection of the 28th Reconnaissance Company noted that "mostly high type men" filled the company's ranks, with many college graduates, and recommended that most of the unit's enlisted men should be sent to Officer Candidate School upon mobilization (Training Inspection Report, 1950, 28th Reconnaissance Company, Department of Military Affairs, Adjutant General 1934–89 general file, box 1, RG 19, PHMC.
39. Berebitsky, *A Very Long Weekend*, p.115.
40. Data is drawn from a comparison of unit officer rosters with the *National Guard Register 1951* and memorandum, 14 Sept. 1950, Subject: "Report of Staff Training Visit," in vol. 5, Second Army Command Report, 1950, box 943, RG 407, NA.
41. The results were: 43d Infantry Division, 1,267; 28th Infantry Division, 968; 40th Infantry Division, 847; 196th RCT, 551; and 278th RCT, 504 new men. See memorandum from National Guard Bureau Information Office for General Fleming, 27 Nov. 1950, "Report on Divisions and RCT's Inducted into Federal Service," file 325.452, general, National Guard Bureau Decimal File 1949–50, box 1083, RG 168, NA; and Gordecki, "From Powder River to Soyang," pp. 18–19. Command Reports for 1950 for mobilized nondivisional units show the shortfall between full TO&E strength and the personnel strength of units brought to active duty. See chaps. 3, 5, and 6 for examples.
42. "Report on Divisions and RCT's inducted into Federal Service"; 1950 Command Reports for nondivisional units.
43. 45th Infantry Division Command Report, 1950; "17-Year-Olds Find Door Out Of Guard Open," *Daily Oklahoman*, 12 Aug. 1950, p. 1; ibid., 24 Aug. 1950, p. 7; and "Report on Divisions and RCT's inducted into Federal Service." Other losses to underage include: 28th, 345; 43d, 235; 196th RCT, 0; 278th RCT, 256.

    Nondivisional units undoubtedly contained some underage boys, but not all of these units' 1950 command reports broke out the causes of why guardsmen did not enter active duty. The 710th AAA Gun Battalion did note that it lost five guardsmen to minority (Command Report, 1950, box 4576, RG 407, NA).

44. Other losses to physicals include: 40th, 484; 45th, 457; 196th RCT, 340; the 278th RCT, 106 ("Report on Divisions and RCT's inducted into Federal Service"). Some examples of losses reported by nondivisional units from guardsmen failing the physicals: 703d AAA Gun Battalion, about 4 percent; 710th AAA Gun Battalion, 14 percent; 746th AAA Gun Battalion, 10 percent; 235th FA Battalion, 25 percent; 171st MP Battalion, 4 percent; 112th Truck Battalion Headquarters Company, 7 percent; and 107th Truck Company (minority and physical), 13 percent (1950 Command Reports for the units listed, RG 407, NA).
45. Commanding general, Sixth Army, to the adjutant general, 6 Nov. 1950, National Guard Bureau Decimal File 1949–50, file 325.452, box 1083, RG 168, NA; 179th Infantry Command Report, 1950, box 4258, RG 407, NA; G-1 Section, 45th Infantry Division, Command Report, 1950; 28th Infantry Division Command Report, 1950, box 3983, RG 407, NA; and Daniel M. Hudelson, Kenneth R. Scurr, and Kenneth F. Cramer, "M-Day . . . The Reality," *National Guardsman*, Feb., 1951, pp. 2–3, 16–21.
46. *Providence Journal*, 14 Aug. 1950, p. 24; and Roberts, "History of the Utah National Guard," p. 494.
47. This and the preceding paragraph are based on "Remarks by Maj. Gen. Raymond H. Fleming, Chief, National Guard Bureau," *Official Proceedings of the National Guard Association of the United States General Conference* 1950, pp. 50–51; "Governor 1947–51" subject file, box 13, Duff Papers; box 45, W. Kerr Scott Papers, North Carolina Department of Archives and History, Raleigh (hereafter Scott Papers); box 8, Lausche Papers, Ohio Historical Society, Columbus (hereafter Lausche Papers); Roberts, "History of the Utah National Guard," pp. 459–60; Hudelson, Scurr, and Cramer, "M-Day . . . The Reality;" "Deferments From 28th Facing Close Scrutiny," *Philadelphia Inquirer*, 5 Aug. 1950, p. 5; *Daily Oklahoman*, 9 Aug. 1950, p. 8; 28th Infantry Division Command Report, 1950; and memorandum, Brig. Gen. Goerge C. Moran to Gov. G. Mennen Williams, 29 Jan. 1951, box 377, Williams Papers.
48. 28th and 45th Infantry Divisions 1950 Command Reports; Hudelson, Scurr, and Cramer, "M-Day . . . The Reality;" 171st MP Battalion, 710th AAA Gun Battalion, and 107th Truck Company 1950 Command Reports; and Grodecki, "From Powder River to Soyang," pp. 18–20. The quote is from the 45th Infantry Division's Command Report.
49. 158th FA Battalion Command Report, 1950, box 4258, RG 168, NA; 28th Infantry Division, 179th Infantry, and 746th AAA Gun Battalion 1950 Command Reports; and Hudelson, Scurr, and Cramer, "M-Day . . . The Reality."
50. See unit command reports for 1950; Hudelson, Scurr, and Cramer, "M-Day . . . The Reality;" and Grodecki, "From Powder River to Soyang," p. 18.
51. See note 50. The quote is from "Penna.'s Own 28th Inducted."
52. Reflecting the elite social status of its members and its history, "the long fa-

mous First Troop Philadelphia Cavalry" ("officially now the 28th Reconnaissance Company") received a breezy, chatty story in the "Features For Women" section of the *Philadelphia Inquirer* ("First City Troop Trains For New Call to Colors," 6 Sept. 1950, p. 40. See also the 1950 Command Reports for the 28th and 45th Infantry Divisions; 703d, 710th, 715th, and 746th AAA Gun Battalions; 194th, 235th, and 272d FA Battalions; and 107th Truck Company; Hudelson, Scurr, and Cramer, "M-Day . . . The Reality;" "Boston N.G. Battalion To Be Inducted Today," *Boston Herald,* 18 Sept. 1950, p. 3; "Engineers' First Day in U.S. Service Filled With Paperwork," *Charlotte News,* 14 Aug. 1950, p. 1B; "378th Fattened on Good Chow Before Starting Active Duty," ibid., 17 Aug. 1950, p. 1B; "MP Battalion From District Is Federalized"; "Guardsmen Train," *Logan Herald-Journal,* 19 Aug. 1950, p. 1; "Guard Unit Federalized"; "Pawtucket Armory Resumes Full-Time Army Role Today"; "Battery D Recruits Put Through Paces"; "Starting Today, State Armory Will Be 'Home' for Co. B Engineers," *Providence Journal,* 3 Sept. 1950, p. 14; and articles in the *Daily Oklahoman* on 3 Sept., pp. 1, 14; 5 Sept., p. 3; and 8 Sept. 1950, p. 1.

53. "378th Farewell Slated Today," *Charlotte News,* 19 Aug. 1950, p. 1B; "Legionnaires to Fete Guardsmen," *Logan Herald-Journal,* 23 Aug. 1950, p. 1; "Send-Off Parties Bid 28th Farewell," *Philadelphia Inquirer,* 10 Sept. 1950, p. 10; "Statesboro Gives National Guard A Royal Send-Off," *Augusta Herald,* 16 Aug. 1950, p. 5; "Departing Soldiers Given Farewell Party, Banquet," *New London Day,* 5 Sept. 1950, p. 5; and articles in the *Providence Journal* on 15 Aug., pp. 12, 13; 20 Aug., p. 18; 24 Aug., p. 13; 26 Aug., p. 10; 5 Sept., p. 12; and 6 Sept. 1950, p. 15.
54. See the following 1950 articles in the *Daily Oklahoman:* 11 Aug., p. 25; 20 Aug., p. 22; and 25 Aug., p. 8; "Alfalfa Goes All-Out With 45th Parties," 25 Aug., p. 20; and "States' Cities Send Their Sons Off To War With Farewell Parties," 27 Aug., p. 18.
55. Many news accounts stressed the similarities with scenes at railroad stations during World War II. This and the preceding paragraph are based on "Kin Bid Farewell to So. End Troops," *Boston Herald,* 28 Sept. 1950, p. 1; "Augusta Guard Unit Entrains for Camp," *Augusta Herald,* 25 Aug. 1950, p. 1; "Old Scene Re-Enacted As Engineers Leave For War," *Charlotte News,* 24 Aug. 1950, p. 1B; "Guardsmen Get Loving Send-Off To Duty", *Nashville Banner,* 6 Sept. 1950, p. 6; "Throngs Wave Goodbye As Famed 28th Departs," *Philadelphia Inquirer,* 11 Sept. 1950, p. 1; "103d Engineers Leave, Kin March to Station," ibid., 12 Sept. 1950, p. 2; "1,000 District Guardsmen Leave Here for Camp Atterbury," *Pittsburgh Post-Gazette,* 11 Sept. 1950, p. 4; "Farewells . . . Tears . . . Wonder"; "1,000 Friends, Relatives Bid Battalion Goodbye," *Canton (Ohio) Repository,* 25 Aug. 1950, p. 1; "M.P. Group Leaves For Active Duty," *Washington Post,* 9 Sept. 1950, p. 1; "Two More D.C. Guard Units Off to Camp," ibid., 20 Sept. 1950, p. 3; "New Call For Troops Made As R.I. Bids 705th Goodbye," *Providence Journal,* 25 Aug. 1950, p. 1; "Relatives Cry As Battery B Leaves Depot," ibid., 25 Aug.

1950, p. 15; and "Youngsters Gay but City's 45th Veterans Ride Quietly Into Night," *Daily Oklahoman,* 9 Sept. 1950, p. 1.

56. The Regular Army corporal's account of combat in Korea is in the *Daily Oklahoman,* 3 Sept. 1950 (2d ed.), p. 1.

Chapter 3. Postmobilization Training

1. Peter R. Mansoor, *The GI Offensive in Europe: The Triumph of American Infantry Divisions, 1941–1945*, pp. 49–83; Christopher R. Gabel, *The U.S. Army GHQ Maneuvers of 1941,* pp. 8–21; Robert R. Palmer, Bell I. Wiley, and William R. Keast, *The Procurement and Training of Ground Combat Troops,* pp. 442–55, 535–39.
2. Office, Chief of Army Field Forces, "Master Training Program For National Guard Divisions," 15 Oct. 1950, copy in National Guard Bureau Decimal File 1949–50, file 353 general, box 1107, RG 168, NA; Col. T. G. Richey, "What Lies Ahead?" *National Guardsman,* Oct., 1950, pp. 18–21. Details on ATPs can be found in unit command reports, RG 407, NA.
3. "Mobilization in the Korean Conflict," pp. 50–52.
4. Memorandum from inspector of artillery to chief, Army Field Forces, 23 Feb. 1951, Subject: "Report of Inspection of AAA Units, Camp Stewart, Georgia, 19–21 February 1951," box 40 (Combat Arms Advisory Group), RG 337, NA; and 197th AAA Group Command Report, 1950, box 4589; 710th, 736th, and 746th AAA Gun Battalion Command Reports, 1950, box 4576; 45th Infantry Division Command Report, 1950, box 4257; 37th Infantry Division Command Report, 1952, box 4024; and 28th Infantry Division, Command Report, 1950, box 3983, RG 407, NA.
5. 163d MP Battalion Command Report, 1950, box 9 (MP Battalions), RG 338, NA; 168th MP Battalion and 51st AAA Brigade Command Reports, 1950, box 4584, RG 407, NA; 197th AAA Group, 28th Infantry Division, and 45th Infantry Division Command Reports, 1950; and 37th Infantry Division Command Report, 1952.
6. 51st AAA Brigade Command Report, 1950; 209th AAA Group Command Report, 1950, box 4815, RG 407, NA; 28th and 45th Infantry Division Command Reports, 1950; Nicholas Kafkalas Oral History, USAMHI; and "28th Is Up and Rarin' to Go," *Pittsburgh Post-Gazette,* 13 Sept. 1950. The quote is from 715th AAA Battalion Command Report, 1950, box 4576, RG 407, NA.
7. 37th Ordnance Battalion Command Report, 1950, box 4725, RG 407, NA.
8. 171st MP Battalion Command Report, 1950, box 4718, RG 407, NA; 163d and 168th MP Battalion Command Reports, 1950; Craig, *Lifer!,* p. 34; Weber Oral History. Respondents to USAMHI's Korean War Veterans Survey who served in guard units often commented on the lack of active duty experience in their position among guardsmen holding NCO and junior officer positions.
9. 45th Infantry Division Command Report, 1950; *Army Register 1951; National Guard Register 1939;* "Wartime 45th Leader Named Chief of Staff," *Daily Okla-*

homan, 30 Nov. 1950, p. 20; David R. Gray, "Black and Gold Warriors: U.S. Army Rangers During the Korean War (Ph.D. diss., Ohio State University, 1992), pp. 54–55. Between August and December 1950, Murphy had spent considerable time at the AFF working on issues related to guard mobilization.

10. 168th MP Battalion Command Report, 1950; and 158th FA Battalion and 279th Infantry Command Reports, 1950, box 4258, RG 407, NA. For World War II examples of this, see Mansoor, *GI Offensive in Europe*, pp. 58–60, 68–69, and Omar N. Bradley and Clay Blair, *A General's Life: An Autobiography*, pp. 108–13.
11. 109th Infantry and 103d Medical Battalion Command Reports, 1951; *Register of Graduates of the United States Military Academy; Army Register 1951;* Strickler, *Memoirs*, p. 168.
12. Johnson, *African American Soldiers*, pp. 169–70, 172–73; *National Guard Register 1951;* 272d FA Battalion Command Report, 1951, box 5192, RG 407, NA; Col. Malin Craig, Jr., "Report of Staff Visit to Units of the Fifth Army at: Camp Atterbury, Indiana; Camp McCoy, Wisconsin; Camp Ripley, Minnesota," 8 Aug. 1951, box 43, (Combat Arms Advisory Group), RG 337, NA; "National Guard Negro Battalion Alerted For Duty," *Boston Globe*, 12 Aug. 1950, p. 1; "Officers Railroaded: Army 'Busts' Top Negro Personnel On Nat'l Guard Unit From Boston," *Pittsburgh Courier*, 6 Oct. 1951, p. 1.
13. 746th AAA Gun Battalion and 37th Ordnance Battalion Command Reports, 1950; Scurr, *Reflections of Service*, pp. 71–72.
14. "Narrative Summary of Unit Activities from Federal Activation Date to First Submission of Monthly Command Report," 1 Oct. 1951, 715th Transportation Truck Company, box 5452, RG 407, NA.
15. Memorandum, Col. James J. Winn to chief, Army Field Forces, 17 Jan. 1951, Subject: "Report of Visit to Artillery Units, Fort Hood, Texas, Camp Carson, Colorado, and Camp McCoy, Wisconsin," box 41 (Combat Arms Advisory Group), RG 337, NA; Berebitsky, *A Very Long Weekend*, pp. 15, 21, 23–24, 46; and Joe E. Whitesides, *204th Field Artillery Battalion in Korea*, p. 12.
16. 37th Infantry Division Command Report, 1952. A rare contemporary public airing of this problem is in a 7 Oct. 1952 story in the *Akron Beacon Journal*.
17. O'Daniel's comments are in the report of an AFF inspection of the 28th on 25–26 Oct. 1950, box 1 (Combat Arms Advisory Group), RG 337, NA. 45th Infantry Division Command Report, 1950; Weber Oral History.
18. 163d, 168th, 171st MP Battalion Command Reports, 1950.
19. Memorandum from commander, 272d FA Battalion, 21 Dec. 1950, Subject: "Status of Training and Equipment" with enclosure from Maj. Gen. George D. Shea to chief, Army Field Forces, 27 Dec. 1950, Subject: "Obstacles to Training, Camp McCoy, Wisconsin," box 15 (Combat Arms Advisory Group), RG 337, NA; 272d FA Command Report, 1950; G1, Army Field Forces, "Personnel Study of Negro Units, Continental United States," 24 July 1951, file 291, Army Field Forces Decimal Files 1951–52, box 471, RG 337, NA.
20. 171st MP Battalion Command Report, 1951, box 5307, RG 407, NA; 45th

Replacement Company Command Report, 1950, box 4258, RG 407, NA; "Army OKs Uniforms of 'Rebels'," *Pittsburgh Courier,* 10 May 1952, p. 5; "'Dixie' Division Band Keeps Confederate Gray," *Army Times,* 12 Apr. 1952, p. 1.

21. The extent of racial integration in the 37th by September, 1952, is based on the photographs of individuals for each company or battery in Richard R. Riehm, ed., *Pictorial History Thirty-Seventh Infantry Division Camp Polk, Louisiana 1952.* The division's 1952 command report noted that the "integration of negroes in the command has taken place without untoward incident except that the Post Exchange barber shops seem to have difficulty providing service for negroes." On the reluctance of many in the army before and during the Korean War to having blacks command whites, see William T. Bowers, William M. Hammond, and George L. MacGarrigle, *Black Soldier, White Army: The 24th Infantry Regiment in Korea,* and Morris J. MacGregor, Jr., *Integration of the Armed Forces 1940–1965,* pp. 440–41.
22. "45th Welcomes First 'Outsiders,'" *Daily Oklahoman,* 8 Oct. 1950, p. 1; Weber Oral History; 158th FA Command Report, 1950; and Scurr, *Reflections of Service,* pp. 71–72. A number of reservists and regulars responding to the USAMHI Korean War Veterans Survey mentioned favoritism toward guardsmen in the guard unit to which they had been assigned, but none provided specific examples.
23. 45th Infantry Division Command Report, 1950.
24. 197th and 209th AAA Group Command Reports, 1950; inspector of artillery, "Report of Inspection of AAA Units"; Shelby L. Stanton, *Order of Battle: U.S. Army World War II,* p. 602; and Walter Hayes to Brig. Gen. George M. Carter, 12 Oct. 1950, Walter Hayes Papers, USAMHI (hereafter Hayes Papers).
25. The first quote is from the 45th Infantry Division Command Report, 1950. "Camp Polk Again Is Getting That Lived-In Look," *Daily Oklahoman,* 15 Sept. 1950, p. 13; 28th Infantry Division Command Report, 1950; Kafkalas Oral History; "28th Is Up and Rarin' to Go," *Pittsburgh Post-Gazette,* 13 Sept. 1950. On the effects of the winter weather on training, see the 109th Infantry and 28th Division Artillery Command Reports, 1951, box 3994; and 628th Tank Battalion, 103d Engineer Battalion, and 112th Infantry Command Reports, 1951, box 3995, RG 407, NA. General Shea's remark is in "Report of Training Inspection," 2 Feb. 1951, box 42 (Combat Arms Advisory Group), RG 337, NA. For conditions at McCoy, see memorandum from Col. Malin Craig, Jr., to chief, Army Field Forces, 13 Nov. 1950, Subject: "Report of Staff Visit to Artillery at Camp McCoy, Wisconsin" box 15 (Combat Arms Advisory Group), RG 337, NA, and Shea, "Obstacles to Training, Camp McCoy."
26. Craig, "Report of Staff Visit to Artillery at Camp McCoy."
27. 28th Division Artillery, 628th Tank Battalion, and 112th Infantry Command Reports, 1951; and 899th AAA Battalion Command Report, 1951, box 3994, RG 407, NA.
28. Many command reports of mobilized guard units comment on the poor conditions on post and difficulties in finding housing off post. For Camp McCoy's

problems, see Provost Marshal Section, Office, Chief of Army Field Forces, memorandum, Subject: "Report of Staff Visit and Inspection of Military Police Units in Second Army," 15 Nov. 1951, box 33 (Combat Arms Advisory Group), RG 337, NA; 171st MP Battalion Command Report, 1950; Craig, "Report of Staff Visit to Artillery at Camp McCoy"; Shea "Obstacles to Training, Camp McCoy"; Col. George D. Crosby to Maj. Gen. George D. Shea, 22 Dec. 1950, enclosure to Shea, "Obstacles to Training, Camp McCoy"; "Camp McCoy Race Policy Vilest in U.S.," *Pittsburgh Courier,* 9 June 1951, p. 1.

29. 37th Infantry Division Command Report, 1952; "37th Troops Face Homes Shortage," *Army Times,* 19 Jan. 1952, p. 8; *Cincinnati Enquirer,* 23 Jan. 1952; memorandum from assistant chief of staff, G3, to chief of staff, U.S. Army, 7 May 1952, Subject: "Request for Information re Installations and Troop Units to be visited," file G3 322, box 197, RG 319, NA.
30. 163d and 168th MP Battalion Command Reports, 1950; and 145th AAA Battalion Command Report, 1 Jan. 1951–30 Apr. 1951, box 4275, RG 407, NA.
31. 107th Transportation Company Command Report, Aug. 1950–Mar. 1951, box 4755, RG 407, NA; and 715th Transportation Truck Company, "Narrative Summary of Unit Activities from Federal Activation Date to First Submission of Monthly Command Report," 1 Oct. 1951, box 5452, RG 407.
32. Grodecki, "From Powder River to Soyang," pp. 24–25, 27–30.
33. Craig, "Report of Staff Visit to Artillery at Camp McCoy"; Grodecki, "From Powder River to Soyang," pp. 21–22.
34. Inspector of artillery, "Report of Inspection of AAA Units"; and 197th AAA Group Command Report, 1951, box 4815, RG 407, NA.
35. Strickler, *Memoirs,* pp. 163–66, 169.
36. 37th Infantry Division Command Report, 1952; "Report of Staff Visit to 37th Infantry Division at Camp Polk, Louisiana to Observe Conduct of ATT No 7-26, 22–25 July 1952," box 64 (Combat Arms Advisory Group), RG 337, NA.
37. The M15 carried a 37-mm gun and two .50-caliber machine guns mounted on a half-track. James A. Huston, *Guns and Butter, Powder and Rice: U.S. Army Logistics in the Korean War,* pp. 32–36, 83–85, 118–36, 173–81, 184–85; Lt. Gen. T. R. Larkin, assistant chief of staff, G4, to Gen. Mark W. Clark, chief, Army Field Forces, 22 Jan. 1951, enclosure 7 to Winn, "Report of Visit to Artillery Units"; 899th AAA Battalion Command Report, 1951; 145th AAA Battalion Command Report, 1 Jan. 1951–30 Apr. 1951.
38. 197th AAA Group Command Report, 1950; Christie file, Korean War Veterans Survey, USAMHI; Hayes to Carter, 11 Aug. 1950 and 1 Feb. 1951, Hayes Papers. The quote is from the 1 February letter.
39. 245th Tank Battalion Command Report, 1 Jan.–30 Apr., 1951, box 4288; and 179th Infantry Command Report, 1 Jan. 1951–30 Apr. 1951, box 4281, RG 407, NA. The quote is from Sfc. Tommy Hawkins, in Berebitsky, *A Very Long Weekend,* p. 122. The M4A3 and M26 both were older designs than the M46.
40. 45th Infantry Division Command Report, 1 Jan. 1951–30 Apr. 1951, box 4259; and 279th Infantry Command Report, 1 Jan. 1951–30 Apr. 1951, box 4285,

RG 407, NA; 179th Infantry Command Report, 1 Jan.–30 Apr., 1951; and Weber Oral History.

41. Winn, "Report of Visit to Artillery Units."
42. G3, "Readiness Dates of Major Units in the U.S.," in file G3/322 (Cases 61–80), box 197, RG 319, NA. Emphasis in Original.
43. Winn, "Report of Visit to Artillery Units"; Berebitsky, *A Very Long Weekend,* pp. 20–21.
44. 45th Division Artillery Command Report, 1 Jan.–30 Apr. 1951, box 4276, RG 407, NA; 179th Infantry Command Report, 1 Jan.–30 Apr. 1951.
45. *Roll On 28th: Twenty-Eighth Infantry Division, United States Army, Camp Atterbury, Indiana, 1950–1951;* 28th Infantry Division Command Report, 1950; Strickler, *Memoirs,* pp. 163–65; Kafkalas Oral History; 28th Infantry Division, Training Memorandum no. 9, 14 Oct. 1950, copy in Daniel B. Strickler Papers, USAMHI (hereafter Strickler Papers); and G1, 28th Infantry Division, "Levy and Fulfillment," 7 Dec. 1950, copy in Strickler Papers.
46. 37th Infantry Division Command Report, 1952; "Report of Staff Visit to 37th Infantry Division, 22–25 July 1952."
47. On the problems the army faced in late 1950 and early 1951, see Blair, *Forgotten War,* pp. 427–556; Schnable, *Policy and Direction,* pp. 294–95, 297–300, 342–45; and John M. Kendall, "An Inflexible Response," pp.193–228.
48. 163d and 171st MP Battalion Command Reports, 1950; 171st MP Battalion Unit Journal, Dec., 1950; and 163d MP Battalion Command Report, 1951, box 9 (MP Battalions), RG 338, NA; 715th AAA Gun Battalion Command Report, 1950, box 4576; and 168th MP and 171st MP Battalion Command Reports, 1951; and box 5307, RG 407, NA.
49. "Commander's Questionnaire," 12 May 1951, copy in 272d FA Historical Files, box 305 (Field Artillery), RG 338, NA; 272d FA Battalion Command Report, 1951, box 5192, RG 407, NA; 163d, 168th, and 171st MP Battalion Command Reports, 1951; memorandum from Provost Marshal Section for chief, Army Field Forces, 5 Apr. 1951, Subject: "Report of Inspection of Military Police and Military Government Units and Staff Sections, Office of the Provost Marshal General; Fifth Army Area; and Second Army Area, 23 March–3 April 1951," box 33 (Combat Arms Advisory Group), RG 337, NA.
50. 197th AAA and 209th AAA Group Command Reports, 1951; 703d and 705th AAA Gun Battalion Command Reports, 1951, box 4789; and 746th AAA Gun Battalion Command Report, 1951, box 4790, RG 407, NA; memorandum, Col. J. F. Howell to chief, Army Field Forces, "Report of Staff Visit to Camp Stewart, Georgia, 8 May 1951," box 40 (Combat Arms Advisory Group), RG 337, NA.
51. 45th Infantry Division Command Reports, Jan.–Apr., 1951; 28th Infantry Division, 28th Division Artillery, 109th Infantry, 112th Infantry, 109th and 229th FA Battalion, 628th Tank Battalion, and 103d Engineer Battalion Command Reports, 1951; Strickler, *Memoirs,* p. 166; Kafkalas Oral History; "Plan of training for 28th Infantry Division, April–June 1951," copy in Strickler Papers;

"Trainees Sailing, Gen. Clark Says," *Philadelphia Inquirer,* 8 Feb. 1951, p. 8; and "U.S. Army Denies Using 'Green' Troops in Korea," ibid., 10 Sept. 1950, p. 1.

52. 158th FA Battalion Command Report, 1 Jan. 1951–30 Apr. 1951, box 4278, RG 407, NA; 179th Infantry Command Report, 1 Jan.–30 Apr. 1951; 45th Infantry Division Command Reports, Jan.–Apr., 1951; memorandum from Maj. Gen. Wayne C. Zimmerman to chief, Army Field Forces, "Report of Inspection of 45th Infantry Division and Non-Divisional Units at Camp Polk, Louisiana, 5–7 March 1951," box 42 (Combat Arms Advisory Group), RG 337, NA.
53. 45th Infantry Division Command Report, 1 Jan.–30 Apr. 1951.
54. Ibid.
55. Ibid. Soldiers in army schools who would not graduate before the 45th sailed would rejoin the division in Japan.
56. 45th Infantry Division Command Report, 1 Jan.–30 Apr. 1951; James H. Weaver, *45th Division Training Regiment.* Weaver commanded the Training Regiment.
57. Schnabel, *Policy and Direction,* pp. 136, 230.
58. The reserve battalion was the 780th FA, an 8-inch howitzer unit. Grodecki, "From Powder River to Soyang," p. 28; Roberts, "History of the Utah National Guard," pp. 472–74, 484–85; Winn, "Report of Visit to Artillery Units;" Berebitsky, *A Very Long Weekend,* pp. 40–41; and 987th AFA Battalion "Activities Report," 4 Mar. 1951, box 388 (Field Artillery), RG 338, NA.
59. The firing battery scores were: A—63.5 percent; B–47.8 percent; and C—74.6 percent. The passing score for ATT 6-1 was 70 percent (272d FA Battalion Command Report, 1951).
60. The quotes are from a memorandum from Lt. Col. C. A. Murphy to the Seventh Army artillery officer, 14 Nov. 1951, Subject: "Chronology of 272nd Field Artillery Battalion," 272d FA Battalion Historical Files, box 305 (Field Artillery), RG 338, NA; and 272d FA Battalion Command Report, 1951. Murphy was the 272d's new commander.
61. The 194th's greatest weakness was its poor ability to mass the battalion's fires. See the unit's 1951 Command Report and Unit Journal, box 293 (Field Artillery), RG 338, NA.
62. 28th Division Artillery, 109th and 112th Infantry Regiment, and 109th and 229th FA, 628th Tank, and 103d Engineer Battalion Command Reports, 1951; and memorandum from commanding general, Fifth Army, to chief, Army Field Forces, 28 May 1951, Subject: "Results of Army Field Forces Training Tests"; and memorandum from Maj. P. G. Walker, Subject: "OCAFF Observer's Report of VI Corps Inspection of 28th Infantry Division, 1–6 July 1951," box 43 (Combat Arms Advisory Group), RG 337, NA. Major Walker praised the 28th Reconnaissance Company, drawn from the elite of Philadelphia society, for its "superior" standard of discipline.
63. Maneuver director's report, Exercise Southern Pine, copy in box 3990, RG 407, NA. Army Field Forces was more concerned with the readiness of the

43d Infantry Division and its commander, General Cramer (Clark, "Suitability of Maj. Gen. Kenneth E. Cramer").

64. Kafkalas Oral History; Maj. Gen. Daniel D. Strickler to Lt. Gen. Stephen Chamberlain, commanding general, Fifth Army, 4 Sept. 1951, Strickler Papers; 109th Infantry Command Report, 1951. A *Pittsburgh Post-Gazette* reporter joined the division for Southern Pine, filing stories much like a war correspondent. See, for example, "District GIs in 'Hot Fight'," 20 Aug., p. 1; "28th's Footballers Get in Shape," 21 Aug., p. 2; "Oil City Troops Doing Fine," 22 Aug., p. 2; "Enemy Objects to Weapon," 23 Aug., p. 4; and "Company A Tanks Attacked," 25 Aug., p. 2.
65. Gen. Mark W. Clark to Lt. Gen. Stephen J. Chamberlain, 23 Aug. 1951 and 5 Sept. 1951, box 43 (Combat Arms Advisory Group), RG 337, NA. The quotes are from the 5 September letter.
66. Lt. Gen. John R. Hodge to Gen. Mark W. Clark, 27 Aug. 1951, box 43 (Combat Arms Advisory Group), RG 337, NA. During World War II, Hodge served in combat as an assistant division commander, division commander, and corps commander. On the 1941 maneuvers, see Gabel, *U.S. Army GHQ Maneuvers.* Hanson W. Baldwin, the *New York Times* military affairs correspondent, also was an observer at Southern Pine. His comments on the 28th and the 43d echoed those of Hodge and the AFF observers. See "110,000 U.S. Troops 'War' In Sand Hills," 22 Aug. 1951, p. 3, and "Army Games Show Many Deficiencies," 29 Aug., 1951, p. 12.
67. Also taking and passing an ATT retest after Southern Pine was the 112th Infantry's 3d Battalion. The 628th Tank Battalion, with the infantry regiment tank companies attached, spent October in the desert at Camp Irwin, California, where the post's unrestricted opportunities for armor offered Keystone tankers their "best training" since mobilization. See 109th and 112th Infantry Regiment, 109th and 229th FA, 899th AAA Gun, and 103d Engineer Battalion Command Reports, 1951; Clark to Chamberlain 5 Sept. 1951; Strickler to Chamberlain, 4 Sept. 1951, Strickler Papers; and Col. W. F. Rehm, "Report of Final Inspection of 28th Infantry Division," 20 Sept. 1951, box 43 (Combat Arms Advisory Group), RG 337, NA.

Chapter 4. In the Land of the Morning Calm

1. Berebitsky, *A Very Long Weekend,* pp. 268–69.
2. National Guard Bureau, "Induction and Release;" and Berebitsky, *A Very Long Weekend,* pp. 268–69.
3. 107th Transportation Truck Company Command Reports, Aug., 1950–Mar., 1951, box 4755; and 715th Transportation Truck Company, "Narrative Summary of Unit Activities from Federal Activation Date to First Submission of Monthly Command Report," 1 Oct. 1951, box 5452, RG 407, NA; and *National Guard Register 1951.*
4. 107th Transportation Company Command Report, Aug. 1950–Mar., 1951;

and 715th Transportation Truck Company, "Narrative Summary of Unit Activities."

5. Ibid.
6. 107th Transportation Truck Company Command Reports, Apr. and May, 1951, box 5446; and 715th Transportation Truck Company Command Reports, Apr. and May, 1951, box 5452, RG 407, NA. For the experience of other truck units during the Chinese offensives, see Westover, *Combat Support in Korea*, pp. 47–49; and Berebitsky, *A Very Long Weekend*, pp. 36–37.
7. 107th Transportation Truck Company Command Reports, June–Dec., 1951, box 5446; and 715th Transportation Truck Company Command Reports, June–Dec., 1951, box 5452, RG 407, NA.
8. Ibid.; 107th Transportation Truck Company Command Reports, Jan.–Mar., 1952, , box 6458; and 715th Transportation Truck Company Command Reports, Jan.–Mar., 1952, box 4753, RG 407, NA. A firsthand account of racial integration in the 715th by a black guard officer from Maryland who took command a month beforehand is in Berebitsky, *A Very Long Weekend*, pp. 253–54.
9. 107th Transportation Truck Company Command Reports, Jan.–Mar., 1952; 715th Transportation Truck Company Command Reports, Jan.–Mar., 1952.
10. On the importance of indirect fire in U.S. tactical doctrine, see Robert A. Doughty, *The Evolution of U.S. Army Tactical Doctrine, 1946–76*, pp. 3–5; Boyd L. Dastrup, *King of Battle: A Branch History of the U.S. Army's Field Artillery*, pp. 241–52; and *FM 100-5, Field Service Regulations: Operations*, pp. 8–11, 93–94, 100–109, 129–37, 147–49. On Eighth Army's need for corps artillery units, see Schnabel, *Policy and Direction*, pp. 96–97.

    By late December, 1950, American and ROK field artillery units had lost 238 howitzers destroyed or abandoned to the enemy (Blair, *Forgotten War*, pp. 576–77). For an analysis of field artillery operations in Korea, see Ronald K. Kyle, "Killer of Communists, Saver of Soldiers: U.S. Army Field Artillery in the Korean War, 1950–1953" (master's thesis, Ohio State University, 1995).
11. Schnabel, *Policy and Direction*, pp. 89–92, 96–97. Much of the General Reserve's 105-mm howitzer strength (a weapon normally used by division artillery units in the direct support role) had to be used to bring direct-support field artillery battalions in Korea and in divisions and regimental combat teams deploying to Korea up to full strength. Before the war, those units had been permitted to field only two of the three firing batteries and only four of the six howitzers per battery called for in the TO&E.
12. In 1950, the National Guard troop list contained the following organized field artillery units: 9 self-propelled 105-mm howitzer battalions; 16 towed 155-mm howitzer battalions; 1 self-propelled 155-mm howitzer battalion; 4 self-propelled 155-mm gun battalions; 2 towed 155-mm gun battalions; 5 observation battalions; 12 group headquarters; and 4 corps artillery headquarters (National Guard Bureau, *Annual Report of the Chief*, 1950, pp. 54–74).
13. National Guard Bureau, "Induction and Release."

14. Berebitsky, *A Very Long Weekend,* pp. 268–69. The quote is from ibid., p.21. See also Grodecki, "From Powder River to Soyang," pp. 1–23; and Winn, "Report of Visit to Artillery Units."
15. Schnabel, *Policy and Direction,* pp. 136, 230; Blair, *Forgotten War,* 576–77; Winn, "Report of Visit to Artillery Units," and Berebitsky, *A Very Long Weekend,* pp. 268–69.

    Those battalions mobilized in 1950 and which deployed in early 1951 were: Pennsylvania's 176th AFA (self-propelled 105-mm howitzer); Tennessee's 196th FA (towed 155-mm howitzer); Utah's 204th FA (self-propelled 155-mm gun) and 213th AFA (self-propelled 105-mm howitzer); Wyoming's 300th AFA (105-mm self-propelled howitzer); Arkansas's 936th FA (towed 155-mm howitzer) and 937th FA (self-propelled 155-mm gun); New York's 955th FA (towed 155-mm howitzer); and Ohio's 987th AFA (self-propelled 105-mm howitzer).
16. Roberts, "History of the Utah National Guard," pp. 474–75, 485–86; and 213th AFA Battalion Command Report, Mar., 1951, box 5192, RG 407, NA. See also Grodecki, "From Powder River to Soyang," pp. 33–39; 955th FA Battalion Command Report, Feb., 1951, box 5217; and 987th AFA Battalion, "Executive and S1 Journal," Mar., 1951, box 5222, RG 407, NA; and 987th AFA Battalion, "Activities Report," 4 Mar. 1951, box 388 (Field Artillery), RG 338, NA.
17. Berebitsky, *A Very Long Weekend,* pp. 40–41. The newly arrived battalions were initially assigned as follows: I Corps—176th AFA, 204th FA, 300th AFA, 936th FA, and 955th FA; IX Corps—213th AFA, 937th FA, and 987th AFA; X Corps—196th FA. These were not permanent assignments; Eighth Army shifted battalions from corps to corps as the tactical situation changed. The reserve battalion was the 780th FA, an 8-inch howitzer unit.
18. 213th AFA Battalion Command Report, Mar., 1951; 955th FA Command Reports, Feb. and Mar., 1951, box 5217; and 987th AFA Battalion Command Report, Apr., 1951, box 5222, RG 407, NA; Headquarters, X Corps Artillery, Command Reports, Dec., 1950–Sept., 1951, copies in USAMHI; Whitesides, *204th Field Artillery,* p. 31–33; and "987th Artillery Group Training In South Korea," *Canton (Ohio) Repository,* 13 Mar. 1951, p. 1.
19. 955th FA Battalion Command Reports, Feb. and Mar., 1951.
20. 213th AFA Battalion Command Report, Mar., 1951; and Grodecki, "From Powder River to Soyang," p. 39.
21. Grodecki, "From Powder River to Soyang," pp. 40–50; Berebitsky, *A Very Long Weekend,* pp. 44–45.
22. Berebitsky, *A Very Long Weekend,* pp. 46–52. After the 936th FA, the guard field artillery battalions entered combat in the following order between 3 April and 22 April: 937th FA, 204th FA, 176th AFA, 196th FA, 955th FA, 987th AFA, and 213th AFA.
23. Ibid., pp.46–48.
24. Ibid., pp.48–53; 955th FA Command Report, Apr., 1951 (the 955th's reporting cycle ran from 6 P.M. to 6 P.M.); Whitesides, *204th Field Artillery,* pp. 36–39;

213th AFA Battalion Command Report, Apr., 1951; and 987th AFA Battalion, "S2-S3" Journal, Apr., 1951. On Operation Dauntless, see Blair, *Forgotten War,* pp.770–71, 797–99, 804, 820–22.

25. Berebitsky, *A Very Long Weekend,* p. 54; Blair, *Forgotten War,* pp. 822–23.
26. 955th FA Battalion Command Report, Apr., 1951; Whitesides, *204th Field Artillery,* pp. 43–46; Berebitsky, *A Very Long Weekend,* pp.54–61; Blair, *Forgotten War,* pp. 823–28, 833–37, 843–55.
27. The following account of the 213th and 987th AFA Battalions' experiences during the April Chinese offensive is based on the units' April, 1951, Command Reports and Berebitsky, *A Very Long Weekend,* pp. 61–68.
28. The quote is from 213th AFA Battalion Command Report, Apr., 1951.
29. The folks back in Stark County learned of the 987th's actions a month later. See "Stark's 987th Routs Reds in Initial Korean Battle," *Canton (Ohio) Repository,* 23 May 1951, p. 2; and "987th Loses Equipment in Rugged Korean Pass," ibid., 24 May 1951, p. 1.
30. The TO&E gave the AFA battalions one liaison officer and three forward observer officers, but no supporting enlisted men or equipment. The 213th found that direct support of infantry regiments or brigades required four liaison officers and nine forward observers.
31. Both the 6th ROK Division commander and the IX Corps Artillery commander called the 213th on 27 April to express their appreciation for the battalion's support, calling it the "largest single factor" in breaking the Chinese attack on the division. Meanwhile, the 987th AFA found it difficult to get "up to date intelligence" from the Marine Corps artillerymen the battalion reinforced because the marine forward observers were "more interested in shooting than in reporting the location nature and activities of either enemy or friendly units" (213th and 987th AFA Battalion Command Reports, Apr., 1951).
32. Blair, *Forgotten War,* pp. 832–33, 851; and Berebitsky, *A Very Long Weekend,* p. 68.

    North Korean units mounted a weak attack along X Corps's front in April. Part of this lack of determination no doubt resulted from the efforts of the 196th FA Battalion, which fired 9,114 155-mm rounds from 22 to 29 April in support of the 7th Infantry and 5th ROK Divisions.
33. 987th AFA Battalion Command Report, Apr., 1951.
34. Ibid., May, 1951, box 5222; 213th AFA Battalion Command Report, May, 1951, box 5192; and 955th FA Battalion Command Report, May, 1951, box 5128, RG 407, NA; Roberts, "History of the Utah National Guard," pp. 478–79; Whitesides, *204th Field Artillery,* pp. 52–56; Grodecki, "From Powder River to Soyang," pp. 53–61; Berebitsky, *A Very Long Weekend,* pp. 71–72; and Blair, *Forgotten War,* pp. 859–60, 868–74.
35. 987th AFA and 955th FA Battalion Command Reports, May, 1951; and *National Guard Register 1951.*
36. Grodecki, "From Powder River to Soyang," pp. 62–67; Berebitsky, *A Very Long*

Weekend, pp. 72–74; and Blair, *Forgotten War,* pp. 871–74, 876, 883. On 17 May, X Corps's divisional and corps field artillery battalions fired thirty-eight thousand rounds. The total climbed to fifty thousand rounds on 19 May.

37. Grodecki, "From Powder River to Soyang," pp. 75–84; and Berebitsky, *A Very Long Weekend,* pp. 75–78.
38. 987th AFA and 955th FA Command Reports, May, 1951; Roberts, "History of the Utah National Guard," pp. 478–79; Whitesides, *204th Field Artillery,* pp. 53–58.

    After the spring offensives, the 987th's operations officer made it clear that a key lesson of this fighting was that 105-mm howitzers lacked the range and power required by battalions serving as corps artillery. He recommended that 155-mm be the minimum weapon size for this role (987th AFA Battalion Command Report, Aug., 1951, box 5222, RG 407, NA). Eighth Army agreed with this analysis and converted the AFA battalions to 155-mm and 8-inch howitzers as the weapons became available. The 213th made the switch in October, 1951, with only a month's notice and only a few borrowed 155-mm howitzers on which to train. The battalion remained in position and continued to fire missions as the M7s were driven out and towed 155-mm howitzers were moved into position. The 987th converted to self-propelled 8-inch howitzers in October, 1952, after it had lost its guard character (213th FA Battalion Command Report, Oct., 1952, box 5192; and 987th AFA Battalion Command Report, Oct., 1952, box 6130, RG 407, NA).
39. 213th AFA Battalion Command Report, May, 1951; and Roberts, "History of the Utah National Guard," pp. 489–90.
40. The following table shows the phase-out of ERC fillers during 1951 in three battalions:

Month	213th AFA	955th FA	987th AFA
June	13	24	24
July	22	48	29
Aug.	30	45	11
Sept.	26	24	35
Oct.	**	48	19
Nov.	**	23	**
Dec.	**	**	**

    By autumn, the ERC fillers, along with other members of the battalions who had arrived in Korea in February, had become eligible for return home under the RCP program. Units thus stopped keeping separate records for fillers who left Korea under the ERC phase-out and those who left because they had accumulated enough points under the RCP program (213th AFA, 955th FA, and 987th AFA Battalion Command Reports, June–Dec. 1951).
41. Grodecki, "From Powder River to Soyang," p. 102.
42. 955th FA Battalion Command Report, Dec. 1951, box 5221, RG 407, NA. The

problems these different phase-out programs presented to units can be seen, for example, in the 987th AFA Battalion, which lost 112 NCOs in its first group of RCP returnees in Nov., 1951 (Command Report, Nov., 1951, box 5223, ibid.).

43. 213th AFA Battalion Command Report, Dec., 1951, box 5192; 955th FA Battalion Command Report, Sept., 1951, box 5220; and 987th AFA Battalion Command Report, Mar., 1952, box 6129, RG 407, NA; Whitesides, *204th Field Artillery*, p. 94; Grodecki, "From Powder River to Soyang," p. 110; *Army Register 1951;* and *National Guard Register 1951.*

    On the army's manpower dilemma during the Korean War, see Stilwaugh, "Personnel Polices in the Korean Conflict." A major drain on the army's manpower quality was the deferment of college students from the draft. By the end of 1952, about two hundred thousand students had received deferments (George Q. Flynn, "The Draft and College Deferments During the Korean War," *The Historian*, May, 1988, p. 383). The war and the draft to support it grew increasingly unpopular during 1952. For a contemporary report, see "Why the Draft Makes Our Young Men Angry," *Collier's*, 13 Sept. 1952, pp. 15–18.

44. Wilfrid O. Boettiger, *An Antiaircraft Artilleryman From 1939 to 1970*, p. 125. 987th AFA Command Reports, Sept., box 5222, and Dec., 1951, box 5223; and 955th FA Battalion Command Report, Sept., 1951, box 5220, RG 407, NA.

45. On the poor skill levels of many of the replacements received by corps artillery battalions, see I Corps Artillery Command Report, July, 1951, box 1588; 213th AFA Battalion Command Report, Mar., 1952, box 6088; 955th FA Battalion Command Report, Feb., 1952, box 6124; and 987th AFA Battalion Command Reports, Jan. and Feb., 1952, box 6129, RG 407, NA; Roster of Officers, 987th FA Battalion, May, 1952, box 394 (Field Artillery Battalions), RG 338, NA.

46. 955th FA Battalion Command Reports, Sept.–Nov., 1951, box 5220; and Command Reports, Jan. and Feb., 1952, box 6124; 213th AFA Battalion Command Reports, Nov. and Dec., 1951, box 5192; and 987th AFA Battalion Command Report, Nov., 1951, box 5223, RG 407, NA.

47. 213th and 987th AFA Battalion Command Reports, Aug., 1951; 987th AFA Battalion Command Report, Dec., 1951; Grodecki, "From Powder River to Soyang," pp. 105–106; and I Corps Artillery Command Report, Oct., 1951, box 1589, RG 407, NA. The 987th AFA's 17 percent black enlisted strength exceeded FECOM's guidance that blacks make up no more than 12 percent of a unit's enlisted strength.

48. Col. Joe E. Whitesides file, Korean War Survey; Grodecki, "From Powder River to Soyang," pp. 105–107; 955th FA Battalion Command Report, Dec. 1951; and Thomas Cacciola file, Korean War Survey. Cacciola was a guardsman in the 955th.

49. 955th FA Battalion Command Reports, Oct.–Dec. 1951; 955th FA Battalion Command Reports, Jan.–Feb., 1952, box 6124; 987th AFA Battalion Com-

mand Reports, Oct.–Dec., 1951; and 987th AFA Battalion Command Reports, Jan. and Feb., 1952, box 6129; and 213th AFA Battalion Command Reports, Oct.–Dec., 1951, and Jan.–Feb., 1952, box 6088, RG 407, NA; Roberts, "History of the Utah National Guard," pp. 481–82, 492–93, 496–97; Grodecki, "From Powder River to Soyang," pp. 104–105; and Berebitsky, *A Very Long Weekend,* pp. 81–83.

50. 955th FA Battalion Command Reports, Oct.–Dec. 1951; 955th FA Battalion Command Reports, Jan.–Feb., 1952, box 6124; 987th AFA Battalion Command Reports, Oct.–Dec., 1951; and 987th AFA Battalion Command Reports, Jan. and Feb., 1952, box 6129; and 213th AFA Battalion Command Reports, Oct.–Dec., 1951, and Jan.–Feb., 1952, box 6088, RG 407, NA; Roberts, "History of the Utah National Guard," pp. 481–82, 492–93, 496–97; Grodecki, "From Powder River to Soyang," pp. 104–105; and Berebitsky, *A Very Long Weekend,* pp. 81–83.
51. Berebitsky, *A Very Long Weekend,* p. 83.
52. Roberts, "History of the Utah National Guard," p. 483.
53. I Corps Artillery Command Report, July, 1951; 213th AFA, 955th FA, and 987th AFA Battalion Command Reports, Oct., 1951–Feb., 1952; Grodecki, "From Powder River to Soyang," pp. 95–97, 104–105, 111–12; and Roberts, "History of the Utah National Guard," p. 483.

    The battalions were not placed in reserve to conduct an intensive training program like the one they had gone through after arriving in Korea because U.S. doctrine held (and still holds) that artillery is never to be placed in reserve.

Chapter 5. The Thunderbirds in Korea

1. Franks, *Citizen Soldiers;* "45th Packed With Know-How," *Daily Oklahoman,* 8 Aug. 1950, p. 3; "Time to Go to Japan!" ibid., 2 Mar. 1951, p. 1; Kendall, "An Inflexible Response," p. 105; and Army Field Forces, "Report of Staff Visit to 45th Infantry Division and the Artillery School, Ft. Sill, Oklahoma, 23 August 1949," box 21 (Combat Arms Advisory Group), RG 337, NA. The quote is from Weber Oral History.

    Bill Mauldin entered federal service with the 45th in 1940, left the infantry to join the division newspaper, and later moved to *Stars and Stripes.* His cartoons, featuring the infantrymen Willie and Joe, won the Pulitzer Prize in 1945. In 1951, a movie based on *Up Front,* a collection of Mauldin's wartime cartoons, was released. The ads for the movie were modified in Oklahoma with additional copy: "'Willie and Joe' Of The Fighting 45th Thunderbirds Come To Life And Step Out Of Bill Mauldin's World Famous Book" (*Daily Oklahoman,* 5 Apr. 1951, p. 10).
2. Background on General Styron is from *National Guard Register 1951;* Franks, *Citizen Soldiers,* pp. 140–41; *Thunderbird Review;* and Jacobs, "Out of the Ashes of Victory," pp. 6–9.

3. Franks, *Citizen Soldiers*, pp. 141–42; *National Guard Register 1951;* and "Division Officers Drop Varied Tasks for Big Job," *Daily Oklahoman*, 2 Aug. 1950, p. 10.
4. *National Guard Register 1951.*
5. Ibid.; *Thunderbird Review;* Clay Blair, *Ridgway's Paratroopers: The American Airborne in World War II*, pp. 70, 197, 275–76, 302; and Weber Oral History.
6. *National Guard Register 1951.*
7. "Veterans of 45th Are Ready for Job," *Daily Oklahoman*, 9 Aug. 1950, p. 9; and *National Guard Register 1951.*
8. *National Guard Register 1951;* and "Division Officers Drop Varied Tasks for Big Job," *Daily Oklahoman*, 2 Aug. 1950, p. 10.
9. On equipment shortages, see "Report of Staff Visit to 45th Infantry Division and the Artillery School." On personnel strength, see "Department of the Army Table of Organization and Equipment 7N: Infantry Division," 7 July 1948, copy in USAMHI; 1950 NGB 115 Reports, box 1, general file, Adjutant General 1934–89, RG 19, PHMC; report from the Oklahoma adjutant general to chief, National Guard Bureau, 7 Aug. 1950, "Strength of 45th Infantry Division units as of 2400 1 Aug. 1950," file 325.44 Oklahoma State Decimal File, 1949–50, box 1199, RG 168, NA.

   The following table shows the strengths of the 45th's major units when they were alerted in August:

Unit	Total	% Guard TO	% Full TO
179th Infantry	1,471	52	39
180th Infantry	1,726	61	46
279th Infantry	1,449	51	8
158th FA Battalion	376	76	56
160th FA Battalion	403	81	60
171st FA Battalion	391	79	58
189th FA Battalion	394	80	59
145th AAA Battalion	398	70	51
245th Tank Battalion	310	66	47
120th Engineer Battalion	344	47	36
120th Medical Battalion	159	58	47

10. Born in 1902, Dulaney graduated from the Infantry Company Officer's Course in 1931 and the Command and General Staff School in 1941. He first joined the 45th in 1942, then left it to command the 645th Tank Destroyer Battalion, created out of artillery units made excess when the 45th went from the square to triangular configuration that year. He returned to the division a year later on Sicily as executive officer of the 180th Infantry. In October, 1943, he took command of the regiment in Italy, leading it until January, 1945, when he was transferred to the 44th Infantry Division as assistant division commander. Dulaney was promoted to brigadier general in March, 1945, but

in 1946, along with many other officers, lost his star when the army demobilized. Among his most notable interwar assignments were command of the 25th Infantry at Fort Benning, graduation form the National War College, and command of the 350th Infantry in Austria (*Army Register 1951; Register of Graduates of the United States Military Academy;* and "Wartime Comrade Gets Post As Assistant 45th Commander," *Daily Oklahoman,* 10 Sept. 1950, p. 1).

Born in Canada in 1901, Murphy served four years in the Regular Army, ending his enlistment in 1925 as a first sergeant. Commissioned the same year into Colorado's 157th Infantry, Murphy became a businessman in Fort Collins and graduated from the Infantry School's National Guard Officer Machine Gun and Howitzer Course in 1930. Mobilized in 1940 with the 157th Infantry, Murphy graduated from the Infantry School's Battalion Commander and Staff Course in 1941. He commanded a battalion of the 157th on Sicily and in the early stages of the Italian campaign. Just before landing at Anzio, he moved to the 179th Infantry as executive officer, taking command of the regiment during the campaign in southern France. Murphy remained on active duty until 1947, mostly as part of the investigation of war crimes in Italy, left the service in August, and then received a Regular Army commission in November. Between August and December, 1950, Murphy spent considerable time at AFF headquarters working on issues related to guard mobilization (45th Infantry Division Command Report, 1950; *Thunderbird Review; Army Register 1951; National Guard Register 1939;* and "Wartime 45th Leader Named Chief Of Staff," *Daily Oklahoman,* 30 Nov. 1950, p. 20).

11. Born in New York in 1909, Wilkes served as an enlisted cavalryman in the guard from 1928 to 1935. Commissioned in 1935, he graduated from the Cavalry School National Guard Officer's Course in 1937, and from the Command and General Staff School in 1941. Born in Virginia in 1910, Throckmorton served as an enlisted cavalryman in the guard from 1931 to 1940. Commissioned in 1940, he graduated from the Cavalry School Squadron Commander and Staff Officer Course in 1942, the Command and General Staff School in 1943, and the Armor Officer Advanced Course in 1950 (*Army Register 1951; National Guard Register 1939; National Guard Register 1943;* and "Two Regular Army Officers Get 45th Jobs," *Daily Oklahoman,* 18 Oct. 1950, p. 8).
12. See the extensive coverage of the 45th in the *Daily Oklahoman* from October to December, 1950. The helmet ad is in the *Daily Oklahoman,* 17 Dec. 1950, p. 14C.
13. *Daily Oklahoman,* 23 Nov. 1950, p. 1; ibid., 8 Dec. 1950, p. 1; and "Santa Claus Arrives Early For 45th Unit," ibid., 10 Dec. 1950, p. 1.
14. "Santa Takes Wings To 45th," *Daily Oklahoman,* 13 Dec. 1950, p. 1; "Air Lift Brings Present-Laden Soldiers Home," ibid., 24 Dec. 1950, p. 1; and 45th Infantry Division Command Report, 1950.
15. *Daily Oklahoman,* 24 Oct, p. 1; and "Army Says No Guard Outfits Going Abroad," ibid., 27 Oct. 1950, p. 1.
16. Ham radio operators in Oklahoma also helped keep the links strong by pass-

ing messages between Thunderbirds and their families. 45th Infantry Division Command Reports, Jan.–Apr., 1951; and *Daily Oklahoman*, 10 Feb. 1951, p. 1.

17. "Protests Over 45th Assignment Cease," *Daily Oklahoman*, 4 Mar. 1951, p. 1.
18. "45TH GOING TO JAPAN IN MARCH," and "Governor Told It's Not Korea," *Daily Oklahoman*, 25 Feb. 1951, p. 1. Murray was elected governor in November, 1950, and Kerr moved from the governorship to a seat in the U.S. Senate.
19. "Division Adds Another To Long List Of Firsts," *Daily Oklahoman*, 25 Feb. 1951, p. 18; "Oklahoma's Own," ibid., 27 Feb. 1951, p. 8.
20. "45th Will Keep Training, Grant Short Furlough," *Daily Oklahoman*, 25 Feb. 1951, p. 18; and "45th Will Walk Ashore This Time," ibid., 26 Mar. 1951, p. 1.
21. "45th Will Keep Training"; "Men At Polk Resigned To Fate; Many Questions Unanswered," *Daily Oklahoman*, 26 Feb. 1951, p. 1; "Korea Duty Called Possible For 45th," ibid., 18 Mar. 1951, p. 1; and "45th Veterans Eye Japan Duty And Their Role In 'Rear Echelon,'" ibid., 22 Mar. 1951, p. 10.
22. Born in Montana in 1902, Maerdian enlisted in the Regular Army in 1924 and received an appointment to West Point the same year. He graduated from the Infantry School in 1935 and the Command and General Staff School in 1941. During World War II, he served as a tactical officer at West Point and commanded the 353d Infantry in Europe. The 353d, part of the 89th Infantry Division, saw far less combat than the 45th, not arriving in France until late January, 1945. Maerdian had been the professor of military science and tactics at Oregon since 1947 (279th Infantry Command Report, 1 Jan. 1951–30 Apr. 1951, box 4285, RG 407, NA; *Register of Graduates of the United States Military Academy; Army Register 1951;* Stanton, *Order of Battle*, p. 250.
23. 45th Infantry Division Command Reports, Jan.–Apr., 1951. For coverage of the final parade, see "45th, Relatives Crowd Chapels; Parade Is Today," *Daily Oklahoman*, 26 Mar. 1951, p. 20; and "Marching Boots Crunch 45th Farewell," ibid., 27 Mar. 1951, p. 1. General Key commanded the 45th when it mobilized in 1940, but was relieved in 1942 as part of the army's purge of senior officers following the 1941 Louisiana Maneuvers.
24. 45th Infantry Division Command Reports, Jan.– Apr., 1951.
25. The *Daily Oklahoman* reporter was Wayne Mackey, a World War II Pacific veteran who received six hours notice that he would be going to Japan. See "GI Life Seems Different Now," *Daily Oklahoman*, 25 Mar. 1951, p. 1. In addition, the editor of the division newspaper was a *Daily Oklahoman* reporter "on Military Leave," as the newspaper described him in the byline for stories he filed. On renewed concern over possible misuse of the 45th by the Regular Army, see "45th Expected To Stay Intact," ibid., 6 Apr. 1951, p. 11, and "Army Renews Promise To 45th," ibid., 9 Apr. 1951, p. 23.
26. 45th Infantry Division Command Reports, Jan.–Apr., 1951; Franks, *Citizen Soldiers*, pp. 144–45; Craig, *Lifer!*, pp. 26–27; "45th In Hokkaido, Japan's Northern Island, Near Reds," *Daily Oklahoman*, 25 Apr. 1951, p. 1; "Last Of Ships Carrying 45th Reaches Port," ibid., 27 Apr. 1951, p. 1; and Berebitsky, *A Very Long Weekend*, pp. 128–29.

27. 45th Infantry Division Command Report, May, 1951, box 4261; 45th Division Artillery Command Report, May, 1951, box 4276; 179th Infantry Command Report, May, 1951, box 4281; 279th Infantry Command Report, May, 1951, box 4285; 145th AAA Battalion Command Report, May, 1951, box 4275; 120th Engineer Battalion Command Report, May, 1951, box 4277; and 245th Tank Battalion Command Report, May, 1951, box 4288, RG 407, NA.
28. See the 45th Infantry Division Command Reports for May–Sept., 1951, in boxes 4261–69, RG 407, NA; and Berebitsky, *A Very Long Weekend,* pp. 130–31.
29. 45th Infantry Division Command Reports, May–Sept., 1951; Allan P. Turner file, Korean War Survey; Robert W. Black Ranger Collection, USAMHI.
30. 45th Infantry Division Command Reports, May–Sept., 1951; "Officer School Discovers GIs Pull Fast One," *Daily Oklahoman,* 24 Jan. 1952, p. 1; and "OCS No Longer Ticket Home," ibid., 11 Mar. 1952, p. 4.

    The men discharged for expiration of enlistment were guardsmen whose guard term of enlistment had ended and who had served one year of active duty. This policy mainly affected junior enlisted men who joined the guard in 1948, the year it switched from six- to three-year enlistments. The policy did not sit well with some World War II veterans, who believed their prior wartime service should be factored into deciding which soldiers were released from active duty first ("National Guard Discharge Plan Irks 45th Men," ibid., 13 Aug. 1951, p. 8).
31. 45th Infantry Division Command Reports, May–Sept., 1951; and 45th Infantry Division Command Report, Oct., 1951, box 4270, RG 407, NA.
32. 245th Tank Battalion Command Reports, July and Aug., 1951, box 4228; 45th Infantry Division Command Reports, May–Sept., 1951; and 158th FA Battalion Command Reports, June and July, 1951, box 4278, RG 407, NA.
33. 45th Infantry Division Command Reports, May–Sept., 1951. The quote from Styron is in the September report. See also 179th Infantry Command Reports, May–Sept., 1951, boxes 4281–82; 279th Infantry Command Reports, May–Sept., 1951, boxes 4285–86; and 45th Division Artillery Command Reports, May–Sept., 1951, box 4276, RG 407, NA. See also these 1951 stories in the *Daily Oklahoman* written by Wayne Mackey during his stay with the division: "45th Is Fit, But Men Have Their Gripes," 12 Aug., p. 1; "Despite Gripes, 45th Training Has A Reason," 14 Aug., p. 20; and "Thunderbirds Are Ready If Korea Duty Comes," 19 Aug., p. 20.

    Regimental combat teams were a standard army task organization for combat composed of an infantry regiment, a field artillery battalion, and an engineer company.
34. 45th Infantry Division Command Reports, May–Sept., 1951. The hard-working public information office (PIO) made sure the folks back home knew of their efforts ("Staff Of 10 Publicizes Life With The Thunderbirds," *Daily Oklahoman,* 16 Aug. 1951, p. 15). In July, WKY-TV began a weekly program titled "The Forty-Fifth," using film sent by the 45th's PIO. (ibid., Sunday magazine, 22 July 1951, p. 20). "McLain Is Told Ridgway Plans No 45th Move," ibid., 4

Nov. 1951, p. 1; "45th Welcomes Jarman To Island," ibid., 17 Nov. 1951, p. 18; and "45th Takes Korea Duty News 'In Good Stride,' Says Jarman," ibid., 16 Dec. 1951, p. 1.

35. The 145th AAA's commander was transferred to the division artillery staff. His replacement was Lt. Col. Carl Santilli, a guardsman from Washington, D.C. Born in 1909, Santilli was commissioned in the D.C. guard in 1933, graduated from the Coast Artillery National Guard Officer's Course in 1940, and was mobilized in 1941 as a captain. He left active duty in 1946 as a lieutenant colonel and graduate of the Command and General Staff School. Appointed a lieutenant colonel in the D.C. guard in 1946, Santilli was mobilized in September, 1950, with the 260th AAA Group's headquarters (145th AAA Battalion Command Report, Sept., 1951; *National Guard Register 1951*).

    The 120th Engineer's new commander was Lt. Col. J. A. Murphy. Born in New York in 1915, Murphy graduated from City College of New York in 1938 and accepted a reserve infantry commission in 1939. He integrated into the Regular Army in 1947 as an engineer and graduated from the Engineer Officer Advanced Course in 1949 (120th Engineer Battalion Command Report, Sept., 1951; *Army Register 1951*).

36. 279th Infantry Command Report, July, 1951; 279th Infantry Command Report, Nov., 1951, box 4287, RG 407, NA; *National Guard Register 1951;* and "Officers Move Up In 45th Division," *Daily Oklahoman,* 25 Nov. 1951, p. 14.

37. For background on developments in Korea, see Hermes, *Truce Tent and Fighting Front,* chaps. 2–9.

38. See the following *Daily Oklahoman* stories "Two-Year Hitch For 45th Is All," 22 July 1951, p. 1; and 8 Aug. 1951, p. 7. On relations between the 45th and the Japanese, see "Japanese Friendly To 45th," ibid., 15 Aug. 1951, p. 19; 45th Infantry Division Command Reports, May–Sept., 1951; Berebitsky, *A Very Long Weekend,* 131–32; and Craig, *Lifer!,* p.26.

39. "Best Bet On 45th Is Korea," *Daily Oklahoman,* 5 Aug. 1951, p. 1; and "McLain Is Told."

40. Hermes, *Truce Tent and Fighting Front,* pp. 202–203; Collins, *War in Peacetime,* pp. 313–14; Collins to Ridgway, 24 May 1951 box 20, Ridgway Papers.

41. 45th Infantry Division Command Report, Nov., 1951, box 4272, RG 407, NA.

42. "Troops Cold To News of Move Into Battle," *Daily Oklahoman,* 31 Dec. 1951, p. 1.

43. "45th Takes Korea Duty News 'In Good Stride'"; "45th Units Going To Korea As Rotation Replacements; Division To Give Weary Troops Chance To Rest," ibid., 30 Nov. 1951, p. 1; "Left In Good Hands," ibid., Dec. 3, 1951, p.24; "45th In Combat Again; Entire Division Moves To Front Line Positions," ibid., 31 Dec. 1951, p. 1; and "Cavalry On Foot Has Unpleasant Memory Of 45th," ibid., 3 Dec. 1951, p. 8.

44. 45th Infantry Division Command Report, Nov., 1951.

45. Ibid., Dec., 1951, box 4274, RG 407, NA. The 189th FA Battalion arrived first because, as the division's general support artillery battalion, it was not paired

with an infantry regiment in an RCT. Also, the battalion's 155-mm howitzers would provide welcome additional firepower for I Corps, especially if the Chinese attempted to disrupt the switch.

46. 245th Tank, box 4288, and 120th Engineer, box 4277, Battalion Command Reports, Dec., 1951, RG 407, NA; 45th Infantry Division Command Report, Dec., 1951; and Berebitsky, *A Very Long Weekend,* pp. 137–38. On the state of bunkers left behind by the 1st Cavalry Division, see Headquarters, 45th Infantry Division, "Minutes of Commanders' Conference," 22 Jan. 1952, box 4289, RG 407, NA.

    The 1st Cavalry was not unique in its approach to fortifying its positions. There were many complaints—from the time the war stalemated in 1951 to its conclusion in 1953—that Americans were not willing to dig in properly (see S. L. A. Marshall, *Pork Chop Hill: The American Fighting Man in Action, Korea, Spring, 1953*).

    However, it is worth noting that the division had occupied its portion of Line Jamestown for only a little more than a month when it handed the position over to the 45th. The 1st Cavalry seized the position from the Chinese during heavy fighting in October at a cost of about 2,900 casualties (Hermes, *Truce Tent and Fighting Front,* pp. 98–102).

47. 45th Infantry Division Command Reports for Nov. and Dec., 1951; and Berebitsky, *A Very Long Weekend,* pp. 142–44.

    On 31 December, the 45th had 946 officers, 125 warrant officers, and 18,657 enlisted men. On CMS and the rotation system, see Hermes, *Truce Tent and Fighting Front,* pp. 186–87, 349–41. In December 1951, an officer needed 40 CMS points for rotation and an enlisted man, 36 points.

48. 45th Infantry Division Command Report, Dec., 1951; and "First 45th Division Casualty Reported," *Daily Oklahoman,* 18 Dec. 1951, p. 1.

49. 45th Infantry Division Command Report, Jan., 1952; and 45th Infantry Division Commanders' Conference, 6 Jan. 1952, box 4289, RG 407, NA. The many and varied problems that afflicted Regular Army divisions dispatched to Korea before the 45th arrived are covered in detail in Blair, *The Forgotten War.*

50. Lt. Gen. Raymond S. McLain to Lt. Gen. James A. Van Fleet, 5 Jan. 1952, and Van Fleet to McLain, 16 Feb. 1952, box 70, James A. Van Fleet Papers, Marshall Library (hereafter Van Fleet Papers).

    Maj. Gen. Henry I. Hodes, whose 24th Infantry Division was replaced on the MLR by California's 40th Infantry Division, wrote: "the men and many officers of this new unit are as fine as I have ever seen" (Hodes to Van Fleet, 28 Jan. 1952, box 69, Van Fleet Papers).

51. 45th Infantry Division Command Reports, Jan.–June, 1952, boxes 4289–304, RG 407, NA. See also Berebitsky, *A Very Long Weekend,* pp. 160–61.

52. This paragraph is based on the following Command Reports: 45th Division Artillery, Jan.–June, 1952, boxes 4324–25; and 158th FA Battalion, Dec., 1951–June, 1952, boxes 4278, 4331–32, RG 407, NA. The quote is from 45th Infantry Division Commanders' Conference, 6 Jan. 1952.

During the period January–May, 1952, the division artillery each month fired an average of 3,403 missions, expending 57,610 rounds. In June, when the division mounted a major effort to seize new outpost positions in front of its MLR, artillery action significantly increased: 5,138 missions expending 154,135 rounds. The 45th's counterbattery efforts were hampered by the failure of infantry units to forward timely shell reports; the age and wear of TPQ-3 countermortar radars inherited from the 1st Cavalry Division; and a shortage of trained counterfire specialists (Command Reports, 45th Division Artillery, Jan.–June, 1952).

53. 45th Infantry Division Commanders' Conferences, 6 and 21 Feb. 1952, box 4292, RG 407, NA. A major problem was bunkers built on the forward slope of hills without a connecting trench built to the hill's reverse slope. This forced troops to expose themselves to enemy fire when crossing the skyline to reach a bunker.

54. 45th Infantry Division Commanders' Conferences, Feb.–May, 1952. The quote is from the 21 Feb. conference.

Much work remained to be done on field fortifications in the division's sector when Maj. Gen. David L. Ruffner succeeded Styron. Four days after taking command, Ruffner noted at the 25 May commanders' conference: "I haven't seen one position that doesn't need a lot of work done on it. The Chinese are building up their artillery fire and a direct hit by a 155mm is not like a hand grenade."

55. Ibid., 22 Jan. 1952.

56. Ibid., 6 Jan. 1952.

57. 179th Infantry Command Report, Jan., 1952, box 4340, RG 407, NA. One fire mission called by the 179th was on a Chinese company unwise enough to assemble during the day in the open in view of their enemy. The 179th's casualties were 69 percent of the division's total battle casualties for January: 27 dead, 126 wounded, and 3 missing (45th Infantry Division Command Report, Jan., 1952).

58. Capt. John W. McClain, "After Action Report of Operation Baldy: Reinforced Company Sized Raid On A Fortified Position Conducted 24 Jan. 1952," copy in 279th Infantry Command Report, Jan., 1952, box 4346, RG 407, NA; 45th Infantry Division Command Report, Jan., 1952; and Berebitsky, *A Very Long Weekend*, pp. 146–48.

59. The quote first appears in the division's March command report and was repeated in the next two months' command reports. While it is counterfactual to place the 45th of 1952 into the war of 1950–51, it is obvious that the Thunderbirds as a unit never encountered situations anywhere near as intense as those faced by the 2nd Infantry Division during the Battle of Kunu-ri in late 1950 and the Chinese 1951 spring offensives, or by the 1st Marine Division at the Chosin Reservoir.

60. 45th Infantry Division Commanders' Conference, 6 Feb. 1952.

61. McClain, "After Action Report Of Operation Baldy"; 279th Infantry Command Report, Jan., 1952.

62. 179th Infantry Command Report, Jan., 1952. An account of the sometimes haphazard patrolling methods used by the 45th early in its service in Korea is provided by the 279th Infantry's 2d Lt. Carl Stevens in Berebitsky, *A Very Long Weekend,* pp. 150–52.
63. 2d Infantry Division Chief of Staff Journal, Jan., 1952, box 2731; and I Corps Command Report, Jan., 1952, RG 407, NA. The 2d Infantry Division's raid cost five dead and thirty-seven wounded. The tendency toward micromanagement became very strong in Eighth Army during the war's final eighteen months. See Maj. Mark M. Boatner III, "Oversupervision," *Military Review* 35, no. 5, pp. 3–5, and Anonymous, "Faithful to Our Trust," *Army Combat Forces Journal* 5, no. 5, pp. 18–21.
64. 45th Infantry Division Commanders' Conference, 21 Feb. 1952.
65. 179th Infantry Command Report, Feb., 1952, box 4340; and 279th Infantry Command Report, Feb., 1952, box 4347, RG 407, NA; 179th Infantry, "Training Memorandum Number 1," 2 Feb. 1952, with Annex 3, 8 Feb. 1952, and Annex 4, 10 Feb. 1952, box 393, RG 338, NA. The quote is from the 179th's command report. For examples from other U.S. divisions, see 25th Infantry Division Command Report, Jan., 1952, box 3876; and 2d Infantry Division Command Report, Jan., 1952, box 2731, RG 407, NA.
66. 179th and 279th Infantry Command Reports, Feb., 1952. The 279th's Raiders were organized and trained by 2d Lt. Carl Stevens. His account of the platoon's training and operations is in Berebitsky, *A Very Long Weekend,* pp. 166–67. For other examples of this phenomena, see William C. Kimball, "We Need Intelligence and Raider Platoons," *Infantry Quarterly,* Jan., 1953, pp. 42–50.
67. 179th Infantry Command Reports, Feb. and Mar., 1952; 279th Infantry Command Report, Mar., 1952, box 4347, RG 407, NA. For an account that shows why good patrolling was vital in the type of combat the 45th encountered in Korea and what proper preparation and good leadership could accomplish, as well as the difficulties patrols faced, see 179th Infantry, "After Action Report of Patrol #5 and Company 'L' Outpost on the Night of 8–9 March 52," 10 Mar. 1952, copy in 179th Infantry Command Report, Mar., 1952.
68. 45th Infantry Division Command Report, Feb., 1952; and ibid. Mar., 1952, box 4295, RG 407, NA.
69. 279th Infantry Command Report, Apr., 1952, box 4349; and 179th Infantry Command Reports, Apr. and May, 1952, box 4341, RG 407, NA; 45th Infantry Division Command Reports, Apr. and May, 1952; and Craig, *Lifer!,* pp. 51–53.
70. 45th Infantry Division Command Report, Mar., 1952 box 4295, RG 407, NA; and 179th Infantry Command Report, Mar., 1952. Accounts of the battle are in Gugeler, *Combat Actions in Korea,* pp. 222–35; and Berebitsky, *A Very Long Weekend,* pp. 162–66. I Corps had ordered the 45th to occupy Eeire over the protests of both Colonel Daugherty and General Styron that the position was too vulnerable.
71. This account of the defense of Hill 200 is based on 6th Historical Detach-

ment, "Night Defense of Hill 200, 26 May 1952, by 2d Battalion, 179th Infantry, 45th Division," copy in 179th Infantry Command Report, May, 1952, box 4341, RG 407, NA; and 179th Infantry, "After Action Report Of A Battalion Size Attack on '200' Night 25–26 May 1952," box 394, RG 338, NA.

72. Robert A. Howes Diary, USAMHI. The next day, Howes received a phone call from Styron congratulating the new lieutenant on his performance. All three of the 45th's general officers attended a critique of the patrol that afternoon.
73. 279th Infantry Command Reports, Mar. and Apr., 1952.
74. The Chinese examples are from 6th Historical Detachment, "Night Defense of Hill 200." A review of the monthly command reports of all U.S. Army infantry regiments in Korea for the period Jan., 1952–July, 1953, shows that the 45th's experience was typical.
75. 6th Historical Detachment, "Night Defense of Hill 200."
76. The 279th's Colonel Murphy complained of the war's "indecisive nature," as did the *Daily Oklahoman* (279th Infantry Command Report, Mar., 1952; and "Flight From Korea," 25 Jan. 1952, p. 10).
77. 45th Infantry Division Commander's Conference, 21 Feb. 1952; 45th Division Artillery Command Reports, Apr. and May, 1952; 279th Infantry Command Report, May, 1952; and Craig, *Lifer!*, p. 52.

    In August, 1952, shortly after the 45th ceased to exist as a guard division, the shortage of qualified replacements meant that some soldiers in the 158th FA Battalion had to be retained beyond their rotation dates in order for the unit to meet the "minimum requirements of combat effectiveness." The battalion noted that this was a "great detriment to good morale and defeats the purpose for which the personnel were held" (Command Report, Aug., 1952, box 4332, RG 407, NA).

    A good account of infantry combat during this period and how the battlefield stalemate and individual rotation affected unit performance is Rudolph W. Stephens, *Old Ugly Hill: A G.I.'s Fourteen Months in the Korean Trenches, 1952–1953*. A draftee, Stephens served in the 2d Infantry Division and fought twice on Old Baldy. Set in 1953, *Pork Chop Hill* (United Artists, 1959) dramatically portrays the nature of the stalemated war. The practice of fixed tours of duty in a combat zone became a major factor affecting unit performance during the Vietnam War. See Ronald Spector, *After Tet: The Bloodiest Year in Vietnam*, chap. 2.
78. In early March, 1952, concerned about a possible Chinese spring offensive, Van Fleet advised Ridgway to replace both guard commanders with regular officers to provide the 40th and 45th with stronger leadership and to increase their combat effectiveness (memorandum for the diary, 11 Mar. 1952, Korean War Jan.–Apr., 1952 special file, box 20, Ridgway Papers).
79. 45th Infantry Division Commanders' Conferences, Jan.–May, 1952. The quotes are from the 22 January and 1 April conferences. Responses to the USAMHI Korean War Veterans Survey from former Thunderbirds vary in their evaluation of the division's leadership. Veterans' comments range from

"excellent" to "fair" to "spotty" to "not adequate." John B. Blount, a 1950 ROTC Distinguished Military Graduate who joined the 45th as a replacement platoon leader in February, 1952, pointed out that "because we were a National Guard division, I had some learning to do about who was in charge. It wasn't always the officer. Their interpersonal relationships were tricky."

80. *Thunderbird Review;* 189th FA Battalion Command Report, Jan., 1952, box 4339, RG 407, NA; *National Guard Register 1951;* and *Army Register 1951.* Fifteen of the 180th Infantry's guard officers were Army Air Forces officers in World War II, and five of the guard officers were not World War II veterans.
81. Ibid. One of the 189th FA's junior officers was a Pennsylvania guardsman stripped from his mobilized antiaircraft battalion and sent to FECOM as an individual replacement. The 180th Infantry had 1 Regular Army officer, 2 guard officers (1 from Florida and 1 from Arkansas), and 29 reserve, ROTC, or OCS officers.
82. Respondents to the USAMHI Korean War Veterans Survey often differed in their evaluations of the leadership provided from each of these commissioning sources, but many commented on the youth and inexperience of ROTC and OCS lieutenants. The problems that army personnel planners faced in providing enough junior officers are described in Kendall, "An Inflexible Response," pp. 210–15, 220–28.
83. 189th FA Battalion Command Reports, Mar.–June, 1952; 179th Infantry Command Reports, Jan.–May, 1952; and Howes Diary.
84. Craig, *Lifer!*, pp. 33–34; John Blount file, Korean War Survey. Also see 158th FA Battalion Command Report, June, 1952, box 4325, RG 407, NA.
85. 45th Infantry Division Command Report, Jan., 1952; and 279th Infantry Command Report, Apr., 1952. The 45th was not the only U.S. division concerned about the quality of enlisted replacements. See 2d Infantry Division Chief of Staff Journal, Jan., 1952; and 40th Infantry Division Command Report, May, 1952, box 4103, RG 407, NA, for examples of what was a widespread concern.
86. 45th Infantry Division Command Reports, Feb. and Mar., 1952. The first quotation is from the 158th FA Battlion's February, 1952, command report, and the second is from Styron's indorsement to the battalion's April, 1952, command report, both in box 4331, RG 407, NA. The 40th Infantry Division also established a school system to train replacements it received (40th Infantry Division Command Report, May, 1952).
87. 45th Infantry Division Command Reports, Mar.–June, 1952. The quote is from the March report. Of the total graduated by 31 May, 310 were from the leadership course. The division artillery complained that not only was it getting few qualified NCOs, but that there were few potential NCOs among the enlisted replacements received (45th Division Artillery Command Report, June, 1952, box 4325, RG 407, NA).
88. 45th Division Artillery Command Reports, Apr., 1952, box 4324; and May, 1952, box 4325, RG 407, NA; and 45th Infantry Division Command Reports,

Apr.–June, 1952. In July, the division consolidated all its schools at Camp Casey, site of the Infantry Training Replacement Center.

89. On Plan Counter, see 45th Infantry Division Command Report, June, 1952, box 4304, RG 407, NA; and Hermes, *Truce Tent and Fighting Front*, pp. 285–94. Division battle casualties in June were 55 officers and 949 enlisted, of whom 8 officers and 176 enlisted were killed in action. The operation's success, according to the June command report, was the result of "adequate training and preparation for the defense of newly-won objectives" and that "platoon and company commanders were directed to take immediate and forceful measures in the defense of newly won objectives." American firepower played a key role in stopping the Chinese counterattacks. In June, the 45th Division Artillery fired 154,135 rounds. Although Plan Counter was implemented after the division had lost almost all of its Oklahoma guardsmen, Oklahomans still took an active interest and pride in the 45th's accomplishments. See "45th Wins Raging Hill Fight With Reds," *Daily Oklahoman*, 13 June 1952, p. 1; and "Red Battalion Smashed on 45th's Hills," ibid., 14 June 1952, p. 1.
90. "45th Veterans Dock in Seattle; Heading for Sill," *Daily Oklahoman*, 14 Apr. 1952, p. 1.
91. See 45th Infantry Division Command Reports, Jan.–June, 1952, for the PIO section's activities. On coverage of the division in Oklahoma, see the following 1952 *Daily Oklahoman* articles: "McLoud 45th Man Wounded in Korea," 16 Jan., p. 15; "45th Shivers As Mercury Dips in Korea," 20 Jan., p. 1; "45th Tastes Blood On Korean Hillside," 27 Jan., p. 1; "Ambush Plan Almost Misfires," 6 Feb., p. 4; "City 45th Soldier Recovering After Wounds in Korea," 9 Feb., p. 2; "16-Year-Old Veteran Home From Korea," 15 Feb., p. 1; "Four 45th Men Receive Medals," 18 Feb., p. 7; "Oklahoma City's Guard Company Lives and Fights in Rugged Korean Mountains," 18 Feb., p. 24; "BY THE WAY, HIS LEGS ARE GONE," Sunday magazine, 9 Mar., p. 22; and "TV Report on 45th To Include City Men," 10 Mar., p. 17.
92. See the following 1952 articles in the *Daily Oklahoman:* "Army to Keep Name of 45th," 1 Jan., p. 6; "45th Soldiers To Get Release Month Earlier," 16 Feb., p. 2; "45th Near the Top On Release Plan," 6 Mar., p. 16; "Men to Replace 45th Begin Duty," 11 Mar., p. 5; Roy Stewart's "Report From Washington" column, 16 Mar., p. 1B; "Plans for 45th Release Speeded Up, First men Start Home in a Week," 17 Mar., p. 1; "They're Coming Home!" 26 Mar., p. 1; "First Homeward-Bound Members of Thunderbird Division Are Listed," 27 Mar., p. 7; and "Praise and Farewell," 28 Mar., p. 4.
93. 45th Infantry Division Command Reports, Jan.–June, 1952.
94. 45th Infantry Division and Division Artillery Command Reports, Apr. and May, 1952.

General Ruffner, a field artilleryman, was born in 1896 and graduated from the Virginia Military Institute in 1917. He took over the 45th after commanding the 5th Armored Division, a training unit, from January to May, 1952. Ruffner's brother, Maj. Gen. Nick Ruffner, commanded the 2d Infantry

Division in Korea from January to September, 1951. Brig. Gen. Dulaney received his second star while commanding the 3d Infantry Division, but in early October, 1952, he was relieved of command and sent back to the ZI, where he took command of the 47th Infantry Division, a mobilized guard division that had lost most of its guardsmen to levies. Dulaney was relieved when his corps commander and General Van Fleet lost confidence in him after the 3d Infantry Division performed poorly in several engagements (File 9, box 87, Van Fleet Papers).

95. MacGregor, *Integration of the Armed Forces,* pp. 442–46. Although General Ridgway followed the army staff's decision to temporarily exempt the 40th and 45th, it caused significant problems for other divisions trying to absorb the large number of black replacements being shipped to Eighth Army from the ZI.
96. 45th Infantry Division Adjutant General's Report, Oct., 1951, box 4271; 45th Infantry Division G1 Report, Nov., 1951, box 4272; 45th Infantry Division Adjutant General's Report, Dec., 1951, box 4274; and 45th Infantry Division Command Reports, Mar. and June, 1952. "Class II" was the army's euphemism for black soldiers.
97. 279th Infantry Command Report, July, 1952, box 4351, RG 407, NA; and 45th Infantry Division Commanders' Conference, 17 May 1952. On the reactions within the division to racial integration, see the USAMHI Korean War Survey; Craig, *Lifer!,* pp. 40–41; and Berebitsky, *A Very Long Weekend,* pp. 254–55.
98. See the following 1952 *Daily Oklahoman* stories: "Thunderbirds Head For Home on Double," 6 Apr., p. 10; "Red Carpet Is Out For Thunderbirds," 13 Apr., p. 1; "45th Veterans Dock in Seattle; Heading for Sill," 14 Apr., p. 1; "No Bands, But Happy Families Are Plenty For 45th Arrivals," 15 Apr., p. 1; "Civvies Just Three Days Away," 18 Apr., p. 6; "Hobart General To Get Welcome With 45th GIs," 13 June, p. 19; and "'Mister' Styron Resumes Golf, Buying Cotton," 22 June, p. 6.
99. "First of Thunderbirds Say 'Call Us Mister'," *Daily Oklahoman,* 23 Apr. 1952, p. 1. The reasons for and the mechanics of the NGUS arrangement are explained by the army chief of staff in J. Lawton Collins, "1 in 1," *National Guardsman,* June, 1952, pp. 2–4. Roy P. Stewart told readers that the NGUS solution to the question of possession of the 45th's lineage was "Solomon-like" and that "both sides win the argument" ("Report From Washington," *Daily Oklahoman,* 6 Apr. 1952, p. 1B).
100. "Praised 45th Gets Battle Flags Back," *Daily Oklahoman,* 26 Sept. 1954, p. 1.

Chapter 6. Back to Europe

1. David T. Fautua, "The 'Long Pull' Army: NSC 68, the Korean War, and the Creation of the Cold War U.S. Army," *Journal of Military History* , no. (Jan., 1997): pp. 93–120. The quote is from page 97.
2. Adjutant general, "Directory and Station List of the United States Army,

4 Sept. 1951," copy in U.S. Army War Center of Military History, Washington, D.C.

3. "Unit History, HQ & HQ DET 37th Ordnance Bn," undated mss., copy in 37th Ordnance Battalion Historical Files, box 13 (Ordnance), RG 338, NA; and *National Guard Register 1951.*
4. 37th Ordnance Battalion Command Report, 1950, box 4725, RG 407, NA.
5. Ibid., 1951, box 5328, RG 407, NA.
6. Ibid.
7. Ibid.
8. Ibid.
9. Ibid.
10. Ibid., 1952, box 6259, RG 407, NA.
11. Murphy, "Chronology of 272nd Field Artillery Battalion"; *Register of Graduates of the United States Military Academy;* and 272d FA Battalion Command Report, 1951, box 5192, RG 407, NA.
12. Murphy, "Chronology of 272nd Field Artillery Battalion."
13. 272d FA Battalion Command Report, 1951. The quotes are from Murphy, "Chronology of 272nd Field Artillery Battalion."
14. 272d FA Battalion Command Report, 1951.
15. Murphy, "Chronology of 272nd Field Artillery Battalion;" and 272d FA Battalion Command Report, 1951.The boards of inquiry were convened in accordance with Army Regulation 605-200, "Officer Demotion and Elimination."
16. *National Guard Register 1951.*
17. 272d FA Battalion Command Report, 1951.The quotes are from Murphy, "Chronology of 272nd Field Artillery Battalion."
18. "Camp McCoy Race Policy Vilest in U.S," *Pittsburgh Courier,* 9 June 1951, p. 1.
19. "Officers Railroaded," *Pittsburgh Courier,* 6 Oct. 1951, p. 1.
20. Ibid.
21. "Officer 'Purge' Probe Launched," *Pittsburgh Courier,* 13 Oct. 1951, p. 1. The Department of the Army had placed racial integration in the ZI on hold while waiting to see how the process worked in overseas commands (MacGregor, *Integration of the Armed Forces,* pp. 453–54.
22. All three captains served as infantry officers during World War II, and were commissioned into the 272d in 1947. Two were in the 372d Infantry when it mobilized in 1941. The lieutenant served as an enlisted man during the war, then enlisted in the 272d in 1949 and was commissioned after the alert notice in August, 1950. None had completed the Field Artillery Officer Basic Course before mobilization (Murphy, "Chronology of 272nd Field Artillery Battalion"; *National Guard Register 1951*). According to George, Col. Edward Gourdin, the former commander of the 372d Infantry and the 272d FA, had brought some of the transferred officers to meet with Governor Dever ("Army Whitewashes Brass Charges At Camp McCoy," *Pittsburgh Courier,* 27 Oct. 1951, p. 1). Gourdin later became the first African American general officer in the National Guard.

23. Murphy, "Chronology of 272nd Field Artillery Battalion."
24. The first quote is from Murphy, "Chronology of 272nd Field Artillery Battalion," and the second is from the 272d FA Battalion Command Report, 1951.
25. Col. W. A. Enemark, 35th FA Group, "Combat Effectiveness Report for Assigned Forces," 25 Dec. 1951, 272d FA Historical Files, box 305 (Field Artillery); and 35th FA Group Command Report, 1951, 35th FA Group Historical Files, box 9 (Field Artillery), RG 338, NA.
26. 272d FA Battalion Command Report, 1952, box 6090, RG 407, NA; 35th FA Group Command Report, 1852, 35th FA Group Historical Files, box 10 (Field Artillery), RG 338, NA; and "Army Removes Colonel Accused Of Railroading Negro Officers," *Pittsburgh Courier,* 5 Apr. 1952, p. 1.
27. Ibid.; the quote is from 272d FA Battalion Command Report, 1952. Memorandum from General Burress to Brigadier General Gard, 18 Jan. 1952, letter file vol. 2, box 11, Withers A. Burress Papers, USAMHI.
28. MacGregor, *Integration of the Armed Forces,* pp. 450–53.
29. 272d FA Battalion Command Report, 1952; 35th FA Group Command Report, 1952; *Army Register 1951;* and "Army Removes Colonel." Available evidence does not indicate whether Murphy was relieved for cause, but his career stalled out after this assignment.
30. 272d FA Battalion Command Report, 1952.
31. Ibid.
32. 194th FA Battalion Command Reports for 1951, box 6083, and 1952, box 6083, RG 407, NA.
33. For the 28th's history before 1946, see Ent, ed., *First Century;* American Battle Monuments Commission, *28th Division Summary of Operations in the World War;* Bradley and Blair, *A General's Life,* pp. 108–13, 287; Stanton, *Order of Battle,* pp. 104–106; Edward G. Miller, *A Dark and Bloody Ground: The Hürtgen Forest and the Roer River Dams, 1944–1945,* pp. 53–92; and Hugh M. Cole, *The Ardennes: Battle of the Bulge,* pp. 173–227.
34. Strickler, *Memoirs,* pp. 2–150; and *National Guard Register 1951.*
After giving up command of the 28th in 1942, Edward Martin remained keenly interested in guard matters and in the division. He kept up a regular correspondence with key guard leaders like Ellard Walsh and Milton Reckord. Martin and Strickler also corresponded regularly during this period. In a 9 Feb. 1945 letter to Martin, Strickler wrote: "it has been a long time since I came into the Division through your efforts. You always said someday I would get a regiment. So I did but by the hard way." See boxes 29, 33, 37, and 39, Official Papers, General Correspondence 1943–46, Martin Papers. The correspondence between Strickler and Martin is in box 37. Martin won a U.S. Senate seat in the 1946 election.
35. Seiverling, "Post World War II–Korean War"; Strickler, *Memoirs,* p. 161; *National Guard Register 1939;* and *National Guard Register 1951.* According to Strickler, just before mobilization the division artillery commander was "lost" to the 28th.

36. Strickler, *Memoirs*, p. 161; Henry K. Fluck Oral History, USAMHI; *National Guard Register 1939;* and *National Guard Register 1951.*
37. *National Guard Register 1951.*
38. Seiverling, "Post World War II–Korean War"; Strickler, *Memoirs*, pp. 150–60; Fluck Oral History; Kafkalas Oral History; 28th Infantry Division Command Report, 1950, box 3983, RG 407, NA; "U.S. Call Adds Fervor To 28th's War Drills," *Philadelphia Inquirer*, 3 Aug. 1950, p. 2; "Duff, Gen. Clark Witness Final Review Of 28th," ibid., 7 Aug. 1950, p. 1; and "28th Breaks Camp; Men On Way Home For 30-Day Leave," *Pittsburgh Post-Gazette*, 8 Aug. 1950, p. 2. The quote from Clark is in "28th Division Proves It's Ready For Duty."
39. 28th Division Artillery, 109th Infantry, and 109th FA, 229th FA, and 899th AAA Battalion Command Reports, 1951, box 3994; 112th Infantry, and 103d Engineer and 628th Tank Battalion Command Reports, 1951, box 3995; and 103d Medical Battalion Command Report, 1951, box , RG 407, NA; Strickler to Chamberlain, 4 Sept. 1951; and Rehm, "Report of Final Inspection."
40. 109th and 112th Infantry Regiment, and 109th FA, 229th FA, 628th Tank, 103d Engineer, and 103d Medical Battalion Command Reports, 1951; Strickler, *Memoirs*, pp. 169–70; "Armistice Day Parade Marks 28th's Farewell," *Pittsburgh Post-Gazette*, p. 4.
41. 109th and 112th Infantry Regiment, and 109th FA, 229th FA, 628th Tank, 103d Engineer, and 103d Medical Battalion Command Reports, 1951; Strickler, *Memoirs*, pp. 170–72.
42. 28th Infantry Division Command Report, 1952, box 3996; 628th Tank Battalion Command Report, 1952, box 4022; and 899th AAA Battalion Command Report, 1952, box 4014, RG 407, NA.
43. 28th Infantry Division Command Report, 1952.
44. 28th Division Artillery Command Report, 1952, box 4015; 109th and 110th Infantry Command Reports, 1952, box 4019; and 112th Infantry Command Report, 1952, box 4020, RG 407, NA.
45. 229th FA Battalion Command Report, 1952, box 4019, RG 407, NA; and 28th Infantry Division and 109th Infantry Command Reports, 1952.
46. The first quote is from 28th Infantry Division Command Report, 1952; the others are from 28th Infantry Division Commanders' Conference, 19 Mar. 1952, box 3996; and memorandum from G1 to Division Chief of Staff, 19 Aug. 1952, box 3997, RG 407, NA.

    The division artillery administered firing battery ATTs to the direct support battalions in March. Two batteries in the 109th FA and one in the 107th FA failed. The 229th FA Battalion's batteries passed their ATTs in January, but the battalion failed its ATT in March (109th FA Battalion Command Report, 1952, box 4019, RG 407, NA; and 28th Division Artillery and 229th FA Battalion Command Reports, 1952).
47. 28th Infantry Division, 28th Division Artillery, 109th and 112th Infantry Regiment, and 628th Tank Battalion Command Reports, 1952.

    In 1952 the division artillery graduated 440 men from its NCO Academy, and 455 graduated from the 109th Infantry's NCO Academy. Units in Germany after World War II pioneered formal training for army noncommissioned officers. See Ernest F. Fisher, Jr., *Guardians of the Republic: A History of the Noncommissioned Officer Corps of the U.S. Army*, pp. 281–300.

48. 28th Infantry Division Command Report, 1952. In 1953 and 1957, groups within the Pennsylvania Republican Party tried to make Strickler the party's candidate for governor, but both efforts failed because of bitter factionalism (Strickler, *Memoirs*, pp. 190–250).
49. 28th Infantry Division Command Report, 1952.
50. Ibid.
51. Ibid.
52. 28th Division Artillery and 899th AAA and 229th FA Battalion Command Reports, 1952. The average Seventh Army soldier had a fifth-grade-level education; it was mandatory that soldiers not at that level take classes during the duty day to reach it.
53. 628th Tank Battalion and 109th Infantry Command Reports, 1952. Nicholas Kafkalas, commanding a battalion in the 110th Infantry by the spring of 1952, said of integration only that "it worked out" (Kafkalas Oral History).
54. 109th Infantry, 28th Division Artillery, and 103d Engineer and 899th AAA Battalion Command Reports, 1952. In October, the 229th FA Battalion received 183 replacements from the ZI without the required MOSs: 100 infantrymen, 60 cooks, and 23 fresh graduates of basic training (229th FA Battalion Command Report, 1952).
55. 28th Infantry Division Command Report, 1952.
56. Ibid.; and 28th Division Artillery, and 103d Engineer, 628th Tank, 899th AAA, and 229th FA Battalion Command Reports, 1952.
57. General Strickler to Colonel Fluck, 2 Oct. 1952, Henry K. Fluck Papers, USAMHI (hereafter Fluck Papers); Kafkalas Oral History.
58. Seiverling, "Post World War II–Korean War;" Fluck Oral History; Lt. Gen. F. A. Weber to Col. H. K. Fluck, 24 Oct. and 2 Dec. 1952, Fluck Papers.

    A major selling point for Fluck was that the position was full-time. In 1953, Pennsylvania was one of the few states to do this. The commander of U.S. Army Europe wrote Weber in early 1953 about Fluck's release from active duty: "While I was reluctant to approve his request because he is such a good man, I felt that in the best interests of everyone concerned it was the thing to do. He was an outstanding commander while he had the 110th Infantry" (Lt. Gen. Manton Eddy to Lt. Gen. Weber, 16 Feb. 1953, Fluck Papers).

Chapter 7. Lost in the Zone of the Interior

1. See Appendix A for the distribution of mobilized Army National Guard units as of Sept., 1951.
2. The army mobilized two other guard MP battalions during 1950: Missouri's 174th, which remained in the ZI, and Kansas's 175th, which deployed to Ger-

many. The five were the only organized MP battalions in the guard in 1950. National Guard Bureau, "Induction and Release"; National Guard Bureau, *Annual Report of the Chief, 1950;* and adjutant general, "Directory and Station List."

3. *National Guard Register* for 1939 and 1951; 163d MP Battalion Command Report, 1950, box 9 (Military Police), RG 338, NA; 168th and 171st MP Battalion Command Reports, 1950, box 4718, RG 407, NA; and William F. Dyer, comp., "168th M.P. Battalion." William Donnegan of Brentwood, Tenn., a veteran of the 168th, kindly provided a copy of Dyer's work.
4. 163d, 168th and 171st MP Battalion Command Reports, 1950; O&M Branch, National Guard Bureau, "National Guard Units Alerted by Order of the Secretary of the Army," file 325.42 general, box 1083, Army National Guard Bureau Decimal File 1949–50, RG 168, NA; *National Guard Register 1951;* Provost Marshal Section, "Report of Inspection of Military Police."
5. 163d, 168th, 171st MP Battalion Command Reports, 1951; Provost Marshal Inspection, "Report of Inspection of Military Police."
6. 163d and 171st MP Battalion Command Reports, 1951.
7. Provost Marshal Section, "Report of Staff Visit and Inspection of Military Police"; 171st MP Battalion Command Report, 1951; 171st MP Battalion Headquarters Journal, 1952, and 163d MP Battalion Command Report, 1952, box 9 (Military Police), RG 338, NA.
8. 163d, 168th, and 171st MP Battalion Command Reports, and 171st MP Battalion Headquarters Journal, 1952, box 9 (Military Police), RG 338, NA.
9. National Guard Bureau, *Annual Report of the Chief, 1950,* pp. 54–74. On early postwar air defense planning, see Moeller, "Vigilant and Invincible," pp. 4–12. I wish to thank Patricia M. Rhodes, Air Defense Artillery Branch Historian at Ft. Bliss, Texas, for bringing this article to my attention. On war planning, see Steven T. Ross, *American War Plans, 1945–1950: Strategies for Defeating the Soviet Union.*
10. National Guard Bureau, "Induction and Release"; inspector of artillery, "Report of Inspection of AAA Units"; *Headquarters Units and Operations Detachments, 51st AAA Brigade,* p. 33; Stanton, *Order of Battle,* p. 430; and *National Guard Register 1951.*
11. 197 AAA Group Command Report, 1950; 209th AAA Group Command Report, 1950, box 4589; and 703d, 710th, and 715th AAA Battalion Command Reports, 1950, box 4576, RG 407, NA; Donald Perkins and Christie files, Korean War Survey; Walter Hayes to Brig. Gen. George M. Carter, 11 Aug. 1950, Hayes Papers; inspector of artillery, "Report of Inspection of AAA Units"; and *National Guard Register 1951.*
12. 197th AAA Group Command Report, 1951; 209th AAA Group Command Report, 1951, box 4589; Command Report, 1951, 703d AAA Battalion, box 4789, RG 407, NA; Command Report, 1951, 705th AAA Battalion, box 4789, RG 407, NA; Command Report, 1951, 713th AAA Gun Battalion, box 4789, RG 407, NA; Command Report, 1951, 715th AAA Battalion, box 4789, RG

407, NA; Command Report, 1951, 736th AAA Battalion; Howell "Report of Staff Visit to Camp Stewart"; adjutant general, "Directory and Station List." Units at other training sites reported similar problems. See 746th AAA Gun Battalion Command Report, 1951, box 4790, RG 407, NA.

13. Adjutant general, "Directory and Station List"; National Guard Bureau, "Induction and Release"; memorandum from Lt. Col. Page E. Smith to chief, Army Field Forces, Subject: "Report of Staff Visit to AAA Units at Fort Totten, N.Y.; Fort Tilden, N.Y.; Fort Banks, Massachusetts; Fort Devens, Massachusetts; Indiantown Gap Military Reservation, Pennsylvania; and Headquarters Eastern Army Antiaircraft Command, Middleton, N.Y. during the period 7–11 August 1951," box 28 (Combat Arms Advisory Group), RG 337, NA. For the experiences of AAA units mobilized in 1951, see 685th AAA Gun Battalion Command Report, 1951, box 4788, RG 407, NA; and 718th AAA Gun Battalion Command Report, 1951, box 4789, RG 407, NA.
14. Moeller, "Vigilant and Invincible," p. 12; 51st AAA Brigade Command Report, 1952, box 5539, RG 407, NA; Christie file, Korean War Survey; and 197th AAA Group and 713th AAA Gun Battalion Command Reports, 1951.
15. 209th AAA Group and 705th AAA Gun Battalion Command Reports, 1951; Smith, "Report of Staff Visit to AAA Units."
16. 197th AAA Group and 703d AAA Gun Battalion Command Reports, 1951; and Smith, "Report of Staff Visit to AAA Units."
17. 197th AAA Group and 713th and 736th AAA Gun Battalion Command Reports, 1951; and 715th AAA Gun Battalion Command Report, 1952, box 5523, RG 407, NA.
18. 197th and 209th AAA Group, and 713th, 736th, and 745th AAA Gun Battalion Command Reports, 1951; Smith, "Report of Staff Visit to AAA Units."
19. 705th, 715th, and 736th AAA Gun Battalion Command Reports, 1951; and Smith, "Report of Staff Visit to AAA Units."
20. 197th AAA Group and 713th, 736th, and 745th AAA Gun Battalion Command Reports, 1951; Smith, "Report of Staff Visit to AAA Units;" and Hayes to Col. L. M. Hart, 18 May and 19 July, 1951, Hayes Papers. The loss of trained personnel to overseas levies also affected AAA units in the western half of the United States (746th AAA Gun Battalion Command Report, 1951).
21. 209th AAA Group, and 703d, 715th, and 736th AAA Gun Battalion Command Reports, 1951.
22. 197th AAA Group and 703d and 736th AAA Gun Battalion Command Reports, 1951.
23. 197th AAA Group and 705th, 703d, 713th, and 736th AAA Gun Battalion Command Reports, 1951; Smith, "Report of Staff Visit to AAA Units"; and Perkins file, Korean War Survey.
24. 703d AAA Gun Battalion Command Report, 1951.
25. 197th AAA Group Command Report, 1952, box 5559, RG 407, NA; and 715th AAA Gun Battalion Command Report, 1952.
26. 197th AAA Group and 715th AAA Gun Battalion Command Reports, 1952; and

713th AAA Gun Battalion Command Report, 1952, box 5523, RG 407, NA.

27. 197th AAA Group and 713th, 715th, and 736th AAA Gun Battalion Command Reports, 1952; Hayes to Col. Elliot C. Goodwin, 30 Jan. 1952, Hayes Papers.
28. 197th AAA Group and 713th, 715th, 736th AAA Gun Battalion Command Reports, 1952; and 745th, box 5524, and 685th, box 5520, AAA Gun Battalion Command Reports, 1952, RG 407, NA.
29. Moeller, "Vigilant and Invincible," pp. 17–18; *Army Times*, 8 Mar. 1952, p. 8; and 685th, 713th, and 715th AAA Gun Battalion AAA Gun Battalion Command Reports, 1952.

    Looking ahead to inevitable postwar budget cuts and hoping to utilize the experience guardsmen gained while in federal service, the army in early 1951 had begun planning for integrating some guard units into the ZI's AAA defense. With expected improvements in early warning systems, the army believed there would be sufficient notice to alert guard units in time to defend against Soviet bombers. However, the first battery assigned to this program did not become operational until March, 1954 (Timothy Osato, "Militia Missilemen: The Army National Guard in Air Defense, 1951–1967" [Ent Air Force Base, Colo.: Headquarters, U.S. Army Air Defense Command, 1968], pp. 13–55).
30. On the many problems the Soviets faced in creating an effective intercontinental bomber force, see Steven J. Zaloga, *Target America: The Soviet Union and the Strategic Arms Race, 1945–1964*, pp. 63–88.
31. Gov. Frank Lausche to Mrs. Bessie Mutersbaugh, 21 Feb. 1952, Adjutant General 1952 general file, box 8, Lausche Papers.
32. Ralph D. Cole and W. C. Howells, *The Thirty-Seventh Division in the World War, 1917–1918*, chaps. 3–7; American Battle Monuments Commission, *37th Division Summary of Operations in the World War;* Riehm, ed., *Pictorial History*, p. 10; Stanley A. Frankel, *The 37th Infantry Division In World War II;* and Donnelly, "Keeping the Buckeye in the Buckeye Division."
33. Information Office, National Guard Bureau, *General Officers of the National Guard of the United States* (Washington: 15 Apr. 1950), pp. 48–49; Ohio adjutant general, General Orders no. 59, 6 Sept. 1973, "Announcement of Death: Maj. Gen. Leo M. Kreber," copy in library of National Guard Association of the United States, Washington D.C.; and *National Guard Register 1951*.
34. *National Guard Register 1951;* NGB, Information Office, *General Officers*, p. 18; Riehm, *Pictorial History*, p. 6; Alden Stilson, Jr., response to author's "37th Division, 1950–1954 Survey," 3 June 1993 (hereafter Stilson, "Survey"); Information Office, *General Officers*, pp. 18, 89; and Riehm, *Pictorial History*, p. 6.
35. Riehm, *Pictorial History*, pp. 18–19; and *National Guard Register 1951*.
36. *National Guard Register 1951*.
37. Ibid.
38. Alden Stilson file, box 8, Lausche Papers; *Columbus Evening Dispatch*, 17 and 18 May 1952.

39. 37th Infantry Division Command Report, 1952, box 4024, RG 407, NA; G3, "Readiness Dates of Major Units." Emphasis in original.
40. 37th Infantry Division Command Report, 1952; "Tac Units to Give Basic," *Army Times*, 6 Sept. 1952, p. 1; "Army Faces Wide Cuts," *New York Times*, 17 July 1952, p. 4; file G3/322 (Cases 141–60), box 197 RG 319, NA.
41. This story faded from public view and no charges were ever filed.
42. "IG Finds 'Buckeye' Spirit OK," *Army Times*, 20 Dec. 1952, p. 1.
43. *Newsweek*'s comment on the letter was that the article "referred to the 37th only to illustrate a situation in several National Guard units. Of course, the 37th, like other divisions, has its excellent officers too."
44. 37th Infantry Division Command Report, 1952; memorandum from assistant chief of staff, G3, to chief of staff, U.S. Army, 7 Mar. 1952, Subject: "Operational Readiness of Major Units in the U.S.," file G3/320.2, box 86, RG 319, NA.
45. 37th Infantry Division Command Report, 1 Jan. 1953–30 Apr. 1953, box 4024, RG 407, NA.
46. Ibid.
47. Ibid.; General Orders file, 37th Division 1953 record set, box 92, RG 338, NA.
48. 4th Army Headquarters, 7 July 1953, Subject: "Reconstitution of the Training Base, Supporting Units and General Reserve During FY 1954," file G3/320.2 (Cases 101–20), box 87, RG 319, NA; file 314.7 Military Histories, Headquarters, 10th Division, 1954, box 80, RG 338, NA; "Kreber Waves 'Bye' At Review," *Army Times*, 26 Dec. 1953, p. 20. *Columbus Evening Dispatch*, 5 Jan. 1954.
49. The 37th moved to Fort Riley when the army deactivated Polk in the postwar drawdown. See the Ohio adjutant general's annual reports for 1953 and 1954 for details on the shadow 37th Infantry Division. On the return of the 37th's colors to Ohio, see *National Guardsman*, Aug., 1954, pp. 20–21; *Columbus Evening Dispatch*, 18 June 1954; and the Ohio adjutant general's 1954 annual report.
50. 37th Infantry Division Command Report, 1952.

Chapter 8. Untold Hardships and Suffering

1. See "Antiquated National Guard," *TIME*, 27 Aug. 1951, p. 22; and "Bleats From the Guard," ibid., 5 Nov. 1951, p. 22.
2. This description is based on a review of the newspapers mentioned in the notes.
3. Although written after the armistice, the best expression of guardsmen who advocated carrying the war to the Chinese mainland is in Hill, *Minute Man in Peace and War*, pp. 503–14. For a review of the literature on why opposition to the Korean War did not create the same turmoil as opposition to the Vietnam War, see Gary L. Huey, "Public Opinion and the Korean War," in Lester H. Brune, ed., *The Korean War: Handbook of the Literature and Research*, pp. 409–17.

4. Gen. Mark Clark, "'. . . the difference between victory and defeat . . .'," *National Guardsman,* Sept., 1950, pp. 12–13.
5. Ellard A. Walsh, "It Might Have Been," *National Guardsman,* Sept., 1950, pp. 10–11.
6. For examples of mobilized guardsmen keeping guardsmen at home updated, see the Hayes and William H. Abendroth Papers, USAMHI; general file, box 39, John S. Fine Papers, PHMC, Pennsylvania; and box 8, Frank Lausche Papers. On politicians and adjutants general visiting units in the ZI, see "Posting the Guard" in 1951 and 1952 issues of the *National Guardsman.* On visits to units overseas, see the discussion in chapter three of the 45th Infantry Division history; Kerry L. Diminyatz, "The 40th Infantry Division in the Korean Conflict: The Employment of the California National Guard in an Undeclared War" (master's thesis, Sonoma State University, 1990), pp. 49–52; 101st Signal, box 5404, and 955th FA, box 5219, Battalion Command Reports, 1951, RG 407, NA. For examples of the NGA's watchfulness concerning legislation, see "Transcript of Conference," 3 Apr. 1952, Subject: "Carrier Unit Bill," Secretary of the General Staff Decimal File 1951–52, box 720, RG 319, NA; and issues of the *National Guardsman* for 1950–53. During the annual hearings on the army's budget held by the House Appropriations Committee, General Walsh and other NGA officials would present testimony designed to protect the guard from what they saw as threats posed by Uptonian regulars.
7. Maj. Gen. Fleming to Gen. J. Lawton Collins, 21 July 1950, National Guard Bureau Decimal File 1949–50, box 1059, RG 168, NA; Ellard Walsh to all adjutants general and commanding generals, 26 July 1950, file 1, box 1, Department of Military Affairs, RG 19, PHMC; memorandum for record, 24 Oct. 1950, Subject: "Remarks of Chief of Staff to the National Guard Association Conference on 23 Oct.," box 16, Ridgway Papers.
8. This and the preceding paragraph are based on the *Official Proceedings of the National Guard Association of the United States General Conference 1950,* pp. 49–50.
9. Gen. Mark Clark to army commanders, 13 Dec. 1950, Army Field Forces Decimal File 1949–50, box 304, RG 337, NA.
10. "Full Call-Up of National Guard Asked To Bar Draft of Lads, 18, and End Doubts," *New York Times,* 17 Dec. 1950, p. 30.
11. For the army's justification of individual rotation in Korea, see Earl D. Johnson, "Rotation," *National Guardsman,* Mar., 1952, pp. 2–6. Johnson was assistant secretary of the army for manpower and reserve forces. On the NGA's position, see Ellard A. Walsh, "The President's Report," *National Guardsman,* Nov., 1951.

    Some lower-ranking guardsmen in units deployed to Korea, and their families, shared Walsh's preference for unit over individual rotation. See file 325, Secretary of the General Staff Decimal File 1951–52, box 720, RG 319, NA.
12. McLain, "Comments on Certain Aspects of the National Guard."
13. Frank Pace to Governor Lausche, 30 June 1952, box 8, Lausche Papers.

14. Memorandum from adjutant general to Governor Lausche, 19 July 1952, ibid.
15. Kreber to Lausche, 22 July 1952, ibid.
16. Assistant Secretary of the Army Fred Korth to Governor Lausche, 22 Aug. 1952, ibid.

    The 37th was not the only mobilized Ohio guard unit that feared destruction of unit integrity; the enlisted men of Battery A, 182d AAA Gun Battalion wrote Lausche asking for his help in preventing the breakup of the unit while in federal service (memorandum from Lausche to Kreber, 7 Aug. 1951.
17. Derthick, *National Guard in Politics*, p. 109. Political figures from other states also complained about levies for overseas service made on their mobilized guard units. See Secretary of the General Staff Decimal File 1951–52, box 720, RG 319, NA; CINCFE Correspondence E–H file, box 18, Ridgway Papers; Roberts, "History of the Utah National Guard," pp. 461–68; and Brig. Gen. George C. Moran to Gov. G. Mennen Williams, 19 Sept. 1951, box 375, Williams Papers.
18. Not as common a request was the one made on behalf of Charles Curtis. Although a major general in the Pennsylvania guard, Curtis returned to active duty with his 51st AAA Brigade as a brigadier general—his federally recognized rank. A fellow Allentown resident wrote Duff's assistant secretary asking if there was any way to get Curtis inducted as a major general, as "we, in Allentown, know that he is most deserving" (Robert Feustermacher to Charles F. Rugaber, 17 Aug. 1950, box 13, Governor 1947–51 subject file, Duff Papers.
19. Examples of this correspondence can be found in subject files, boxes 7 and 8, Fine Papers; box 8, Lausche Papers; and box 373, Williams Papers.
20. Mrs. Ann Martin to Governor Fine, Sept. 16, 1951, file 15, box 8, subject file, Fine Papers. Lieutenant Allan was in the 967th AFA Battalion, which had entered federal service in May, 1951. The correspondence on this case is in file 13, ibid.

    With the battle lines in Korea largely static after mid-1951, the army was more likely to approve hardship and dependency discharges. See the command reports of units discussed in chaps. 4 to 7.
21. This story can be followed in the Alden Stilson file in box 8 of the Lausche Papers. The quotes are taken from Stilson's 2 Dec. 1952 letter to Lausche and Lausche's 4 Dec. 1952 reply. Kreber's first recommendation concerning future mobilizations was that the "period spent at service schools prior to activation be in addition to the period of service for which the unit is inducted" (37th Infantry Division Command Report, 1952, box 4024, RG 407, NA).
22. Sgt. Ellsworth Linker to Governor Fine, 19 Aug. 1951, file 14, box 8, subject file, Fine Papers; and Sgt. George Harris to Governor Scott, 4 Sept. 1951, box 80, Scott Papers.

    Some in the Utah field artillery battalions sent to Korea had similar sentiments. See Sen. Arthur Watkins to Secretary of the Army Frank Pace, 18 Sept. 1951, file 325, box 720, Secretary of the General Staff Decimal File 1951–52,

RG 319, NA. A variation on this theme arose from the army's decision to allow enlisted guardsmen to leave active duty a year after their guard enlistment expired. This meant that some young men who had enlisted in 1947 and 1948 returned home in 1951 and 1952 before many World War II veterans were eligible to do so. See Sgt. Percy Snater to Governor Fine, 5 Jan. 1952, file 16, box 8, subject file, Fine Papers. Thirteen other members of the 28th Infantry Division cosigned Snater's letter.

23. First Lt. F. J. Noecker to Governor Fine, 12 Apr. 1951, file 15, box 8, subject file, Fine Papers. See also Mrs. Edna Everette to Governor Fine, 2 Aug. 1951, file 12, ibid. On the draft, see Flynn, "Draft and College Deferments," pp. 369–85. About 78 percent of all students who took the test qualified for deferment. Flynn cites public opinion polling showing that angry guardsmen and their families were in the minority concerning this issue—particularly after the war stalemated in mid-1951—when a majority of Americans approved of student deferments.
24. Although the 31st never left the ZI, many of its guardsmen were levied as individual replacements for service in Korea. Stennis's letter is in Case 276, file 353, Assistant Chief of Staff G3 Decimal File 1951, box 495, RG 319, NA. See also Case 608, box 501, ibid.; "G.I. Kin To End Protests," *New York Times,* 27 Feb. 1952, p. 2; Mrs. Celeste Rau to Governor Fine, 28 Sept. 1951, file 16, box 8, subject file, Fine Papers; and Mrs. Ruth E. Fetzer to Governor Lausche, 21 Feb. 1951, box 8, Lausche Papers.
25. Ridgway, memorandum for record, 8 Mar. 1951, Subject: "General MacArthur's 7 Mar. 51 Visit," special file Dec. 50–Mar. 51, box 20, Ridgway Papers. Congressman Tackett's telegram to Ridgway is in box 17, Ridgway Papers. Department of the Army involvement is in Case 346, file 353, Assistant Chief of Staff G3 Decimal File 1951, box 497, RG 319, NA. See also the following 1951 articles in the *Northwest Arkansas Times:* "Guard Training Being Pushed Says Trimble," 28 Feb. p. 1; "Guard To Receive Full Training Says MacArthur," 3 Mar., p. 1; "Proud Of Honor In Going To Korea Says Member of 936th National Guard Unit," 20 Mar., p. 1; and "Sergeant in Korea Reports Guard Units Well Supplied With Rations and Equipment," 21 Mar., p. 1.
26. O'Daniel to Lt. Gen. James A. Van Fleet, 21 Sept. 1951, box 71, Van Fleet Papers.
27. "Hanna, Who Scored Korea Policy, Out," *New York Times,* 6 May 1951, p. 3; "Army Relieves General," *New York Times,* 7 May 1951, p. 3; "Pace Disputes Doubt U.N Can Defeat Reds," *New York Times,* 10 June 1952, p. 1; and "U.S. Army Reprimands Hudelson On Korea," *New York Times,* 14 June 1952, p. 2.
28. For the return of guardsmen from federal service, see chaps. 4 to 7. In one instance, it was a state politician—not the army—who triggered an uproar on this issue. Illinois's governor proposed dropping the mobilized 44th Infantry Division from the state's troop list, merging its returned guardsmen into the 33d Infantry Division, which had not been mobilized. A regimental commander in the 44th resigned his guard commission, charging that the gover-

nor and the state's adjutant general were turning the Illinois National Guard into "nothing more than a political football" ("Protests Rip Illinois Guard," *Army Times*, 16 Jan. 1954, p. 18.

29. Letters, telegrams, and petitions opposing this policy are in file 325, box 720, Secretary of the General Staff Decimal File 1951–52, RG 319, NA.
30. This paragraph is based on Brig. Gen. John E. Walsh to Brig. Gen. William H. Abendroth, 30 Jan. 1952, personal file Oct., 1951–Mar., 1952, Abendroth Papers; and Harris to Scott, 4 Sept. 1951. For comments from adjutants general concerning the harmful effects of partial guard mobilization and stripping of mobilized units, see Rose, "Training the National Guard." Rose solicited comments on this issue from adjutants general, although he does not identify which adjutants general made which comments. Also see the Kafkalas and Weber Oral Histories.
31. Memorandum from Col. Philip C. Pack to Gov. G. Mennen Williams, 8 Nov. 1951, box 375, Mennen Papers; Governor Williams to General Moran, 7 Nov. 1951, ibid.; General Moran to Governor Williams, 11 May 1953, box 380, ibid.; "Status of Enlisted Pers (Army National Guard)," copy in box 384, ibid.; memorandum from Earl D. Johnson to the army chief of staff, 6 Mar. 1951, and memorandum from Gen. Wade H. Haislip to Johnson, 18 May 1951, both in Chief of Staff Decimal File 1951–52, box 720, RG 319, NA; Milton A. Reckord to John A. Hannah, 7 May 1953, Chief of Staff Decimal File 1953, box 815, ibid.; and Walsh, "Address to the Army War College," pp. 70–74.
32. "'Dixie' Division Band Keeps Confederate Gray"; and "Army OKs Uniforms of 'Rebels'." The *Pittsburgh Courier*'s Collins George, touring posts in the ZI to check on the status of Jim Crow in the army, visited Fort Jackson, the 31st's postmobilization training site. He did not bother checking on the 31st, "where the policy of white degeneracy runs full blast" (*Pittsburgh Courier*, 21 Apr. 1951, p. 1).
33. Gov. W. Kerr Scott to Sgt. George H. Harris, 10 Oct. 1951, box 80, Scott Papers.

BIBLIOGRAPHY

Archives

National Archives, College Park, Md.

Record Group 168. National Guard Bureau.

Record Group 319. Army Staff.

Record Group 337. Headquarters Army Ground Forces/Army Field Forces.

Record Group 338. Army Commands.

Record Group 407. The Adjutant General's Office.

U.S. Army Military History Institute, Carlisle Barracks, Pa.

W. H. Abendroth Papers.

Army War College Student Theses Collection.

T. L. Berry Oral History.

Robert W. Black Ranger Collection.

Withers A. Burress Papers.

Henry K. Fluck Papers and Oral History.

Francis S. Greenlief Oral History.

Walter J. Hayes Papers.

Robert A. Howes Diary.

Nicholas P. Kaflalas Oral History.

Korean War Veterans Survey.

Matthew B. Ridgway Papers.

Daniel B. Strickler Papers.

LaVern Weber Oral History.

Stewart Yeo Papers.

Bentley Historical Library, Ann Arbor, Mich.

G. Mennen Williams Papers.

George C. Marshall Library, Virginia Military Institute, Lexington, Va.

George C. Marshall Papers.

James A. Van Fleet Papers.

National Guard Association of the United States, Washington, D.C.
Official Proceedings of the NGAUS General Conference, 1947–52.
Ellard A. Walsh Papers.
North Carolina Department of Archives and History, Raleigh, N.C.
W. Kerr Scott Papers.
Ohio Historical Society, Columbus, Ohio.
Robert S. Beightler Papers.
John W. Bricker Papers.
Frank Lausche Papers.
Pennsylvania Historical and Museum Commission, Harrisburg, Pa.
James H. Duff Papers.
John S. Fine Papers.
Edward Martin Papers.
Record Group 19. Department of Military Affairs.
Rhode Island State Archives, Providence, R.I.
Records of the Adjutant General's Office.

Manuscripts

Black, Lowell D. "The Negro Volunteer Militia Units of the Ohio National Guard, 1870–1954." Ph.D. diss., Ohio State University, 1976.

Diminyatz, Kerry L. "The 40th Infantry Division in the Korean Conflict: The Employment of the California National Guard in an Undeclared War." Master's thesis, Sonoma State University, 1990.

Dolph, Cyrus A. III. "The National Guard." Student thesis, U.S. Army War College, 1951.

Gandy, Raymond E., Jr. "Are the 'Minute Men' Fast Enough? A Historical Look At Pre and Post Mobilization Training." Individual study project, U.S. Army War College, 1991.

Gray, David R. "Black and Gold Warriors: U.S. Army Rangers During the Korean War." Ph.D. diss., Ohio State University, 1992.

Grodecki, Thomas S. "From Powder River to Soyang: The 300th Armored Field Artillery in Korea, A Case Study of the Integration of the Reserve Components into the Active Force." U.S. Army Military History Institute, Carlisle Barracks, Pa. (Hereafter USAMHI.)

Heymont, I., and E. W. McGregor, "Review and Analysis of Recent Moblizations of U.S. Army Reserve Components." Study prepared for the U.S. Army Strategic Studies Institute by the Research and Analysis Corp. of McLean, Va., 1972.

"Historical Resume, Division Force Structure, Active and Reserve, 1935–1963." Washington: Office of the Chief of Military History, 1963.

Kendall, John M. "An Inflexible Response: United States Army Manpower Mobilization Policies, 1945–1957." Ph.D. diss., Duke University, 1982.

Kyle, Ronald K. "Killer of Communists, Saver of Soldiers: U.S. Army Field Artillery in the Korean War, 1950–1953." Master's thesis, Ohio State University, 1995.

McLain, Raymond S. "Comments on Certain Aspects of the National Guard, 8 August 1951." USAMHI.
"Mobilization in the Korean Conflict." Study prepared for the Office of the Assistant Secretary of Defense for Manpower, Reserve Affairs, and Logistics by the Historical Evaluation and Research Organization of Dunn Loring, Va., 1982.
National Guard Bureau. "Induction and Release of Army National Guard Units, 1950–1956." U.S. Army Center of Military History, Washington, D.C.
O'Donnell, Thomas W. "Training the National Guard." Student thesis, U.S. Army War College, 1955.
Osato, Timothy. "Militia Missilemen: The Army National Guard in Air Defense, 1951–1967." Ent Air Force Base, Colo.: U.S. Army Air Defense Command, 1968.
Roberts, Richard C. "History of the Utah National Guard: 1894–1954." Ph.D. diss., University of Utah, 1973.
Rose, William B. "Training the National Guard." Student thesis, U.S. Army War College, 1954.
Stilwaugh, Elva. "Personnel Policies in the Korean Conflict." Washington: Office of the Chief of Military History, n.d.
Southward, Charles L. "Training the National Guard." Student thesis, U.S. Army War College, 1954.

Books

American Battle Monuments Commission. *28th Division Summary of Operations in the World War.* Washington: U.S. Government Printing Office, 1944.
———. *37th Division Summary of Operations in the World War.* Washington: U.S. Government Printing Office, 1944.
Berebitsky, William. *A Very Long Weekend: The Army National Guard in Korea, 1950–1953.* Shippensburg, Pa.: White Mane, 1996.
Blair, Clay. *Ridgway's Paratroopers: The American Airborne in World War II.* New York: Dial Press, 1985.
———. *The Forgotten War: America in Korea, 1950–1953.* New York: Times Books, 1987.
Boettiger, Wilfred O. *An Antiaircraft Artilleryman From 1939 to 1970.* N.p., 1990.
Bowers, William T., William M. Hammond, and George L. MacGarrigle, *Black Soldier, White Army: The 24th Infantry Regiment in Korea* (Washington: Center of Military History, 1996).
Bradley, Omar, and Clay Blair. *A General's Life.* New York: Simon and Schuster, 1983.
Chief, Army Field Forces. *The National Guard Manual Basic.* Washington: Government Printing Office, 1948.
———. *Notes for Instructors and Adviser-Instructors, Army National Guard.* Washington: Army Field Forces, February, 1950.
Civilian Components Policy Board, Office of the Secretary of Defense. *Progress and Status of the Civilian Components U.S. Armed Forces, 1 July 1950.* Washington: Office of the Secretary of Defense, 1950.

Cole, Hugh M. *The Ardennes: Battle of the Bulge.* U.S. Army in World War II. Washington: Office of the Chief of Military History, 1965.

Ralph D. Cole and W. C. Howells, *The Thirty-Seventh Division in the World War, 1917–1918.* Columbus, Ohio: 37th Division Veterans Association, 1923.

Collins, J. Lawton. *War in Peacetime.* Boston: Houghton Mifflin, 1969.

Controvich, James T. *United States Army Unit Histories: A Reference and Bibliography.* Manhattan, Kans.: Military Affairs/Aerospace Historian, 1983.

Conversations with General J. Lawton Collins. Fort Leavenworth, Kans.: U.S. Army Combat Studies Institute, 1990

Cooper, Jerry. *The Militia and the National Guard Since Colonial Times: A Resource Guide.* Westport, Conn.: Greenwood Press, 1993.

———, with Glenn Smith. *Citizens as Soldiers: A History of the North Dakota National Guard.* Fargo: The North Dakota Institute for Regional Studies, North Dakota State University, 1986.

Craig, William T. *Lifer! From Infantry to Special Forces.* New York: Ivy Books, 1994.

Cropp, Richard. *The Coyotes: A History of the South Dakota National Guard.* Mitchell, S.D.: Education Supply, 1962.

Crossland, Richard B., and James T. Currie. *Twice the Citizen: A History of the U.S. Army Reserve, 1908–1983.* Washington: Office of the Chief, Army Reserve, 1984.

Dastrup, Boyd L. *King of Battle: A Branch History of the U.S. Army's Field Artillery.* Fort. Monroe, Va.: U.S. Army Training and Doctrine Command, 1992.

Davis, Oscar E. *The Thunderbird: A 45th Division History.* Tokyo: Toppan, 1953.

Day, William W. IV, *The Running Wounded: A Personal Memory of the Korean War.* Riverton, Wyo.: Big Bend Press, 1990.

Department of the Army. *Field Manual 100-5, Field Service Regulations: Operations.* Washington: Government Printing Office, August, 1949.

Department of the Army. *Official Army Register for 1951.* Washington: Government Printing Office, 1951.

Derthick, Martha. *The National Guard in Politics.* Cambridge, Mass.: Harvard University Press, 1965.

Directory and Station List of the United States Army, 4 September 1951. Washington: Adjutant General's Office, 1951.

Doughty, Robert A. *The Evolution of U.S. Army Tactical Doctrine, 1946–1978.* Fort Leavenworth, Kans.: U.S. Army Combat Studies Institute, 1979.

Ent, Uzal W., ed. *The First Century: A History of the 28th Infantry Division.* Harrisburg, Pa.: 28th Infantry Division, 1979.

Epley, William W. *America's First Cold War Army, 1945–1950.* Arlington, Va.: Institute of land Warfare, 1993.

Fisher, Ernest F., Jr. *Guardians of the Republic: A History of the Noncommissioned Officer Corps of the U.S. Army.* New York: Ballantine Books, 1994.

Fogelson, Robert M. *America's Armories: Architecture, Society and Public Order.* Cambridge: Harvard University Press, 1989.

Fowles, Brian D. *A Guard in Peace and War: The History of the Kansas National Guard, 1854–1987.* Manhattan, Kans.: Sunflower University Press, 1989.

Frankel, Stanley A. *The 37th Infantry Division In World War II.* Washington: Infantry Journal Press, 1948.

Franks, Kenny. *Citizen Soldiers: Oklahoma's National Guard.* Norman: University of Oklahoma Press, 1984.

G3 Historical Section, 45th Infantry Division. *Thunderbird: 45th Infantry Division.* Tokyo: Toppan, 1953.

Gabel, Christopher R. *The U.S. Army GHQ Maneuvers of 1941.* Washington: Center of Military History, 1991.

Gifford, Jack J. "The U.S. Army in the Korean War." In *The Korean War: Handbook of The Literature and Research,* ed. Lester H. Brune. Westport, Conn.: Greenwood Press, 1996.

Gough, Terence J. *U.S. Army Mobilization and Logistics in the Korean War: A Research Approach.* Washington: Center of Military History, 1987.

Gross, Charles J. *Prelude to the Total Force: The Air National Guard, 1943–1969.* Washington: Office of Air Force History, 1985.

Gugeler, Russell A. *Combat Actions in Korea.* 1954. Reprint, Washington: Center of Military History, 1987.

Haraty, Peter H., ed. *Put the Vermonters Ahead: A History of the Vermont National Guard, 1764–1978.* Burlington, Vermont: Queen City Printers, 1978.

Hawk, Robert. *Florida's Army: Militia/State Troops/National Guard, 1565–1985.* Englewood, Fla.: Pineapple Press, 1986.

Headquarters Units and Operations Detachments, 51st AAA Brigade. Atlanta: Albert Love, 1951.

Heller, Charles E., and William A. Stofft, eds. *America's First Battles, 1775–1965.* Lawrence: University Press of Kansas, 1986.

Hermes, Walter G. *Truce Tent and Fighting Front.* U.S. Army in the Korean War. Washington: Office of the Chief of Military History, 1966.

Hill, Jim Dan. *The Minute Man in Peace and War: A History of the National Guard.* Harrisburg, Pa.: Stackpole, 1964.

Huey, Gary L. "Public Opinion and the Korean War." In *The Korean War: Handbook of the Literature and Research,* ed. Lester H. Brune. Westport, Conn.: Greenwood Press, 1996.

Huston, James A. *Guns and Butter, Powder and Rice: U.S. Army Logistics in the Korean War.* Toronto: Associated University Presses for Susquehanna University Press, 1989.

Index To Tables of Organization and Equipment and Tables of Organization. Washington: Adjutant General's Office, 1 August 1950.

Information Office. *A Review of Progress of the National Guard Through a Continuous Program of Public Information, 1 September 1947–1 January 1950.* Washington: National Guard Bureau, 1950.

———. *General Officers of the National Guard of the United States.* Washington: National Guard Bureau, 15 Apr. 1950.

Johnson, Charles, Jr. *African American Soldiers in the National Guard: Recruitment and Deployment during Peacetime and War.* Westport, Conn.: Greenwood Press, 1992.

Kunz, Virginia Brainard. *Muskets to Missiles: A Military History of Minnesota.* Saint Paul: Minnesota Statehood Centennial Commission, 1958.

Little, Roger W. "Buddy Relations and Combat Performance." In *The New Military: Changing Patterns of Organization,* ed. Morris Janowitz. Chicago: Russell Sage Foundation, 1964.

MacGregor, Morris J. *Integration of the Armed Forces, 1940–1965.* Washington: Center of Military History, 1981.

Mahon, John K. *History of the Militia and the National Guard.* New York: Macmillan, 1983.

Mansoor, Peter R. *The GI Offensive in Europe: The Triumph of American Infantry Divisions, 1941–1945.* Lawrence: University Press of Kansas, 1999.

Marshall, S. L. A. *Pork Chop Hill: The American Fighting Man in Action, Korea, Spring, 1953.* New York: William Morrow, 1956.

Miller, Edward G. *A Dark and Bloody Ground: The Hürtgen Forest and the Roer River Dams, 1944–1945.* College Station: Texas A&M University Press, 1995.

Mossman, Billy C. *Ebb and Flow: November 1950–July 1951.* U.S. Army in the Korean War. Washington: Center of Military History, 1990.

National Guard Association of the United States. *The Nation's National Guard.* Buffalo, N.Y.: Baker, Jones, Hausauer, 1954.

National Guard Bureau. *Annual Report of the Chief, National Guard Bureau.* Washington: Government Printing Office, 1946–54.

———. *Official National Guard Register Army for 1951.* Washington: Government Printing Office, 1952.

Nelson, Guy. *Thunderbird: A History of the 45th Infantry Division.* Oklahoma City: 45th Infantry Division Association, 1970.

Newland, Samuel J. *The Militia's Role in National Defense: A Historical Perspective.* Carlisle Barracks, Pa.: U.S. Army Strategic Studies Institute, 1987.

Oldham, Donald E. *The Finance Section: World War II and Korean War.* Oklahoma City: 45th Infantry Division Museum, 1994.

Palmer, Robert R., Bell I. Wiley, and William R. Keast. *The Procurement and Training of Ground Combat Troops.* Washington: Office of the Chief of Military History, 1948.

Paxton, A. G. *Three Wars and a Flood: The Memoirs of Lieutenant General A. G. Paxton.* N.p., n.d.

Pictorial History, Thirty-Seventh Infantry Division, Camp Polk, Louisiana, 1952. Columbus, Ohio: F. J. Heer, 1952.

Pogue, Forrest C. *George C. Marshall: Education of a General, 1880–1939.* New York: Viking, 1963.

Register of Graduates of the United States Military Academy. West Point, N.Y.: Association of Graduates United States Military Academy, 1974.

Report of Mobilization of the North Dakota National Guard, Korean Emergency. Bismarck, N.D.: Office of the Adjutant General, 1952.

Roll On 28th: Twenty-Eighth Infantry Division United States Army, Camp Atterbury, Indiana, 1950–1951. Atlanta: Albert Love, 1951.

Ross, Steven T. *American War Plans, 1945–1950: Strategies for Defeating the Soviet Union.* Reprint, London: Frank Cass, 1996.
Schnabel, James F. *Policy and Direction: The First Year.* U.S. Army in the Korean War. 1972. Reprint, Washington: Center of Military History, 1992.
Scurr, Kenneth R. *Reflections of Service: 147th Field Artillery Group, 1917–1977.* N.p, n.d.
Seiverling, Richard. "Post World War II–Korean War." In *The First Century: A History of the 28th Infantry Division,* ed. Uzal W. Ent. Harrisburg, Pa.: 28th Infantry Division, 1979.
Sligh, Robert Bruce. *The National Guard and the National Defense: The Mobilization of the Guard in World War II.* New York: Praeger, 1992.
Spector, Ronald. *After Tet: The Bloodiest Year in Vietnam.* New York: Free Press, 1993.
Stanton, Shelby L. *Order of Battle: U.S. Army World War II.* Novato, Calif.: Presidio Press, 1984.
Stephens, Rudolph W. *Old Ugly Hill: A G.I.'s Fourteen Months in the Korean Trenches, 1952–1953.* Jefferson, N.C.: McFarland, 1995.
Strickler, Daniel B. *The Memoirs of Lieutenant General Daniel Bursk Strickler.* Lancaster, Pa.: Forry and Hacker, 1972
Sullivan, John A. *Toy Soldiers: Memoirs of a Combat Platoon Leader in Korea.* Jefferson, N.C.: McFarland, 1991.
Thunderbird Review. Atlanta: Albert Love, 1952.
Twenty-Eighth Infantry Division, United States Army: Europe 1951–1952. Atlanta: Albert Love, 1953.
War Department Pamphlet no. 20-6, *Command of Negro Troops.* Washington, D.C.: War Department, 29 February 1944.
Weaver, James H. *45th Division Training Regiment.* Oklahoma City: 45th Infantry Division Museum, 1989.
Weigley, Russell F. *Towards an American Army: Military Thought from Washington to Marshall.* New York: Columbia University Press, 1962.
———. *History of the United States Army.* Enlarged ed. Bloomington: Indiana University Press, 1984.
Westover, John G. *Combat Support in Korea.* Washington: Combat Forces Press, 1955; Washington: Center of Military History, 1987.
Whitesides, Joe E. *204th Field Artillery Battalion in Korea.* N.p., n.d.
Williams, Warren J., ed. *A Revolutionary War: Korea and the Transformation of the Postwar World.* Chicago: Imprint, 1993.
Witt, Tillman P. *Moving On: The Story of the 279th Infantry Regiment.* Oklahoma City: 45th Infantry Division Museum, 1980.
Zaloga, Steven J. *Target America: The Soviet Union and the Strategic Arms Race, 1945–1964.* Novato, Calif.: Presidio Press, 1993.

Articles

Anonymous, "Faithful to Our Trust." *Army Combat Forces Journal* 5, no. 5 (December, 1954): pp. 18–21.

"Antiquated National Guard." *TIME*, 27 August 1951, p. 22.
"Bleats from the Guard." *TIME*, 5 November 1951, p. 22.
Boatner, Mark M. III. "Oversupervision." *Military Review* 35, no. 5 (August, 1955): pp. 3–5.
Bryer, Paul J. "Campus on the Carpet." *National Guardsman* 4, no. 7 (July, 1950): pp. 17–20.
Cocklin, Robert F. "Fish Or Cut Bait." *Combat Forces Journal* 4, no. 1 (August, 1953): pp. 26–27.
Colby, Elbridge, "What of the National Guard?" *Infantry Journal* 60, no. 2 (February, 1947): pp. 9–15.
Collins, J. Lawton, "1 in 1." *National Guardsman* 6, no. 6 (June, 1952): pp. 2–4.
Clark, Mark W. "'. . . the difference between victory and defeat . . .'" *National Guardsman* 4, no. 9 (September, 1950): pp. 12–13.
Cramer, Kenneth F. "M-Day and the New National Guard." *Army Information Digest* 2, no. 9 (September, 1947): pp. 2–7.
———. "The National Guard in the Post-War Military Establishment." *Military Review* 28, no. 3 (June, 1948): pp. 3–9.
———. "The National Guard—Our Modern Minutemen." *Coast Artillery Journal* 91, no. 4 (July–August, 1948): pp. 27–29.
Dixon, Sherwood. "A Militiaman's Farewell to Arms." *Infantry Journal* 58, no. 5 (May, 1946): pp. 15–18.
———. "The Impossible Takes Longer." *Infantry Journal* 62, no. 4 (April, 1948): pp. 27–30.
Donnelly, William M. "Keeping the Buckeye in the Buckeye Division: Major General Robert S. Beightler and the 37th Infantry Division, 1940–1945." *Ohio History*, no. 106 (winter–spring, 1997): pp. 42–58.
Edmonds, Maj. Gen. James E. "It's Up To Congress." Pt. 2. *National Guardsman* 3, no. 1 (January, 1949): pp. 8–10, 29.
Fautua, David T. "The 'Long Pull' Army: NSC 68, the Korean War, and the Creation of the Cold War U.S. Army." *Journal of Military History* 61, no. 1 (January, 1997): pp. 93–120.
"The First to Fight." *Newsweek*, 22 September 1947, pp. 27–28.
Flynn, George Q. "The Draft and College Deferment During the Korean War." *The Historian* 51 (May, 1988): pp. 369–85.
Hudelson, Daniel M., Kenneth R. Scurr, and Kenneth F. Cramer. "M-Day . . . The Reality." *National Guardsman* 5, no. 2 (February, 1951): pp. 2–3, 16–21.
Hunter, Bob. "Southern Pine." *National Guardsman* 5, no. 10 (October, 1951): pp. 5–8.
Jacobs, Bruce. "The National Guard: Our Really Ready Reserve." *ARMY* 7, no. 1 (August, 1956): pp. 19–26.
———. "The National Guard: Policy-Makers and Policy Problems." *ARMY* 7, no. 2 (September, 1956): pp. 49–55.
———. "Out of the Ashes of Victory." *National Guardsman* 25, no. 8 (August–September, 1971): pp. 2–13.

———. "Tensions Between the Army National Guard and the Regular Army." *Military Review* 73, no. 10 (October, 1993): pp. 5–17.

Johnson, Earl D. "Rotation." *National Guardsman* 6, no. 3 (March, 1952): pp. 2–6.

Kimball, William C. "We Need Intelligence and Raider Platoons." *Infantry Quarterly* 42, no. 1 (January, 1953) pp. 42–50.

Kirkland, Farris R. "Soldiers and Marines at Chosin Reservoir: Criteria for Assignment to Combat Command." *Armed Forces and Society* 22, no. 2 (winter, 1995–96): pp. 257–74.

Markle, Harry A. "We Did It, But—." *National Guardsman* 3, no. 2 (February, 1949): pp. 24–26.

Martin, Thomas L. "New National Guard Training Plan." *Infantry Journal* 62, no. 9 (September, 1948): pp. 32–36.

Milton, Hugh M. "A Respectable Posture of Defense." *Military Review* 33, no. 9 (December, 1953): pp. 3–8.

Moeller, Stephen P. "Vigilant and Invincible: United States Army Air Defense Command." *Air Defense Artillery*, May–June, 1995.

"National Guard Gets New Boss." *LOOK*, 18 November 1947, pp. 104.

"No Other Choice: A Statement of the Army's Position Regarding Replacement Levies Against National Guard Units." *National Guardsman* 5, no. 11 (November, 1951): pp. 2.

"Operation 88,888." *Collier's*, 8 November 1947, pp. 94.

Richey, T. G. "What Lies Ahead?" *National Guardsman* 4, no. 10 (October, 1950): pp. 18–21.

Scurr, Kenneth R. "Is The RCT A Stepchild?" *National Guardsman* 4, no. 1 (January, 1950): pp. 16–17.

"Silver City Goes To War Again." *LIFE*, 7 August 1950, pp. 25–29.

Stevenson, Charles G. "The Federally Recognized National Guard." *Infantry Journal* 61, no. 1 (July, 1947): pp. 40–43.

"The Troubled 43rd." *TIME*, 4 June 1951, pp.

Walsh, Ellard A. "It Might Have Been," *National Guardsman* 4, no. 9 (September, 1950): pp. 10–11.

Weber, Richard E., Jr. "Manpower Economy." *Military Review* 31, no. 11 (February, 1952).

Whitman, Richard, "Why the Draft Makes Our Young Men Angry." *Collier's*, 13 September 1952, pp. 15–18.

Williams, R. C., Jr. "National Guard Instructor." *Infantry Journal* 62, no. 2 (February, 1948): pp. 11–13.

———. "Details With the National Guard." *Field Artillery Journal* 38, no. 4 (July–August, 1948).

———. "The Colonel Calls a Meeting." *National Guardsman* 3, no. 1 (January, 1949): pp. 5–7.

———. "In Conclusion . . ." *National Guardsman* 4, no. 3 (March, 1950): pp. 10–11, 20.

INDEX